LORD of BEASTS

LORD of BEASTS

The Saga of

BUFFALO JONES

ROBERT EASTON

and

MACKENZIE BROWN

Foreword by Jack Schaefer
Illustrations by Mac Schweitzer

THE UNIVERSITY OF ARIZONA PRESS TUCSON

FIRST PRINTING, OCTOBER, 1961
SECOND PRINTING, NOVEMBER, 1961

To Charles Franklin Parker

"To the frontier the American intellect owes its striking characteristics. That coarseness and strength combined with acuteness and inquisitiveness; that practical, inventive turn of mind, quick to find expedients; that masterful grasp of material things, lacking in the artistic but powerful to effect great ends; that restless, nervous energy; that dominant individualism, working for good and for evil, and withal that buoyancy and exuberance which comes with freedom — these are traits of the frontier."

— Frederick Jackson Turner
The Significance of the Frontier in American History

Foreword

IT TOOK TWO MEN several years to rope Buffalo Jones and tie him down in this book. Not surprising. He was a bigger, tougher, more rambunctious quarry and he led them a longer chase than any buffalo or musk ox or lion or rhino or gorilla he ever looped with his own rope.

There were giants in the land in the old days. Buffalo Jones was one of them. Much in this book about him is unbelievable. That all the facts are as accurate as careful scholarship can make them and all interpretations are roundly reasoned does not in itself induce belief. The man simply does not fit into the framework of the modern welfare state, into the context of life as we frailer mortals know it today. He is something big in more than size, exaggerated, pushed past the limits of contemporary cribbed credibility about the capabilities of the lone man, out of a past that is far-gone in more than time. He fits and with a cramped fit only into his own period, that of the brash, arrogant, over-confident, rashly individualistic, reckless, bumptious America of between-the-wars, the two epoch-making wars, the Civil War and the First World War. He came to manhood with the one and he died with the other. He can be grasped in proportion only against that garish oversize exaggerated background. His two captors, tying him down here, have tried to present him in that way. I do not think they have quite succeeded. He still breaks loose occasionally, right out of their pages, a Gulliver snapping bonds, escaping the last final absolute belief. His career was the stuff of which legends can be made — and they were made during his lifetime. But his captors have tried. Manfully, somewhat in his own tradition.

There is something ironic here. Two modern men, quite

at home and at ease in the modern overstuffed overcivilized world, settled in the sedentary profession of teaching as well as writing, living in the soft comfort of the softest most comfortable part of the United States, southern California, from the quiet serenity of armchairs and desks pursue a man whose whole life was a negation of softness and comfort, who made his friend Teddy Roosevelt's notion of the strenuous life seem mild and tame, who, till age and jungle fever took him, courted danger as another man might have courted a woman. They turn to, are attracted to, a pioneer period that contrasts sharply with their own, to subject matter much different from and outside their professional specialties, to a man whose life in condition and intent and the actual living was wholly unlike their own lives. I throw no stones. I embrace the same irony. I do the same, in my way, with my fictional quarries, in my books. But why this backward look, from the lush plush gadget-bolstered today to a rougher tougher more adventurous time and a man who deliberately sought the rough and the tough and the personalized adventure? Is this done solely to provide interesting reading? To make a contribution to that piling up of printed facts and opinions about them called history? Those goals are well met here. But is there something more? The attempt to recapture, if only vicariously, journeying from the armchair if only in spirit with Buffalo Jones into silly grandiloquent yet somehow superb feats, something of the zest for living, something of the strong juices of life, which advancing civilization seems to be squeezing out of contemporary existence?

If so, what better quarry to pursue, loop of words swinging free, than Charles Jesse Jones, lord of beasts, man among men?

And about time. He was a westerner. Though he courted danger and fame and won both in far parts of the world, he did so with the cowboy's rope and the western cowpony.

Whether in the Arctic Circle or on the high veldt or in the equatorial jungles of Africa, he was always a true product of the American west. He was *Buffalo* Jones, first and last and longest, at his finest galloping across the Texas panhandle to rope buffalo calves and preserve the breed from extinction. Too long have writers about the west slipped past him, preferring to play around with the Buffalo Bills and the Jesse Jameses and the Wild Bill Hickocks and the General Custers and the Wyatt Earps and the Billy the Kids — most of whom had considerable fakery involved in their careers and subsequent literary treatment. Even without the fakery, they represented only a few facets of the west, primarily the bang-bang bullet-bouncing breed. Buffalo Jones used his share of bullets in his early days, but he went on to compass far more of the vast and varied and the real life of the west — and of its spirit transported into other arenas.

Oh, Zane Grey and Emerson Hough, in their times, wrote about episodes in his life. He himself perpetrated, in period style as these pages reveal with judicious quotes, a few pieces about himself. But through recent decades and the rise of more serious interest in western history and more earnest attempts at sound scholarship, there has been nothing even remotely adequate about him. And that has been downright aggravating, particularly to writers like myself who depend upon the scholars in the field for authentic background material for our own lesser fictions.

Continually in our own reading of old sources we have come on casual references to Buffalo Jones — casual in that the knuckle-headed writers of those old books and diaries and personal accounts simply took for granted that we would know all about him. They did. He loomed large, like a landmark, to them. Tantalizing references, remarkably scattered in time and place and activity, building to the general impression that the man must have been triplets with all three of him going everywhere and doing almost everything possible in the west of his period — meanwhile tucking in somehow those fabulous roping excursions to other lands. Now at last the record is here, reasonably complete, documented against argument. He was one man — one man who in his time played many parts yet was always that one man. He was Buffalo Jones.

Just the other day, for a minor example, I was digging for facts about the longest horse race ever run in this country, a mere 1800 miles, from Galveston, Texas to Rutland, Vermont. I found a brief account by the man who won it. Suddenly this sentence: "My friend Buffalo Jones induced me to enter and backed me to win." Just that. Again the apparent assumption that I would know this Jones out of all the multitudinous Joneses. A few weeks before I would have cursed softly and muttered: that man again! how did he sneak in here? Now, with galley proofs of this book in hand, I knew it was inevitable he would pop up there, that with such a race in the making he would inevitably have had a hand in it. I knew too that at the time he himself was off in western Texas outdoing even himself running down the last remnant of the once-great buffalo herds to capture the calves and save them from the last of the hunters. Yet a thousand miles to the east another man, urged to it by this same Jones, was racing north to prove that a western horse could outperform the best of the eastern and imported wellbred hotbloods and Jones money was riding with him. I saw nothing surprising in that. He was Buffalo Jones.

Seventy years old and just out of Africa battered by the roughest and most dangerous expedition of them all and weakened by jungle fever and a series of heart attacks — and promptly planning to go back to capture one thousand zebras! Yes, he was Buffalo Jones! It took a world war to stop him.

There is a larger irony here, implicit in the whole book, in the man's whole life. He was a man with an obsession, the central obsession of his time and of ours, to conquer and subdue the environment, to fulfill the Biblical injunction to have dominion over all of nature. In his case, primarily but not wholly, of wild beasts. In this, like many another, he was the repentant sinner. The obsession to preserve, to subdue and domesticate, started in him after he had done as much as any other man in the slaughter of the buffalo herds. It remained with him to the end. And at the same time he loved the wilderness, the untamed and unsubdued. He was caught in his own contradiction. Wilderness, to him, in his own words, was both "challenge and refuge." But to regard it as a challenge, to be subdued and tamed, is to destroy it as a refuge. There was wilderness enough in his time. There is little left now in what was his land and it dwindles fast — and he was one who helped vigorously in the dwindling process. He was one of those who, with the best of intentions and contrary purpose, helped kill the very thing they loved.

Perhaps that is why, after reading this book, I find I have little affection for him. Tremendous respect and unlimited admiration. But not affection. He now looms large, like a landmark, to me too. But something of essential humanity seems to be missing. I find more of that, though only in slight suggestions, in the Sousie Barromie, the Yellow Knife, the Ahtena Indian, who saw to it (in the finest passages in this book) that this Jones did not get his musk ox calves out of the Arctic alive. In Ambrose Means, the southwestern cowboy, who went to Africa with him without the comparable grandiliquent gesture and showmanship and flung his loop over a lioness in the first real test of the possibility with the same deft sureness with which he roped tame Herefords on his New Mexico ranch. Even in the

English lord, briefly mentioned, who gave a festive dinner for the Jones party to celebrate their conquest of a rhino — without disclosing he had just lost 5,000 pounds betting it couldn't be done.

But I see that Jones' captors have anticipated me, foreseen such a reaction. They have fitted him into his period. "But if we note his foolishness, we note the foolery of an epoch. If we see his manhood, we see the manhood of a frontier that a softer age has relegated to the paperback and the viewing screen."

And I see too that in the one passage in which they have freely used their imaginations (cheerfully admitting as much in their notes) they have caught their Jones more accurately, in summing symbol, than in all the carefully accumulated precise facts. Charles Jesse Jones at one end of a rope and a male gorilla at the other end. The lone man with the single subduing tool up against the ultimate in the untamable. That was Buffalo Jones.

Jack Schaefer
Cerrillos Flats, N. M.

Contents

LORD of BEASTS

CHAPTER ONE

Young Man, Young Nation

ONE MORNING in London in 1910, a tall man with gray hair and gray v-shaped beard walked into a Piccadilly hardware store. He might have been mistaken for an ordinary customer in business suit, except that there were boots on his feet, a broad-brimmed hat on his head, his eyes were keen, commanding, his face brown and rugged, his look that of an outdoorsman — with something more. He might have been an officer returned from India or a famous scout from Africa.

"I'd like to see a pair of handcuffs, please," he said. His voice gave him away. It was plain American.

The clerk — a regular English "clark" in wing-tipped collar and three-button suit — showed him a pair of handcuffs.

"Not large enough," he said.

"How large would you like them, sir?" asked the clerk, slightly surprised.

"Oh, twice that size."

"May I ask what you intend to use them for?"

"For lions."

"Ah, precisely! Handcuffs for lions! To be sure you'll need

large ones! We have none in stock just now," said the flabber-
gasted clerk, "but we can make them for you by the end of
the week."

"The end of the week is when I'll need them," the tall
customer said quietly, "thank you," and leaving his name and
address, he walked out.[1]

The man behind the counter didn't know whether he'd
been talking to an escapee from an insane asylum or not. He
glanced down at the scrap of paper on which was written:

C. J. Jones

It didn't sound very original, though the handwriting was
mature and polished. And the address?

Boma Trading Company

Was he a fraud?
The clerk shrugged — and ordered the handcuffs.

It was a wise decision. He didn't know it but he'd been
talking to one of the most celebrated characters of his time:
Charles Jesse ("Buffalo") Jones, often called Colonel Jones,
frontiersman, Indian fighter, business man, buffalo hunter,
who had lately been devoting his time and fortune to preserving the buffalo he had once slaughtered, crossing them with
domestic cattle to produce a new breed, called "the cattalo;"
Buffalo Jones, who on a previous visit to London had been unable to accept an invitation to call at Buckingham Palace and
meet the Prince of Wales so he had sent the Prince a buffalo
robe; Buffalo Jones who had camped out with Teddy Roosevelt in the Rockies and had gone alone to the Arctic Circle to
capture a wild musk ox, who had lassoed mountain lions on the
Grand Canyon's rim, and who — becoming annoyed at a bully-
ing grizzly bear in Yellowstone Park — lassoed the animal by
a hindleg and strung it over a tree limb and paddled its behind

with a pole to teach it manners;[2] Buffalo Jones, adviser to presidents, sought after by princes, now at age sixty-five about to embark on the most fantastic episode of his fantastic career, lassoing an African lion from an Arizona cow pony.

At the week's end he left for Nairobi in Kenya with the handcuffs, a cordial greeting from the clerk who'd been reading the newspapers, a pack of hounds, a half-ton of gear and supplies, two photographers, and a pair of iron tongs for clamping shut the mouths of lions while he slipped muzzles over them.

News media around the world carried the news. Millions of people awaited the outcome. Few knew it was an adventure that had begun sixty-five years before in an Illinois log cabin, and that it symbolized the pioneer personality of a young nation — wrapped up in one man.

He was born in Tazewell County in January, 1844, and grew up on Money Creek in backwoods McLean County, not far from the Abraham Lincoln residence in Springfield. He was the son of a Southern woman and a Yankee man.

When he was three the event occurred which shaped his life. His father, Noah Jones, woke one cold winter morning, snow on the ground, to remember the deacon was coming for dinner and there was no meat in the house. "I'll shoot me a buck before you can bake hot biscuits!" he challenged his wife Jane, who weighed a mere two hundred and fifty pounds. He picked up his muzzleloader, mounted his pony, and trotted away to the nearby woods. The first thing he saw when he got there was a buck's antlers sticking up above some tall dry grass.

Carefully Noah dismounted, raised his gun and fired. The buck slumped to the ground. Pleased with his prowess, the hunter found the animal apparently quite dead. The ball had gone clean through its neck. Jones took the rope from his horse and tied the buck by the horns to the pony's tail, then jumped to the saddle and trotted homeward, dragging the buck behind him over the snow.

But the animal had been merely creased — stunned by the passage of the bullet over its spinal cord — and the drag on the cold snow revived it.

Jane Jones was busy in the kitchen when she heard her husband shouting, "Quick, Jane, the butcher knife! The butcher knife!"

She was a strong-minded person, used to the ways of the frontier, and did not panic when she heard her husband's next exclamation, up a notch:

"Quick, Jane, the axe, the axe!"

She stepped to the window. Galloping across the field she saw Noah, pursued, not by a band of robbers, but by a buck deer who seemed to be tied to his horse's tail and was threatening to root the life out of the pony.

Grabbing the butcher knife she ran outside. Just as she reached the yard gate, Noah maneuvered the charging buck against the wheel of a nearby wagon, and the animal slipped and fell. She threw her two hundred and fifty pounds upon it and held it down while Noah got off, grabbed the butcher knife, and completed the subjugation of the buck.

Then they heard a burst of childish laughter, turned and saw standing in the doorway their second son (in a family of twelve), aged three, dressed all of one piece in baby's tow frock. He had witnessed the proceedings and evidently found them much to his liking. He never forgot them. He grew up to subjugate more animals in more strange places in more strange ways, than probably any other man who ever lived, and he did it without a two hundred fifty-pound wife to help him.[3]

He grew up like most frontier boys, split rails, picked

corn, hunted wild turkeys, fished, and caught crawdads from the still pools of the central Illinois streams of the 1850's. The story goes that Charlie Jones' father once employed Abraham Lincoln as attorney. It was during the election that sent Stephen A. Douglas, later Lincoln's opponent in the famous series of debates, to Washington as congressman-at-large, and Noah Jones was one of the election judges and became fistically involved with the best fighter of the neighborhood over the conduct of the election. Noah won, but such was the nature of the altercation that he felt it best to go to the local magistrate and pay his fine for fighting in public. His opponent didn't let matters rest there but demanded a trial by district court. Noah retained two attorneys to defend him. One was Abe Lincoln. The fee was ten dollars, the verdict acquittal. Thereafter Abe and Noah were friends. Since Abe owned real estate in nearby Bloomington, young Charlie Jones, growing up, came to know the tall somber-faced circuit-riding lawyer who was rapidly making a name for himself.[4]

Charlie, like Abe, had a slender but tough physique and seldom let others outdo him at assigned tasks. By modern standard he might have been called maladjusted because he shunned the crowd and preferred solitary walks in the woods. Birds and animals fascinated him. He caught them at every opportunity and brought them home. The more his parents forbade this pursuit, the more he became attached to it.

They were afraid he would grow up dreamy and no-account, always mooning about animals. For example, his father sent him into the woods one day to saw logs with the hired man.

"I'll be along later in the sled and pick up what you've done," Noah said sternly.

As they began work Charlie looked up and saw a red squirrel in the tree above. Something about that squirrel drew him on. Before he knew it, he was climbing the tree.

"Where you going?" demanded the hired man. The boy didn't hear.

The squirrel jumped to the next tree. Charlie climbed down the first tree and up the second. So it went, through the woods, tree after tree. The squirrel finally took refuge in a hole twenty feet up the rough-barked trunk of a great oak. The boy climbed the tree and, holding on with his right hand, put his left carefully into the hole. He felt the sharp teeth close on his finger. But at the same time his fingers closed around the soft warm furry body. He held firm despite the pain. On the ground he thrust the squirrel into the pocket of his jacket, pinned shut the pocket with a honey-locust thorn, stopped the bleeding of his injured finger by wrapping it in a leaf, and now, remembering his obligations, hurried back toward the job.

He found his father waiting for him in a fit of temper.

"Young man, why aren't these logs sawed?"

There was no reply. He took his thrashing but managed to keep his arm over the pocket so that the blows fell on him and not on the squirrel.

Eventually the squirrel, whom he named Dickie, became quite tame and one day Charlie took him with him to Bloomington, twelve miles, walking barefoot on the dusty road, Dickie riding his shoulder. He thought he might sell or trade the squirrel because on the frontier it was necessary to think about selling and trading and getting ahead, and Bloomington was a market town.

"Would you like to buy a squirrel?" he asked shyly as he passed people in front of Moore's harness shop and Benjamin's general merchandise store.

They laughed at him. What would anyone want with a squirrel? The woods were full of squirrels.

But a kindly faced man with good clothes stopped and said, "Would you like to sell that little animal? My boy's about your age but he's paralyzed. I know he'd get a lot of enjoyment out of a pet like that."

For two dollars Charlie parted with his squirrel. Two whole dollars. He'd never had more than one bit (twelve and a half cents) before in his life. Vistas of wealth opened before him. "If I can sell every squirrel I catch for two dollars, I'll be a rich man in no time," he thought.

Within a year after selling Dickie he had a menagerie that consisted of practically every wild creature inhabiting central Illinois, including a rattlesnake and a bullfrog, and was doing a thriving business with new arrivals in the town, and even with friends and neighbors, trading for barlow knives, peppermint candy, and now and then, hard cash.

The affinity between him and animals grew. He began to feel deep down that God had spoken to him and said, "Go thou and subdue all animals in my name." Perhaps the feeling came from hearing his father read the Bible, the stern authoritative man's voice pronouncing the words of Genesis: "Be fruitful and multiply, and replenish the earth, and subdue it; and have dominion over the fish of the sea, and over the fowl of the air and over every thing that moveth upon the earth."[5]

Then one day his father and two hired men tried to yoke a pair of unbroken young oxen to a plow. They tried all morning. In the afternoon when they had given up and gone to town, leaving the oxen in the pasture, Charlie tried his hand. The animals were far from in a cooperative mood thanks to the morning's mishandling, but he managed to drive them from the pasture into the barnyard and then into the barn. There he lassoed one by the horns and drew its head up close

against a rafter; then he got another rope and lassoed one
of its hind legs and stretched the beast out, head and foot.
Leaving it trussed, he picked up the heavy wooden ox-yoke
and locked one of the bows on the animal's neck. Then he
treated the second ox likewise.

When Noah came back from town he was amazed to
see the animals that he had given up as impossible to handle,
standing yoked in the corral. He was more peeved than
pleased when he learned a thirteen-year-old boy had accomplished what he and two grown helpers had failed to do in
half a day. It ended with him giving Charlie a thrashing because the oxen proved so wild and mean that the bows had
to be sawed from their necks and were ruined.

By the time he was twenty-one, Charles decided he had
had enough. He'd worked for his father to the best of his
ability in repayment for room and board, and there was a
dark-eyed girl who would like him better, he felt, if he had
an education, so he set off for Bloomington and entered Wesleyan University there. Until then he had had only the backwoods schooling: slab bench, no map, no blackboard, a "blab"
schooling. However he was far from obtuse and liked to
associate with bright minds. Friends from these days included
Joseph Fifer, who became governor of Illinois, and Elbert
Hubbard, who became a well-known author. Natural history,
as it was called — the study of birds, plants, and animals and
all the things that come of the earth — took up most of his
time. He spent two years at Wesleyan and then caught ty-
phoid fever which impaired his eyesight so that he was obliged to give up his studies. He went back to his father.

"I've decided to go west, and I want you and Mother
to know."

Noah, by now a prosperous farmer, begged him not to go.

"Son, I'll give you one of my best farms fully stocked with horses and cattle if you'll stay with us."

Charles shook his head. "I'm grateful for your generosity, but I've got it in mind to go beyond the Missouri to the Far West."

"That's a wild region. You can't tell what's going to happen out there. Now with the war over (it was 1866) and ex-soldiers flocking west from both North and South, it's going to be a pretty rough life. Why don't you settle down here and be secure? Marry Rebecca. Your mother and I'll be proud to have you near us."

"I appreciate your offer but I'm afraid I'd never be satisfied if I stayed."

The father did not argue further. He saw in the decision the qualities that had brought his own pioneering father from Massachusetts to Illinois, and his wife's father from Virginia. It was Pilgrim and Quaker stock, North and South, that were merged in the young man who stood before him.

"Go to it and don't look back," Noah growled.

They shook hands. Charles did not say that he was going beyond the Missouri to find that most exciting of all discoveries: himself.

CHAPTER TWO

Westward

DONIPHAN COUNTY, eastern Kansas, in the spring of '66 was the edge of the frontier, and in the village of Troy things were stirring. Along the dusty street that ran from the railroad depot to the courthouse white-hooded "mover wagons" were rocking westward, and people were in the stores buying things, because the war was over and goods were on the shelves again, new-fangled friction matches and women's silk dresses.

Down at the depot a young man got off the noon train from St. Joseph, Missouri. He was six feet tall and weighed a hundred seventy pounds. His facial structure was bony and his light blue eyes clear and penetrating. His muscles stood out through the tight-fitting suit with the peg-bottom trousers and high-buttoned coat. He moved with the air of a young fellow going places who is not afraid of what he meets on the way. He carried a small duffel bag in his right hand. In it were his worldly belongings, a change of shirt and underwear, two pair of socks, the Bible, and a quantity of Osage orange seeds. The Osage orange, a shrub-like tree, was then thought to be the answer to the plains settlers' needs for fencing.[1] Barbed wire had not been invented yet, and there were no trees on the plains to provide fence rails. It was thought that hedges of Osage orange, spiny and quick growing, would take the place of posts and rails. The hedges grew and are still growing, with hard bright orange wood and yellowish apple-shaped fruit, but barbed wire came along and outmoded the idea. But in '66 it was a red-hot scheme, the sort of thing a wide-awake young man might cash in on. Jones had bought a quantity of seed from a dealer in St. Joseph.

He parlayed his purchase first into a nursery, and then into a wife.

First he sold Osage orange seed in Troy. Then he established a nursery where he grew not only Osage oranges but many kinds of fruit. Next he built himself a stone house and married Martha Walton, descendant of the seventeenth-century fisherman and author, Izaak Walton, and daughter of a well-to-do settler just arrived from Indiana. She was shy and lady-like, Jones exuberant and forward-looking, he the rising young man, she the gentleman's daughter. They were married in the Christian Church in Troy and before the year was out they had a son, and Jones helped to establish the basis for the nursery and orchard industries that still flourish in eastern Kansas and western Missouri, and then the grasshoppers came and instead of having a nursery he had a crop of bare poles. Instead of being a young man with a promising future, he was broke.

With characteristic determination he turned around and grafted fifty thousand fruit trees, developed grapevines, and got going again. It was a young land, full of possibilities. Anyone who would work would get ahead. He geared himself to its optimism.

His stone house is still standing in Troy and the "C. J. Jones Addition" to West Troy is a permanent feature of real estate maps. But he was not happy in his business success. The wilderness was calling and at every opportunity he wandered off into the raw prairie to the west.

The animals out there fascinated him, the air-light antelope, the menacing wolves, above all the buffalo which he had never seen before, the Red Man's Cattle. The buffalo epitomized the wildness, majesty and mystery of the plains — of the primitive "Out There" that always drew Jones. The little curly-red calves particularly fascinated him. He vowed he'd catch one some day.

Martha did not approve of these restless wanderings but she was learning that she was married to a man who had something more than nurseries and orchards on his mind.

That winter he disposed of his interests in Troy. Next spring they were moving west in a white-hooded wagon, man and wife and baby, leaving civilization behind and passing into the lonely grassland, and at night coyotes ringed the campfire and kept the baby awake with their din. Martha was afraid.

"Pshaw," he reassured her, "a coyote won't hurt you. He's just a nuisance at worst!"

Next morning they found The Nuisance had chewed through the tie ropes that picketed their two horses. The hoof-prints led homeward. They were in a fix, miles from anywhere, on foot, and there was always the possibility of marauding Indians riding over the nearest rise.

"I'll run those horses down" he said finally. "It may take all day. But they'll be stopping to graze, while I won't waste any time."

"Let me go with you!" she begged.

"No," he said, "I've got to travel fast. You stay here with the baby," and as he was talking he was making a comfortable place for her on the wagon seat, under the hood, "you'll be in the shade up here, and it'll be airier than on the ground." He did not say that she would be out of reach of marauding wolves.

He kissed her and started into the sunrise at a trot, two tie ropes in his hand. At the first crest he stopped and looked back. The wagon was small and lonesome against the empty land. She made a tiny figure under the arch of the hood, holding the baby. He waved. She waved. He turned and trotted on.

Like most frontiersmen he was accustomed to covering long distances on foot and felt he had a good chance of running down the horses despite their headstart. Hour after hour he followed the tracks, alternating trot and walk, five, ten, twenty miles. He began to wonder if the horses intended to stop before reaching Troy. Around him was a wilderness of grass, the bluestem three feet high, meadowlarks rising from it, antelope and buffalo grazing in the distance with their accompanying predatory fringe of wolves and coyotes. Now and then he passed a skull.

Toward midday he jogged down a slope, rounded a corner and came full on the runaways. The bay stood still, ears pricked forward. The buckskin took a step toward him. But before he could move, they threw up their tails and departed.

Looking at the sun he saw he must turn back soon in order to reach the wagon before dark. He remembered that the trail ahead curved to the south, then swung north. He took a short cut down a valley, running at top speed, planning to intercept the horses, came to a creek too wide to jump and too deep to wade, and he did not want to plunge into it, hot as he was, so he sprang into a young tree that grew on the bank, climbed till the top bent under him, chose just the right moment — and jumped across.

He ran on over a low divide and saw the horses walking two hundred yards away. They hadn't seen him. But if he approached they'd run off and be lost for good. Changing tactics he slipped out of sight, ran two miles, approached the trail again. Had they passed? His eyes read the ground. No homeward hoofprints.

He walked back along the trail, singing one of his favorite tunes so as not to alarm the runaways. Within a few yards he met them. They walked right up to him, ears pricked forward, seeming to recognize their master's voice.

Twenty-five miles now lay between him and the wagon. He jumped on the bay gelding and set off at a gallop, leading the buckskin mare. When the bay tired he changed to the buckskin. He covered more than fifty miles that day, half of them on foot, half on horseback.[2]

At dusk he topped the last rise and saw the fire by the wagon. In front of it the lone figure of a woman was moving. She was calmly getting supper — as if in the whole raw wild prairie there were no hostile Indians, no marauding wolves, no renegade white men — only she and her husband and the baby.

"Hello, Mattie!" he called triumphantly as he raced down the slope.

CHAPTER THREE

Buffalo and Indians

THEY SETTLED on a one hundred sixty-acre homestead in what was to become Osborne County, Kansas, in the center of the buffalo range, and Jones built a house of sod and timbers, plowed, and planted corn in the bottom by the creek, put in a vegetable garden of potatoes, onions, turnips, and then took up hunting as a means of survival while his farm developed.

His first experience hunting buffalo had been painful. It had occurred back at Troy when a veteran plainsman named Schultz had taken him out on the prairie. They spotted a herd of twenty bulls grazing toward them and lay flat in hopes of getting a shot.

By the time the huge brutes were within three hundred yards Jones found himself sweating profusely. The bulls looked as big as elephants.

"Let's compromise," he whispered. "If they let us alone, we'll let them alone!"

He was shaking so that he couldn't have hit a whole flock of barns broadside.

Schultz grinned and laid his eye along the barrel of his Civil War musket.

The bulls came so close Jones could hear the grinding of their teeth as they chewed.

The farthest thought from his mind was damaging a buffalo in any way. In panic, he buried his face in the grass.

Schultz's gun went off. Jones looked up, shamefaced, to see a bull falling.

"You've been through the sweat," Schultz said, "you'll be all right."

Now he shot coolly, killing for use, meat to eat, hides for harnesses, blankets, and buffalo hair garments for himself and his wife and children; and then he killed for the market. He lived by the buffalo, as the demand for buffalo products shot sky high. Here on the hoof on the prairie was an animal that could be turned into money. The hides made leather for industrial beltings, boot and shoe uppers, and bags. The meat was delicious fresh or smoked. A buffalo robe was just about the warmest thing yet invented and it was "romantic" — it brought the wild west into your Eastern living room, bedroom, buggy or sleigh, or you could buy one of the fashionable buffalo's hair overcoats and think of yourself wearing the garment a buffalo had worn, and all of it gave you the feeling of having been on the frontier — without any risk at all. Money could buy it.

The newly-built railroads made access to the buffalo range easy. They advertised hunting excursions. They hauled away the products of the slaughter. Slaughter it was. 200,000 hides were sold in Fort Worth in a single day. One St. Louis firm bought 250,000 in one season. They say that in the seventies you could walk one hundred miles along the Santa Fe Railroad west of Fort Dodge, stepping from one buffalo carcass to another.

To be specific: a pair of men and team of horses could

earn from thirty to fifty dollars a day hunting buffalo — big
money for those days. Bull hides brought you more, though
they were harder work. Hunting alone, Jones killed and
skinned ten bulls a day, pegging the hides out on the prairie
to dry, nicking each hide with his knife to show it was his.
The animals averaged two thousand pounds in weight. He
sold the hides for $2.50 each — at the stations where Eastern
buyers had their agents — and the hams brought three cents
a pound when he was hunting near the Union Pacific railroad
or a settled community or smokehouse. The tongues, considered a great delicacy fresh or smoked, were worth twenty-
five cents. Thousands of buffalo were killed for their tongues
alone.

He preferred to kill the bulls because each bull grossed
him eight dollars under optimum conditions, or eighty dollars
for a good day's work, the equivalent of at least $250 today.
Fabulous income. No wonder men left their farms to go buffalo hunting. When the depression of '73 came along, it merely
accentuated the fact that out in Kansas you could make money
despite the hard times.

Jones abhorred the slaughter, but went along with it,
rationalizing, as did many, that if he didn't kill the buffalo,
someone else would; and it was a living for his wife and two
small sons. When the pinch was really bad, he collected
bones and sold them by the cartload to be hauled East and
ground up for fertilizer.

The big kill came in the years 1871 — '72 — '73. They
killed two to four million a year in those years, by Jones'
estimate, and the prairie looked like a slaughterhouse floor,
dotted with the carcasses left to rot or butchered and the
choice pieces removed, and the hides pegged out to dry.[1]

Each outfit, he says in his journal, *could be traced over
the prairie by its peculiar method of skinning its game. Some
would take off the hide in excellent shape, leaving the head*

on the carcass, and then turn it over by main strength, while others cut off the head and rolled the carcass on its back using the decapitated mass to block up the carcass, thus facilitating the process of skinning. Some would drive a sharp steel rod through the neck of the animal and into the hard ground about eighteen inches, cut around the head back of the horns, split the skin on the belly, skin around the legs, then hitch a rope to the hide at the neck, and attach the rope to the doubletrees or rear of the wagon, fasten horses, crack the whip, and peel the hide off the buffalo as you peel the skin off an onion.[2]

Jones' method of hunting was to place himself in the herd's line of advance, lie down on a knoll or behind a ridge-top, and wait until the animals were within two hundred yards. He preferred a small herd of twenty to sixty animals, a fragment of the almost-numberless "main herd."

Everything depended on the accuracy of the first shot, he wrote, in order to get a "stand" on the herd, and it was always aimed for the heart or backbone of the leader, if you were within one hundred yards of the animal; or at the lungs if farther away. If the heart or vertebrae were hit, the animal fell in its tracks; if in the lungs, it ran from one to two hundred yards before dropping, which took the herd much farther off. After firing the first shot, I would wait until the animals stopped, which would be about a hundred yards from the place where the wounded one had fallen. I would remain perfectly quiet and motionless until one of their number had assumed leadership and led off in the original direction of the herd, they taking care to avoid the dangerous place where their leader had fallen. No sooner were they started than a bullet would be sent into the leader's vitals. The herd would run back a few yards, gather into a compact mass, and appear to hold a council, grunting and moving about in as small a range as possible. Then another would lead off to the other *side of the danger-point, but keeping as near the old direction as he considered safe, when a well-directed shot would bring it down. If these three shots were fatal, the herd was mine. If either one failed to kill, they went on their way rejoicing, excepting what few could be brought down by the shots sent after them as they ran. If the three were killed, the herd became completely demoralized, and none would venture to lead, knowing danger to be in front of them, and that death was certain to any which attempted to go to either side. Their stubborn natures would not allow a retreat. They would naturally bunch together, and stand still until the last one was killed, provided the hunter did not get excited and fire too rapidly, or did not rise up so high as to betray his whereabouts.*[3]

Visualize Jones as he lies on his belly in the grass on the crest of a knoll: two cartridge belts wound around his waist. He fires and reloads, one cartridge at a time, moving slowly so as not to alarm the game. At his right hip is the flat leather scabbard such as television repairmen wear today. It contains his thin-bladed ripping knife, skinning knife, and butcher's steel. He fires steadily but not fast. A shot every minute or two will get the job done and will not alarm the buffalo.

He will kill from six to sixty, depending on his luck, sometimes cooling his Sharps .44 sporting rifle (called "sporting" to differentiate it from military models) by urinating down the barrel or with water from his canteen. The Sharps was a sixteen-pound gun that could be rested on a tripod, forked stick or mound of snow (much hunting was done in fall and winter when skins were prime) or on the ground, or even fired offhand. It took a cartridge four inches long containing seventy-seven grains of black powder. Most of the cartridges were paper patched to give greater accuracy. The paper "took to the bore," it was believed — gave the projectile purchase by sticking to the rifling.

Often the results of a stand were pitiful. Jones wrote:

Often I've crippled a calf, so that it was impossible for it to follow the rest of the herd. Its pitiful bleating would hold the family till I had killed all I needed. If the calf were wounded in the fore or hindquarters, old cows would actually support the crippled parts with their horns and snouts, and the calf would walk away on three legs by such aid. . . .[4] Often in those bloody years at the height of the buffalo slaughter, I would determine to "swear off" and would promise myself to break my gun over a wagon wheel when I got back to camp, yet always hesitated to do so until several hours had elapsed. Next morning I would hear the guns of other hunters booming and would say to myself that even if I did not kill any more the buffalo would soon all be killed anyway. Again I would shoulder my rifle, to repeat the previous day's murder. I am positive it was the wickedness committed in killing so many, that impelled me to take measures for perpetuating the race. . . .[5]

He experienced physical as well as mental hazards in his buffalo hunting.

Once, while camping on the headwaters of the South Fork of the Solomon River, in western Kansas, I had wandered about six miles from my wagon, and had killed five buffaloes. It was an hour before sundown, and as may be imagined, I was very busy stripping the hides off the animals. I was leaning over the carcass of the last of the five, just putting the finishing touches to my work, when, happening to glance under my left arm toward the rear, I saw two Indians approaching, tiptoeing along in a crouch. I did not rise, but walked in my cramped position to the opposite side of the beast I was skinning, picked up my rifle, and leveled it on the red devils before they were aware their presence was discovered. They were not more than seventy yards distant, when I exclaimed "Halt!" The Indian in front raised himself to his full height and cried, "Good Injun, me!" at the same instant striking himself on the breast with his right hand while holding his gun in his left. "Vamoose!" I thundered out, as he continued to approach.

"Big Indian, me; good Indian, me," he said again.

"Good Indian goes around," I replied; but he still advanced. I brought my rifle on the old chief in such a determined manner that he knew very well what to expect next. He halted, and fairly danced up and down, chattering all the time like a monkey that had been struck in the eye with a quid of tobacco. He yelled out three times, "Red man's cattle; do, do!" But all I did was to yell back at him, "Vamoose, or I'll kill you!" He immediately led off to the right, and the young buck followed.

I then resumed skinning the buffalo I was engaged on, and appeared terribly brave, while really I was disturbed, and guarantee there were more holes in that hide as I nervously handled my knife than there are in the bottom of a sieve, and I kept my eyes on the Indians continually, for I did not know how many of the devils might be in the vicinity, and my scalp might be in serious danger. After the savages had withdrawn, and were about half a mile distant, an antelope commenced to circle around them, presently stopping to gaze on the red blankets which both wore. Soon, "bang!" went one of the guns, and I plainly heard the ball spat, and saw the poor animal attempt to dash away. He reared, walked a few steps backward on his hind feet, and fell dead. The Indians each cut off a quarter of the animal, packed them on their shoulders, and leisurely sauntered off toward the northwest. I watched them until they were out of sight, finished my work, and walked six miles to camp, congratulating myself that I did not meet the fate of the antelope.[6]

On another occasion, while out hunting, one of Jones' horses fell over an embankment and was killed. Jones could not keep up with the hunt with only one horse to draw his wagon, so he rode boldly to a camp of Kiowas nearby. He recalls:

There must have been a thousand of them on a great buffalo hunt, laying in meat for winter. At my approach there was quite a scramble among the half-naked outfit. An old chief came out to meet me, with bow strung and arrow in place. My salute to him was, "Good Injun?" He replied, "Good Injun." I dismounted, and by that time a half-dozen lesser chiefs and braves surrounded me. I said to the chief, "Sell pony?" He answered "Big Chief, me. Heap ponies. Got money?" "Yes," was my reply. He immediately reached out his hand, saying "Me see." I had not been accustomed to doing business in that way, and shook my head, giving him to understand that when I got the pony, he got the money, and not before. I held four five-dollar bills in my hand, but was careful he did not grab them. He made a reach for them but I quickly drew them back. Upon this he gave a characteristic "Ugh! Ugh!" grasped his arrow and pulled the string until his bow was nearly double, and sent the arrow into the soft marshy ground, nearly out of sight, and walked directly toward his tent, never looking back, skulking off like a spoiled child.

Presently another chief spoke up: "Heap chief, Big Bow, much mad; sell no ponies. One sleep, come back; heap money, good pony." This was very easily understood, and I made straight for my camp; took pains not to return, but moved about ten miles to where some men were camped on a hunt, and bought a pony for less money than the Indians wanted, and already broke to harness."[7]

Jones' attitude toward Indians was probably typical of that shared by most of the plainsmen. He comments:

The American savage exercises the utmost precaution in regard to his self-preservation. None have been known to boldly measure prowess with the white man when the chances were about equal; nor would a half-dozen of these "braves" attack a single old plainsman openly, though they were armed with the latest and most approved repeating rifles, and their tactics and strategy equal to the enemy. They blustered and dashed in such a bewildering manner, however, that they received credit for courage and prowess which they did not possess, and stories are related of them which never had the least basis of truth. . . .

How often have we read of 'outfits' crossing the Plains in the early days being surprised and surrounded by Indians. How the savages, it was told, encircled the hapless band of travelers. Running around on their ponies in a circle, the Indians gradually closed in upon the excited little group of whites, constantly pouring a shower of arrows into them, while the latter vainly essayed to drive the Indians off. . . . How brave and daring this account of the Indian method of warfare sounds! Yet I could take the same number of white men, and all sitting erect in their saddles, encircle the same number of "tenderfeet" for an hour or more, and not one of us receive a scratch. . . .

The explanation of the perfect immunity from danger on the part of the Indian while circling around the enemy as described, drawing the fire of a hundred or more rifles, is this: The "tenderfoot," aiming directly at the pony or its rider while moving rapidly, misses the object intended, the ball falling in the rear, as no allowance is made for the velocity of the Indian dashing ahead at a tremendous rate; consequently the ball arrives at the spot where the savage has been, when he is at least a rod or two in advance (according to distance from the shooter). The next Indian was always careful to keep full ten times that distance behind his leader, so that all balls intended to stop the first man, had passed on before the second reached the place where they struck. . . .

As an Indian-fighter, I must admit that I never especially desired to get into battle with the savage; nor do I care to boast of scores of scalps, as some self-styled plainsmen do. . . . I may have killed an Indian or two; if I did, no one will ever be the wiser. . . . I must confess, that in those troublesome days I would as soon have killed an Indian as a rattlesnake.

Some people will doubtless say I was a hard-hearted and strange sort of frontiersman. To all such let me say that they have never passed through the scenes, trials, and tribulations incident to a life on the plains. . . . If you had been with me from 1869 to 1886, hounded and haunted by these savages; compelled to go hungry, thirsty, and sleepless; losing cattle and horses through their devilish machinations; and had seen with your own eyes, as I have, scores of innocent people mutilated, tortured, and even butchered, simply because they were of the hated white race — it would be indeed a strange thing not to have sworn eternal vengeance against the perpetrators of such hellish deeds. . . . I have ever dealt with them in the sternest and most determined manner, always demanding my legitimate rights under almost every circumstance, yielding to them an equally honest adjustment of theirs, believing that by thus acting I have warded off many a severe encounter and saved myself and party much suffering, to say nothing of possible death.[8]

There was one occasion when he achieved fame as an Indian fighter despite his natural aversion to human strife and bloodshed.

His friend Marshall Sewall had got a stand on a herd of buffalo on the Staked Plain not far from where the last of the militant Comanche chiefs was hiding with his band of warriors. . . . In December, 1876, Old Chief Black Horse and one hundred and seventy Comanche braves, together with their families, had escaped from the reservation at Fort Sill, Oklahoma Territory, during a snowstorm, traveled south and west, eluding pursuit, and gone into camp in their ancestral hunting grounds at a place called Pocket Canyon on the edge of the Staked Plain. The Custer Massacre had taken place in the summer of that year and the Plains Indians were on edge and the whites even edgier. The escape of the Comanches from Fort Sill looked like a new outbreak.

The Indians stayed hidden till February and then as good weather came, began murdering and pillaging. Sewall, unaware of their presence, was knocking over the animals on his stand one by one with his Sharps Creedmor .45, a new long-range gun that could bring down a buffalo at two hundred yards.

Attracted by the sound of his rifle, the Comanches stalked him, as the two Kiowa braves had done Jones. Sewall, however, did not have the luck to see them coming.

His body was found by fellow hunters several days later. Roundabout at varying distances were the carcasses of twenty-one bloated unskinned buffalo, the results of his stand. The Comanches had taken two scalp locks from Sewall's body, had stretched it out naked and cut a gash in each temple and one at the navel; and in each gash they had placed a point of the three-pronged rest-stick on which he had been steadying his rifle as he shot the buffalo.[9]

The hunters immediately organized. Led by Smoky Hill Thompson, a white-headed mountain man of the Kit Carson type, Pat Garrett, John R. Cook, Jones, and others, they formed into two separate companies, one to fight the Indians, the other to guard a central base camp with its food, supplies and livestock.

Aided by a Mexican scout named Hosea who had scouted the country with Colonel McKenzie in the 1874 campaign against the Kiowas, the plainsmen of the fighting company tracked the Comanches to a point near "Casa Amarilla," (Spanish for "yellow house," so called by reason of the rugged bluff with natural and excavated caverns dug out by Comanches thirty years before) near the present site of the city of Amarillo.

On top of the escarpment here was a stone half-circle breastwork, a place where once the entire Sioux nation is said to have come down and fought the Cheyenne, Arapaho, Kiowa, and Comanche alliance.

Early on the morning of March 18, 1877, the plainsmen attacked. They did not know that a band of Apaches had united with the Comanches, bringing the total number of Indians to about three hundred. There were forty-five hunters.

The fight began at daybreak and the outnumbered plainsmen soon found themselves on the defensive. By noon they were forced back to the prairie at the mouth of Pocket Canyon. The Indians, with the memory of Custer's Massacre fresh in mind, hoped to repeat the success of the Sioux the previous June. Speading out in double wings of skirmishers, they set fire to the prairie grass, and began an envelopment of the beleaguered whites.

Under cover of the smoke, a large party crept toward the hunter's right flank, slipping through the breaks of the canyon side, while another group, led by a young chief on a snow-white horse, dashed out onto the floor of the canyon to draw the plainsmen's attention.

The Comanches had not reckoned on the range of the buffalo guns. The young chief was shot from his horse at three hundred yards. At the same time Jones' voice bellowed out: "It's a ruse, boys. Watch this flank. They're creeping down on us through the smoke."

He had been stationed on the far right and as he spoke the wind changed, the smoke dispersed, and the attacking braves were exposed in plain view on the slopes of Pocket

Canyon, where the hunters picked them off one by one.

The Indians lost thirty-five killed, twenty-two wounded; the hunters one killed and half a dozen wounded.

The Comanches withdrew discouraged and were never again a fighting force of consequence, while the Apaches fled back to their reservation in New Mexico.

That night in camp on the scene of the victory, the young hunter who had shot the young chief from the snow-white horse and first chilled the courage of the enemy, stood up among the other plainsmen as they relaxed by the fire, licking their wounds and discussing the fight. He lifted his tin cup of whisky toward the other man who had been most responsible for the day's success.

"Here's to Buffalo Jones!" he said.

And the name stuck.[10]

They called him Buffalo Jones to differentiate him from Dirty-Face Jones and Wrong-Wheel Jones who were also on the buffalo range, and because he was so closely identified with the buffalo. Even in the early days of the slaughter, he had been catching the curly-red calves and gentling them, selling them as pets as he'd sold Dickie the squirrel, though for a higher price — as much as $7.50 — or taking them to county fairs and betting fellows they couldn't lasso them.

There was an identity between him and the buffalo. Men sensed it. They called him Buffalo Jones.[11]

Where was Martha all this time? And the children?

The sod house was whitewashed inside and snug and warm, just one room. The ceiling was of woven willow boughs and sod on top of that, and in spring, flowers grew on the sod. It was built into the bank overlooking the stream. Inside was warmth, life and hope, the core of the family. Outside in the cornfield the corn had sprouted, then most of it died in the drouth, and the grasshoppers and crows got the rest.

Sometimes Martha thought of the good stone house they had had in Troy and of the promising nursery. Here there was talk of riches and comforts that were to come, through the pursuit and capture of wild animals — through the development of land — speculation — promotion — bumper crops — but she already sensed that it was in the pursuit and capture of a dream that the riches were to come; and the dream might not be captured, and the riches might not come; but still Jones would have to go on his way.

After the Pocket Canyon fight he came home brim-full of enthusiasm.

"We're going to move southwest," he said, "out along the Arkansas River. Conditions are safe down there now. The railroad's a-building. Things are bound to boom."

CHAPTER FOUR

Prairie Town

ONE DAY'S TRAVEL west of Dodge City, where Wyatt Earp was marshal, was a place where the buffalo crossed the river, a pretty place, between low bluffs, knee-deep in grass. Indians had bivouacked there and Santa Fe traders had camped there. It was on the Santa Fe trail west of Cimarron Crossing and east of the crossing of the Purgatoire River, west of Fort Dodge and east of Bent's Fort, as near the heart of the big country as you could get. There four men came together to make a town.

They were bearded men, fierce-looking, if the old photographs are to be believed. Not one of them is smiling. They are J. A. Stevens, J. R. Fulton, W. D. Fulton, C. J. Jones, buffalo hunters, Indian fighters, plainsmen.

Their conversation went something like this. Stevens: "With the Santa Fe building west, this here's an ideal place for a town. It's just the right distance from Dodge City, fifty-one mile. If we homestead here, each of us take a quarter section, put up a house, give the place a name and then persuade the railroad to build a station, why, we'll have a town."

"Town means money," said J. R. Fulton. "The way people are pouring West, they'll take building lots off our hands, quick."

"A fellow can't hunt buffalo or wild horses for a living all his life," said Jones, "that's certain."

"Trouble is," said Stevens, "railroad owns every other section of land on both sides of the track from here to the mountains. . . ."

"Here to the Pacific," W. D. Fulton corrected.

"Biggest give-a-way Congress ever made," growled Jones.

"And they'll want the station on *their land*," continued Stevens. "They're already promoting Sherlock on the section west of here."

"I'll talk to them," Jones said, "maybe we can work out a deal. Let me go to Topeka."

He was a good talker so they chipped in and paid his expenses to Topeka. He'd come last to the partnership — buying in for a $150-note and a gold watch — but he was first now. He went to Topeka. He talked to the railroad. He came back with a station. In exchange for approximately half of two homesteads the Santa Fe agreed to build a station on their land. It's practically the only station built on non-railroad land between Chicago and the Pacific.[1]

Around the station, Garden City sprang up. Why "Garden City"? One day a hobo walked over to the fence of Mrs. Fulton's yard and said, "Mam, that's a pretty green garden you got there!" So they named the town Garden City.

Stevens and the Fultons laid out the streets of their homesteads at right angles to the railroad, "square with the Santa Fe," as one newcomer joked. Jones, on the other hand, laid his streets out square with the North Star, "square with Heaven," as another citizen commented. They angled off sharply from Stevens' and the Fultons'. The contest was on, each partner trying to outdo the others in improvements and benefits.

Jones laid out Jones Avenue ten miles long. (It's still ten miles long.) With money from his first land sales, he built the Buffalo Block — of solid limestone building blocks hauled miles overland on railroad cars. It was three stories high and known also as the Marble Block, because of the marble-like appearance of the limestone, and it had a life-size stone buffalo on top of its three-story facade.

Stevens went Jones one better. He built the Windsor Block of brick made in Garden City and it was *four* stories high, and it housed the Stevens Opera House and the Windsor Hotel. Stevens brought culture to town.

Jones put in shade. There were no trees so he imported a carload and had them planted, all at his own expense.

Stevens donated a block of land for a public park.

Jones donated a block of land for a courthouse, built the courthouse and gave the whole thing to the city for one dollar.

"Jones, you're square with Heaven," they said.

"Yeah, but Stevens is square with the Santa Fe."

The town split into two factions. It was a jim-dandy competition — all stemming from buffalo money, all based on wild horses. It had heroic dimensions. It was a John Bunyan tale come true. And yet despite his business interests Jones kept his hand in that primitive background he'd sprung from. . . . F. E. Lothringer was living in a shanty out on Section Twelve. One day Jones walked out there.

"Heard you had a new repeating rifle, Lothringer," he said.

Lothringer showed him the gun. It was a Winchester .45 caliber, 75 gunpowder, twelve shot, lever action, with a barrel twenty-eight inches long.

Jones missed a weed an inch at a hundred yards. Lothringer said, "Try again."

Jones missed again by an inch on the other side.

The weed was about the size of a lead pencil.

"That's a pretty good gun, Lothringer."

A week later, Jones had one, .45-75, Winchester's latest, popularly called "The Centennial" because it appeared in that centennial year of United States' history, 1876.[2]

They elected Jones mayor by a majority of the thirty-four votes cast. Next they sent him to Topeka to the Legislature. There he continued to promote Garden City — and Jones. He liked to carry a basket of oversized vegetables around with him as an advertising stunt, beets, carrots, potatoes. Holding up an eighteen-inch carrot, he would say, "Anything shorter than that is illegal where I come from!" and to a skeptic who doubted the availability of water in supposedly bone-dry western Kansas, he said that every time you pulled a beet out of the ground, water gushed up through the hole — which was very nearly true — along the bottomlands at Garden City.

He dreamed of water, land flowing with milk and honey, harvest home and corncribs bulging. He suggested the site for the diversion ditch that is in use today as a basis for Arkansas River Valley irrigation, and he proposed diverting the rivers at their sources high in the Rockies, but the state of Colorado beat him to it and passed a law saying its rivers belonged to itself.

Turning his attention the other way, he heard that in Chicago horse-drawn cars were running on the streets, and two Garden City-ites were dispatched to the windy city to see if this was the case. They came back and proposed a horse-drawn railway company, but Jones balked at joining. "It's an unsound scheme," he said, "and I won't put a dime into it," he stated flatly.

Instead he drove a cart hitched to a pair of buffalo up and down the streets, stampeding the streetcar horses and terrifying newcomers. "That's Buffalo Jones," people said, "biggest man in this part of the West. He's got Wyatt Earp's brother working for him, and you know how high Wyatt stands in Dodge."

George Earp, Wyatt's half brother, was office man for Jones and helped him sell real estate to immigrants. They got speedy wire reports from the government land office in Larned, brought their maps up to date, measured off homesteads by tying a white rag to a buggy wheel and counting the revolutions of the wheel over the raw prairie. So that if you wanted to know what land was vacant and how much of it you were getting, and how to fill out the papers, it was good to deal with Jones.[3]

He persuaded the land office to move to Garden City, established it in his Buffalo Block, and the people stood in line all night to get a chance to buy a piece of property in the morning from Buffalo Jones and Uncle Sam. His wealth was reckoned into six figures. He was said to be able to write a check for ten thousand dollars at any time. Ten thousand in those days was the equivalent of forty-thousand now.

Bad men, good men, peace officers, real estate promoters, pretty girls, loving wives, all mingled in the dust of Garden City under his omniscient eye, and there was no law-and-order problem.

Whereas at Dodge City, fifty miles away, there was nothing but trouble. Wyatt Earp, Bat Masterson, a whole series of peace officers couldn't keep the peace. But Garden City was synonymous with peace and quiet. Maybe the difference lay in the founding fathers. One look at the faces of Jones, the Fultons, and Stevens would be enough to give a bad man a bad dream. But it was also typically Jones' way: peace by establishing a climate of peace, not by strife; tame a man or an animal by moral suasion, don't kill him.

Not that there wasn't a little friendly shooting. Newsboy

Edwards, having flopped on the floor of his father's hotel, papers in hand, saw H. P. Myton and Old Man Stotts, two prominent citizens, shoot it out over his head. Myton got it in the shoulder, Stotts in the knee.

Shortly afterwards Ross and Scarlet, two lodgers, were observed to come downstairs in the hotel. Ross said: "I'll get you for this!" A few minutes later Ross strode along the street with a shining .38 in his right hand. Scarlet was sitting on a box whittling a stick. Scarlet jumped up, knife in hand, and ran to meet Ross. Ross was aiming the pistol at him, saying, "I told you I'd get you!" Scarlet grabbed the gun with one hand and began stabbing Ross with the the other. The gun accidentally went off and shot Ross through the head.

Aside from a few friendly disturbances such as these, all was quiet in Garden City. However, John W. Gibson, looking with clear boyish eyes, saw two civic leaders use each other as targets in front of Buffalo Jones' office. No arrests made. "Another day," says Gibson, "I saw a covered wagon surrounded by five or six U. S. marshals, back into a livery barn across the street. Curious, I crossed . . . in time to see them unload four dead outlaws wrapped in old horse blankets."

What impressed Gibson most was "the politeness of these western men. I seldom witnessed any quarreling. Only once did I hear the short, ugly word used, and the user was knocked out with a punch in the eye before he could grab his weapon. They seldom used an offensive expression unless looking for trouble."[4]

Handy as Jones was with a gun, there is no record that he ever killed a man in private fight.

At his two-story white frame house at the edge of town, the family was growing. He had two sons and two daughters.

Blight hit the growing family. The two sons died, one of them the tiny tot Martha had held in her arms that day Charles ran back twenty-five miles to catch the horses, and they were buried in Valley View Cemetery on the slope of the bluff overlooking the town and the river, and Jones went on.

Some skinflints built a bridge across the river and charged exhorbitant prices to let people over. Jones got mad, harnessed his team, and hauled people across free in his wagon until public opinion was roused high enough so that a subscription could be taken and a bridge built free for the use of all.

He loved children. There was a little girl whom he used to visit at this time, and she wrote years later, "We always used to love to see Uncle Charlie coming. He would take us on his knee and tell us stories of his adventures. What impressed me most was the way his muscles stood out in his lean straight body and the way he looked straight through you. . . ."

He attributed his great strength to clean living and total abstinence from tea, coffee, tobacco, and liquor of all kinds. His main drink at meals was hot water with one-half teaspoonful of sugar and a little cream added. He spoke in a well-modulated voice, good English, seldom used profanity and it only of the mildest variety.

People respected his moderation, though they might be heavy indulgers themselves. When he was in Abilene during the period of transition from Osborne County to Garden City he met Buffalo Bill Cody, the town marshal.

"We've organized a law-and-order league, young man," Cody said, "are you with us or against us?"

"I'm with you."

"Have a drink, then?"

"No thanks."

Cody respected his temperance habit and never again pressed him to drink during a friendship that lasted nearly fifty years.[5]

Towering figures were emerging here and there on the plains. Buffalo Bill Cody, Wyatt Earp at Dodge, Bill Hickok at Hays City, Buffalo Jones.... They were supplanting the older order: Kit Carson, Jim Bridger, William Becknell.

Meanwhile, there was an Indian scare and nearly everyone in Garden City crowded into the skating rink on Main Street where the men were drilling with muskets and rifles, to the accompaniment of a brass band, while the throng of women and children got hysterical. Jones put his head in the door. "What sort of nonsense is this?" he demanded in a ringing tone. "If the men must drill, let it be in the street, and let it be done quietly." He pooh-poohed the Indian scare and the scare subsided.

Now and then he would get away on a hunt. Picture him leaving his office in the Buffalo Block, a lean, sinewy, forceful-looking man of forty-two, stepping from the high double doors under the stone-solid statue of the buffalo, dressed in grey stovepipe trousers, grey suitcoat, high-crowned black hat, clothes he doesn't bother to change for an afternoon's hunt. He has a tuft of chin whiskers like Uncle Sam; his whole figure is in fact that of a lean, athletic Uncle Sam. Trotting after him is a grey staghound that's been lying on his office floor.

Outside a light wagon is waiting. In it is his hunting partner, N. F. Weeks.

Jones takes the reins. Weeks sits beside him holding the guns and they go for a hunt along the Arkansas bottoms, the hound scouting ahead. It jumps a buck. Jones stands up in the wagon and urges the horses to full speed. They race gloriously across country, hit rough ground, the wagon begins to pitch, Jones and Weeks are thrown out. Jones somehow manages to hit ground running, and when the buck takes refuge on an island in the river Jones comes splashing through the water and is there almost as soon as the staghound and dispatches the buck with his knife, just as his father and mother did the deer in the dooryard so long before.

He was transformed in the hunt, Weeks said, became like somebody else, all wildness and fury, and so alert that even when pitched out of a careening wagon he hit the ground running.[6]

And after a hunt like this, he was a new man. In his own words:

The sun has gone down and the stars are already blinking. It is fully six miles home. I have to go rapidly to keep up the circulation or freeze, as I am in my shirt sleeves. Away to the northeast I see a dim light and know how anxiously my wife and two little daughters await my return. . . .

A half mile more and home. The dog sees me, hear him bark. Here he comes whining for joy. They all know who it is by the dog's actions. The door flies open and I shout, "All right, girlies, venison galore." The ice rattles on my trousers as I step on the porch, but what matters about ice or anything else when one faces such a joyous greeting? This is the kind of hunting that brings pleasure and enjoyment. One short year of such a life is worth an ordinary lifetime pent up in a great city, which must be abhorred by all true sportsmen.[7]

All the time he had buffalo in the back of his mind. The herds no longer covered the prairie black as far as eye could see. Market hunting had destroyed the species, almost. Hides had reached seventy-five dollars apiece and the hunt was a series of isolated murders.

He thought the time had come to do something about the last survivors. If he didn't, perhaps nobody else would, and the buffalo would perish from the face of the earth.

Other ideas were fighting for his attention: financing the

boom, expansion, railroads to build,[8] irrigation, legislative problems such as the boundaries of counties as large as old-world nations, the death of his sons, the frailty of his wife's health, interest, enemies. . . . Not everybody liked him. He was imperious, proud, strong-willed, rich.

Oddly enough, it was a catastrophe that brought him to the point of action on the buffalo. The winter of '86 was the most disastrous the West had ever known. He himself was caught out in one of its blizzards while hunting antelope horseback and only survived by leaving his floundering horse and making for the railroad on foot, and following the rails back to Garden City. The blizzards blew up in a matter of minutes, so heavy you couldn't see your hand in front of your face, and they continued three and four days. Thousands upon thousands of range cattle froze to death, many of them drifting as much as a hundred miles before the storms.

The following March, driving over the prairies, Jones saw the carcasses.

"Every one of them," he wrote, "had died with its tail to the blizzard."

But when he reached the buffalo range not a buffalo carcass was visible. It seemed miraculous that any living thing could have survived unsheltered in such storms.

As Watts meditated over the mystery of steam lifting the lid of the teakettle, Jones wrote, *I commenced to ponder upon the contrast between the quality of the white man's domestic cattle and those of the red man's cattle. Young Watts exclaimed, as he watched the effect of the powerful vapor, "Why not chain this great giant?" I thought to myself, "Why not domesticate this wonderful beast which can endure such a blizzard, defying a storm so destructive to our domestic species? Why not infuse this hardy blood into our native cattle, and have a perfect animal . . . ?"*[9]

Jones then jotted down the assets of the buffalo.

1. Made for the Great Plains climate.
2. Flesh superior to any domestic animal's under similar conditions.
3. Tallow rich and tasty as butter.
4. Hide makes good shoes, rope, leather.
5. Fur softer than lamb's wool. When woven into cloth it makes the lightest, warmest fabric known.
6. The "underfur" as soft as swan's-down and makes a perfectly waterproof hat.
7. The buffalo are impervious to rattlesnake bite. They receive the fangs on their long hair and fur, then stamp the life out of the reptile.
8. Their yearly fleece may be carded off each spring and woven into hosiery, robes, and blankets.
9. Their endurance is second to none.
10. Their milk is richer than a Jersey cow's.
11. They do not stray. Neither can they be driven off their range by blizzards.
12. Their sense of smell is so keen they can smell a bunch of grass a foot under the snow and root it out.
13. Their sinews make excellent thread.
14. Their horns make excellent goblets and receptacles and buttons.
15. Their bones can be converted into handles for ladles and cutlery. And when ground, they make ideal fertilizer. And when charred they can be used by sugarworks in the process of refining.

Where then, he asked himself, *is the animal that can compare with the buffalo . . . ? I will chain him, and domesticate a race of cattle equal to, if not superior to all ruminants heretofore known. I will attire myself entirely in clothing made from the product of the buffalo; even the buttons of my clothes shall be made of horns and hoofs of that wonderful animal. I will not rely on the ravens for my food and raiment, and all may rest assured I will never suffer from the howling blizzard nor for meat go hungry.*[10]

He told Martha when he returned from the trip across the blizzard-bound, carcass-strewn prairies, that he was going to catch some buffalo calves as soon as good weather came.

CHAPTER FIVE

Lassoing Buffalo Calves

THE POINT of departure was Kendall, a village on the Arkansas River, the date April, 1886. The party consisted of Jones and two helpers, Charlie Rude and Newt Adams, and two wagons, each drawn by a span of mules and loaded with provisions for man and beast for a six-weeks' trip. The first obstacle was the river which was half a mile wide, in flood, choked with blocks of floating ice, treacherous with quicksand. Jones summoned workmen and teams of horses from the nearby "marble quarries" where stone was being hewn for his Garden City buildings. Hitching teams in tandem and taking the reins in his own hands, he pioneered the crossing with his usual disregard for difficulty.

From Kendall the route lay southwestward into wilderness toward the Texas Panhandle. It was un-buffalo-like country, arid, in part desert, but here the last remnant of the race had taken refuge.

One morning, Jones was in the driver's seat as usual when they approached a crest of the prairie. Old hunter that he was, he made it a rule when on an expedition after game on the

Plains, never to cross a ridge in sitting position, always standing on the seat, so as to be able to see animals or Indians before they saw him. Rude was lying in the rear of the wagon holding the lead ropes of two saddle horses that were being reserved for the chase when the proper time came. Adams was following in the second wagon.

"Holy Smoke, it's an elephant sure!" Rude heard Jones exclaim. Jones sat down, gave the off horse a crack with the whip, whirled the team so abruptly Rude nearly spilled out of the wagon. Away they went lickety-split for two hundred yards. Then Jones jumped down, gave Rude the lines, grabbed his Winchester, and crawled back to the top of the divide. Bang. Jones waved. Rude hurried to the crest.

Three hundred yards beyond was a huge buffalo bull lying stretched out on his belly on all four legs. He had been killed instantly and had not rolled over as is usually the case but remained upright. Rude who stood six feet could barely see over the top of him. He was meat for camp and a robe to help pay for the trip.

Where was the main herd? At dawn next morning Jones walked to the crest of a knoll and discovered a beautiful pool of water close by. From that crest he could see an unbroken panorama of virgin wilderness, little groups of antelope grazing at either hand, bands of wild horses here and there in the distance, a solitary wolf or coyote skirting about these herds, but no buffalo.

Suddenly far in the distance he saw a herd of perhaps twenty huge shaggy beasts appear from behind a shoulder of the land. With his glasses he searched them for signs of calves.

But the herd was so far away he couldn't tell what it contained. Returning to camp he gave orders for hurried departure. He led as usual in the light wagon, Kentuck, his Kentucky thoroughbred, tied behind, saddled and bridled, lasso carefully coiled at the horn, and plenty of small rope to tie the calves. Rude went with him and would follow up the chase in the wagon and collect the calves, if any were caught.

Mile after mile they rolled northward till about ten o'clock they neared the crest of a divide, against the clear April sky, and saw in a valley beyond, twenty buffalo, lying down for the midday rest.

A detour was necessary to gain advantage of the wind. Then Jones turned the wagon over to Rude and took Kentuck and approached on foot, masked by the horse till he was as close as he dared go, then quickly mounting he lay flat on Kentuck's back and raced straight at the herd.

His strategy worked. Buffalo, like other wild animals, are not able to distinguish a moving object from a stationary one, providing that it is moving straight at them. To them it appeared merely that a solitary wild horse had entered their field of vision, a familiar sight. He was within two hundred yards when they began to rise slowly and move away. As they stood up, he saw with delight four yellow-red calves which had been hidden by their shaggy mothers' bodies.

For good measure he had anchored his lasso around Kentuck's neck — so that in the confusion of roping and tying the calves the horse would not run off and leave him.

The cows ran with the calves almost under their bellies. The adult buffalo threw their hindfeet up alongside their heads at every bound, and their noses were close to the ground. Only the fastest horse could catch them.

The nearer Jones got, the faster they ran. But Kentuck was fresh, and gained. The lasso was whirling. It shot out. A curly-red three-months-old calf was plucked from the herd. It struggled. Jones hit ground, grabbed the youngster and in three or four quick motions lashed its hind legs close up to its front, slipped the noose off its head, and was back in the saddle and away at full speed.

The soft turf flew high in the air from the horse's feet.

Kentuck was a runner and he gained on the buffalo. Zing went the lasso again. Jones got down as quickly as before and was rapidly tying the legs, when he was interrupted by a furious bellow. Glancing up he saw the mother of the calf bearing down on him. Her eyes were green. Her hair was on end. And she had nothing but murder at heart.

He jumped into the saddle and spurred Kentuck. The horse dashed away, came to the end of the rope that was tied to the calf, and Kentuck was spun around by the impact and Jones nearly thrown off. The cow had missed her first charge and was coming back. He ran the horse in a circle, tied to the calf, firing with his .45 at the enraged cow a few feet behind. It was a Colt single action. Four of six shots were gone. He waited till she was about three feet from Kentuck's rump. Then he let her have the fifth shot square in the face. She gave a furious snort and leaped away, shaking her head. Off a hundred yards she stopped and pawed earth.

Jones, taking advantage of the lull, slipped off, tied the calf's hind legs, drew the noose from its neck, mounted, and started for the herd again. He decided not to try any more catches with the rope tied to Kentuck's neck. Reaching down he attempted to untie it. But the struggle with the calf had pulled the knot so tight it wouldn't come undone. Realizing if he stopped to untie it he'd lose the herd, he decided to catch one of the calves by hand — by the tail — throwing it down and jumping on it before it could get up — in the time-honored Western manner — *colear del toro,* the Spanish originally named it, tailing the bull.

Dashing between the calf and the herd, he attempted to part it out, it bawled, the herd grunted a response, whirled, and presented a solid row of heads and horns.

But when they turned and ran on he spurred Kentuck, reached down, grasped the curly-red tail of the calf — buffalo when pressed run with their tails curled over their backs — and

Kentuck being well trained knew what to do: he knew that when you leaned to the right, it was a signal to veer in that direction. He veered, stumbled against the calf — and next instant Jones, Kentuck, and calf tumbled in a confused heap on the prairie.

The calf bawled lustily at this mistreatment. The herd charged back. Jones was in immediate danger of his life. Striking the horse a terrific cut with the end of the rope, he brought Kentuck to all fours and pitched himself into the saddle. The oncoming horns practically jingled the rowels of his spurs as Kentuck raced away.

He was soon pressing the herd again so hard that one calf fell behind. He continued pressing the adult buffalo till they were far away and could not hear the calf bleat, then swung back to pick up his prize. It was an easy catch. A kicking buffalo calf was left for the wagon to pick up.

After this sort of thing had been repeated four times — during three hours and across fifteen or twenty miles of country in the broiling sun — the horse was too winded to go on, so Jones unsaddled it, tied the animal to the saddle, and went on foot in search of the wagon, walked half a day, found it, led it to the calves, and to the exhausted horse — and eighteen hours after beginning the hunt, having put in eighty miles, they arrived back in camp with the calves and the wagon.[1]

"Four calves aren't enough," commented Jones next morning, surveying the four red beauties tied by short ropes to a line strung between two upright posts. "We've got to have more, as insurance against loss, or else our whole trip has been in vain. We've got to find the main herd."

He had brought condensed milk to feed the calves, but there was no guarantee that they would live.

"We'll go on into the Staked Plain," he said, and they did, until the sand stretched clear to the horizon blowing in waves as the wind howled. Adams and Rude refused to continue.

"All right," said Jones, "I'll go alone."

They gave up their mutiny and followed him, and at two o'clock that afternoon when he was sitting on Kentuck on a high promontory, sweeping the horizon with his field glasses, he saw, far to the westward, a lone buffalo cow running. He knew she was hurrying to join the herd.

He made the agreed-on signal: two quick dashes with his horse in the direction taken by the cow. Adams and Rude whipped up the teams. The chase began. Twenty miles and the sun was going down, and not a living thing had they seen, and then in the far horizon nine dark objects were moving against the sunset, nine buffalo, practically the last on earth.

Jones and Rude cantered off until near them. They turned out to be nine bulls. The men dismounted and approached on foot, keeping their horses between them and the buffalo. So far as the bulls could tell, two wild horses of the plains were approaching, grazing towards them, nothing extraordinary. Masked in this way Jones and Rude got to within two-hundred yards.

"You keep on walking with the horses till I shoot," whispered Jones, handing the reins of Kentuck to Rude. Rude continued, leading the horses, while Jones dropped to the ground. As soon as the horses passed from in front of him he fired. The nine bulls rushed off.

"Shoot, shoot," cried Rude, "you missed. Shoot again."

"Watch!"

As Jones spoke, one of the rushing bulls began to stiffen in stride. Next moment it toppled over dead. The shot had penetrated the lungs and the bull had run the usual hundred yards before falling.

They cut out the choice parts — the portion forward from

the shoulders to the neck, including the juicy hump — two-hundred pounds of delicious meat.

While Rude was completing the job Jones slipped away to a nearby ridge. Peeping over he saw about six hundred buffalo, the last herd, grazing peacefully, among them dozens of reddish-yellow calves.

This was all that was left of sixty million that once roamed North America from the Gulf Coast to the Arctic Circle and from Pennsylvania to Oregon. It was known also as the Southern Herd, remnant of the north-south division of the buffalo caused by the railroads and the advance of civilization. But there was no time to make a run at them now. Night was falling.

Hoping they'd stay put till morning, he rejoined Rude and they carried the meat back to Adams and the wagons.

His thoughts that night were of imponderables. Part of him was waiting Fate out there in the dark with each of those buffalo. In the morning he would begin to catch himself, as it were, to preserve himself, the wild primitive Jones that was becoming a thing of the past, like the wild primitive buffalo. . . . And he would carry out the atonement of his slaughter of the species, an atonement begun with the capture of the four living calves.

But bad weather blew down, a spring norther, that dropped the temperature from sixty to twenty before morning. Sleet and snow poured out of the sky. The men lay all day under the tarpaulin propped up by the wagon tongue, wrapped in their buffalo robes.

During breaks in the storm he would slip out and observe the herd standing facing the rain and sleet, huddled where he had left it. Night came on again, sleepless and cold and wet.

At dawn the weather lifted and Jones started. He took two horses this time, both saddled, tied together by a short rope connecting the cinch rings. He would change from one to the other without stopping. It would double his range of action and, he hoped, his effectiveness.

He did not repeat his mistake of tying the lasso to Kentuck's neck. He did repeat his former successful tactic of riding straight at the herd. But his lasso was stiff with cold and he needed four throws to catch the first calf.

As he was tying it he noticed that the wolves and coyotes were unusually bold. Cold weather had sharpened their hunger. They seemed to realize this was the last herd, and their food supply, like the Indians', doomed. They sat around him on their haunches. He couldn't leave the calf to their tender mercies. But if he delayed, he might lose the herd.

"Can I leave this calf and take chances of a wolf devouring it?" he asked himself. "I'll have to. I've traveled five hundred miles for this opportunity. I've spent thousands of dollars on it. I'm not going to muff it." He whipped off his Stetson, knowing that the odor of articles of human clothing renders them and anything associated with them taboo to wolves and coyotes, and tucked it under the rope that tied the calf; then was onto Kentuck and away.

A second calf was caught. His handkerchief was left to protect it. A third cost him his coat, a fourth his vest. In effect he was playing strip poker with the wolves. At the sixth calf he took off one boot. At the seventh another. In stocking feet, hatless, coatless he came to the eighth calf, having changed horses and driven the herd headlong forty miles.

His horse was nearly done, loose in the knees, lathered with sweat, and Jones half naked as he raced through this raw spring day, in a performance undreamed of before and probably unequalled since. He caught the eighth calf. But that was all he could do. He remounted after tying it, reached down and hoisted the baby onto his saddle bow, then started back on his tracks. He could see a band of wolves circling the seventh calf and arrived just in time. The wolves had closed in.

He reached down and picked up the calf (first repossessing himself of a boot) and on he went, a calf under each arm, a band of some fifty wolves and coyotes trotting around him in the twilight.

The next calf had been left in a clump of grass and the wolves had missed it. Here Jones' ingenuity for the first time failed. He simply didn't have arms enough to carry three buffalo calves on horseback.

He set down the two calves, put on his other boot, made a dash at the wolves, revolver in hand, shooting right and left. He killed some and crippled others. The rest paid little or no attention. Hunger crazed, they came back around him and waited. Had they eaten the other calves? Where was the wagon? It was back somewhere on the endlessly rolling prairie over which night was coming.

He had to stand almost astraddle of the little group of three calves to prevent the huge gray buffalo wolves from rushing them. Just before dark he heard a shot and the wagon appeared over the edge of the nearest hill.

Rude found him besieged by what appeared to be all the wolves of the Staked Plain, he half dressed, gun in hand, standing guard over three helplessly tied calves. Rude had collected the others and the castoff clothes. Eight calves were the trophies of that day.

He was atoning, and he was not yet done.

In all, fourteen calves were caught on that trip to make up in part for the thousands he had killed. They were fed on condensed milk and ten lived to reach Garden City and be the nucleus of Jones' buffalo herd, ancestors of the majority of the buffalo we have in the world today.[2]

It was while returning from the trip, at a point between the Canadian Rivers, in the Texas Panhandle, that Jones saw what he declared was the most wonderful sight of his long experience on the Plains.

He was plodding along on foot, leading a tired horse, picking out a route for the heavily loaded wagon and its precious calves. As he came to the top of a divide, he saw what appeared to be a herd of buffalo and domestic cattle, mixed. He stopped, and telling Rude to keep on a straight course with the wagons, made a detour and went up a ravine to a point near the grazing herd.

When he got to within a couple of hundred yards of the supposedly mixed band, he found that the white animals in it were not cattle at all. They were *white buffalo,* a three-year-old, a two-year-old, and a yearling. He didn't know whether he was awake or dreaming. He had read and heard the superstitions of the Indians, about white buffalo, and had considered them a phantasy. Now he saw the proof, under the noon sun, chewing their cuds. White buffalo.

His horse was completely used up. But P. T. Barnum would pay him ten thousand dollars if a penny for one of those white buffalo. If only he had a fresh horse!

Not having one, he decided to make the best of the one he had. Mounting and lying flat in his usual way, he got quite close, but the white cow saw him. She threw up her tail and led the herd away at a terrific clip to the south. They sailed out of sight over a far divide, but not before Rude and Adams had seen them too, white buffalo, unbelievable, floating across the distant green hills of the prairie.

CHAPTER SIX

Colonel Jones

HIS FACE shows many men: the con man, the promoter; the prophet man, the visionary; the fighting man, the plainsman; the sensitive man, the atoner and preserver expressed in features in which there is a strange delicacy, a most unfrontierlike sensibility, the gentleness of a man who could establish a nursery and graft fruit trees as well as fight Indians. A strange complicated deep-running man. He was a writer too and could express himself in words that had validity. Comes another writer, now, to see what he is all about.

Jones' calf-catching exploit made him famous. It caught the public's attention: a man who had slaughtered buffalo, now preserving them! It made good newspaper copy.

Emerson Hough, a budding western writer, later famous as the author of *The Covered Wagon*, came to see for himself. In fact Hough invited himself to go along on the next calf hunt. It was rather as though Zane Grey had invited himself to go along on somebody's hunting trip.

"All right you can go," Jones told him, unimpressed, sitting in his office in the Buffalo Block, "but only if you will promise to obey orders and not get in the way."

While the great man attended to last minute affairs, Hough knocked about town, collecting material.

"The Hon. C. J. Jones," he wrote, "is 'The gentleman from Finney County' when he is in the legislative halls at the capital of Kansas; but when out of his legislator's desk he is just 'Buffalo Jones,' all over Kansas and the West. There is no man in Kansas so well known, perhaps no private citizen better, in the entire United States. He has built a city, made a fortune, and has gone to the Legislature; but still his old name sticks to him, and will stick so long as time shall last. There is no use of his trying to escape it: he is and will always be 'Buffalo Jones.' "[1]

This was heady praise. They'd begun calling him "Colonel," Hough discovered, the title awarded in the Old West when a man reached a certain level of popular esteem.

What impressed Hough as much as anything was the preparations for the trip, heavy equipment, camp supplies, tents, etc. that left town a week ahead by rail, continued by means of two mule-teams, three men, extra saddle horses, into the buffalo range. Included were two thousand pounds of grain for livestock feed and twelve milk cows to nourish the calves that might be caught. It was like an army on the march. Jones and Hough followed in a light two-seated buggy drawn by a big black horse named "States" and a little gray horse named "Gray Devil."

If Jones in person amazed Hough, Jones in action when they reached the buffalo country left him breathless.

"I heard him call for his rope, call for his charger like a knight of old going out to battle, and his voice roared over the plain till it was enough, alone, to have terrified the buffalo and brought them to a standstill."[2]

He saw the Colonel thrown from his horse, fly through the air, land smack on the calf over which his horse had stumbled, clasp the calf in both arms in a flying tackle and hold it down till a rider dashed up and lassoed it.

But this was small doings. Luckily, Hough went along on this trip or nobody would have believed what happened. They ground their coffee beans in a hollow buffalo skull, they used a buffalo's shoulder blade as shovel, their stove was the cavity where a buffalo's brains had been, and Hough got so manly he forgot he was merely a writer, seized a gun and shot a buffalo bull before he had time to be afraid.

He thought he'd seen everything until he saw a mare drink a bucket of whiskey. "The poor creature had been ridden a hundred miles, made three tremendous runs after calves, all in a day," he wrote. "She stood with head down, legs wide apart, wet with sweat, and trembling like a leaf. In her misery at trying to breathe, she blundered and stumbled about the camp, and we soon found she was quite blind, or could see only imperfectly. A moment later she attempted to lie down but we caught her and held her up, a dead weight between us. Then we poured a straight pint of raw whiskey into a pail. Before we could dilute it with water, the mare felt the rim of the pail, and at once drank its contents at a gulp. Whether the Kentucky mare recognized the Kentucky product or not, I do not know; but she drank that whiskey 'straight' and it was the best thing she could have done. She did not get down at all after that; and in a little while we gave her a quart or so of water, then half a pailful; and after blanketing and rubbing down her legs, she began to prick up her ears and whinny a little. Then we knew she would pull through; and we held a general jubilee, hugging the game old animal and calling her all sorts of pet names.[3]

Here was the raw stuff of which a hundred Westerns could be made. No need to romanticize. Hough labored to put down the truth. In describing how the calves were fed:

"Jones would go out and rope a red range cow from the

herd he'd brought along, one that most nearly resembled a mother buffalo in color, and then he would hobble her securely fore and aft, and bring the calf up to her — the calf kicking and butting with all his might. The cow would turn her head, and promptly kick so hard that she sometimes broke the hobbles and sent the calf in a somersault backwards."

This did not daunt the calves in the least because a strange thing had happened: they had recognized maternity; they had smelled milk! Back they would come. And in a few minutes the best of relations would be established, and the calf would be lying down beside its foster mother, chuck full.

"The calf was never wild afterwards, but could be approached easily and was perfectly docile," wrote Hough. "In the morning we let it loose near the cow and it followed her about, kicking up its heels and bawling out of very exuberance of spirits."[4]

Some of the calves were temperamental. One would drink from nothing but a beer bottle covered with a rag, another only from a bucket, and it so happened the bucket was painted white. Afterwards the calf would drink from that bucket only. Give him one of another color and he would butt it over.

Hough and Jones wound up the trip in typical Jones whirlwind fashion, covering one hundred miles in a buggy in twenty-four hours. Hough wrote with a final gasp: "Could . . . the calf-hunt be duplicated by other parties? Hardly! for the reason that men having sufficient knowledge of the haunts and habits of the game, and an inclination to secure it, are very few; and of these few, fewer yet are able financially to organize such a hunt. It cost Mr. Jones over one thousand dollars in preparatory and current expenses for the short time which our trip lasted."

Hough's publicity helped focus the public's eye on Jones and Garden City.

CHAPTER SEVEN

The Buffalo Ranch

HIS DREAM was coming true. There were buffalo calves in his backyard and he would be remembered as the preserver of the American Bison. He had fulfilled a promise to himself. But as usual with Jones, there was a practical overtone — a commercial wrinkle — something untried as yet — something in which he could be first, and maybe turn an honest penny. He wanted to create a new species by crossing buffalo and domestic cattle.

First he bought land across the Arkansas River and there, a few miles southeast of Garden City, in acreage sloping back from the green bottomlands, he established his buffalo ranch, and there, if you go out today, you can see the big shaggy cottonwoods, gems of shade in that hot land, that sheltered his buffalo — and his "cattalo."

The cattalo were the result of the union of a domestic cow and a buffalo bull. He arrived at the word by combining the first three letters of "cattle" with the last three of "buffalo." But the dictionaries have given it an extra "t" — cattalo.

He bred his buffalo bulls to Galloway (a black, hardy,

Scottish-highland breed), Angus, Hereford, and range stock. He found that the hybrids were as large or larger than the parents on either side, cattalo cows weighing from twelve to fifteen-hundred pounds, nearly twice as much as ordinary cows, and cattalo bulls — which he had some trouble producing — weighing over a ton.

But what of it? What good was a cattalo? This: Stockmen had lost fortunes in the recent terrible blizzards. Jones expressed their general attitude when he said, writing of his cattalo experiments in the *Farmers' Review*, Chicago, August 22, 1888:

1. *We want an animal that is hardy.*
2. *We want an animal with nerve and endurance.*
3. *We want an animal that faces the blizzards and endures the storms.*
4. *We want an animal that will rustle the prairie and not yield to discouragement.*
5. *We want an animal that will fill the above bill, and make good beef and plenty of it.*

The cattalo seemed to be the answer.

Not only were they tractable and good "keepers" — they produced beef in abundance, and it was as tasty and nourishing as domestic beef. Furthermore cattalo robes were as good as buffalo robes, especially in the case of the three-quarter and seven-eighths buffalo hybrids. Where the maternal strain was black, the cattalo fur was as rich and compact as black beaver.

Anything that smacked of beaver or buffalo fur in those days had money in it. The future looked promising for the cattalo and Jones.

George Bird Grinnell, distinguished author, naturalist, student of Indian and plains lore, visited the Buffalo Ranch, and wrote in *American Big Game Hunting*, the book of the Boone and Crocket Club which he and Theodore Roosevelt edited:

"Mr. Jones is the only individual who, of recent years, has made any systematic effort to cross the buffalo with our own domestic cattle. As far back as the beginning of the present century, this was successfully done in the West and Northwest; and in Audubon and Bachman's *Quadrupeds of America* may be found an extremely interesting account, written by Robert Wyckliffe, of Lexington, Kentucky, giving the results of a series of careful and successful experiments which he carried on for more than thirty years . . . but no systematic efforts to establish and perpetuate a breed of buffalo cattle were afterward made until within the past ten years. . . . A half-breed cow of Mr. Jones' that I examined was fully as large as an ordinary work-ox, and in spring, while nursing a calf, was fat on grass. She lacked the buffalo hump, but her hide would have made a good robe. . . . If continued, these attempts at cross-breeding may do much to improve our Western range cattle."

And as for the domesticating of buffalo, Grinnell said: "Mr. Jones is perhaps the only man living who knows enough of this subject to carry on an experimental farm with success."[1]

This was high praise from a responsible source. It brought Jones to the attention of intellectuals and to a man not then so famous as he, Theodore Roosevelt. T. R. was a progressive member of the U. S. Civil Service Commission and had his western ranch experience behind him, but he was still years away from the White House and eventual intimacy with Jones.

All the while the former buffalo killer, now hailed as The Preserver of the American Bison, was adding to his original herd by purchase and capture.

He went to Canada and created an international incident by purchasing the then famous Stony Mountain, Manitoba, Herd from a Major Bedson. For days Bedson and Jones dickered, while wires carried the news, Bedson demanding

that the Dominion Government top Jones' offer of twenty
thousand dollars in order to keep the bison in Canada. People
felt strongly about buffalo in those days: the idea of a
damyankee relieving Canada of its biggest, best, and practically its only buffalo herd did not sit well with Canadians.
But the Dominion would not top the offer, at least not by
much, and Jones closed the deal for a cool twenty-five
thousand, moving fast lest Canada pass a law or take execu-
tive action to prevent him from removing his buffalo.[2]

Said the Chicago *Times:*

It is understood that the Dominion Government made a bid, but
the recent transfer shows Colonel Jones on top, at a cost of about
twenty-five thousand dollars. A week ago Saturday, the first consign-
ment from the famous herd was loaded at Winnipeg, on the cars of
the St. Paul, Minneapolis, and Manitoba Railroad, and they are now
en route to the Kansas Ranch.

Among those who witnessed the loading of the animals were
several "old-timers" in the Northwest, who ten years ago thought
nothing of a sight of great herds of buffalo in a stampede across the
country, and there was a feeling of sadness at parting with the shaggy
monsters; and well there might be, for specimens on the far North-
western plains are now as scarce as hen's molars.

The distance from Stony Mountain to Winnipeg is about twelve
miles, and when thirty-three of the ninety-five had been separated
for shipment, they were driven across the open prairie to the Winnipeg stockyards. Three or four naughty old bulls, when half-way on
their journey, sniffed the air, saw trouble, and with a sudden "right
about" threw down their heads, and with their tails high in the air
took the crow-line for their old quarters.

Horsemen armed with heavy cowboy whips and steel prongs
charged after the truants, but the animals, their ancient vigor having
returned to them, soon reached home.

When the others arrived at Winnipeg yards, they too turned
tail, but were headed off, and soon driven across the railroad. Jones
ordered, as soon as the herd was across, that a train of freight cars a
mile long be pulled up to the end of the railroad fence, and thereby
prevent a stampede back across the railroad.

Everything worked exactly as the great general had planned. The stockyards were on the north side of the road, and how to get the buffalo into such a trap was apparently beyond human skill; but Jones is the most wonderful schemer ever seen in the Queen's domain, beyond question.

He had a hasty fence built from the north side of the gate on the west side of the yards, in a circular fashion, and made it fast to the east end of a car, then ordered the coupling-pin pulled and the east end of the train moved to the east one car-length. As soon as the buffalo saw daylight between the cars, they made a furious dash for their old home to the north.

Jones was well mounted, and pushed those in the rear up into the herd. Every buffalo leaped clear over the track, and the circling fence guided them through the great gate into the stockyards.

Jones then jumped from his mount upon the gate and gave himself a mighty push from the fence, and swung in front of the whole herd, which had reached the limits of the pen, realized the trap, and were retreating — but too late. The mighty gate had closed, and Jones was standing triumphant upon it, as calm and composed as if nothing unusual had occurred, while crowds of people enjoyed this greatest victory our people ever witnessed.[3]

So Canada knew him. His reputation had become international. The trip homeward was no joyride despite the triumph of the "great general." Three buffalo, worth upwards of $1000, were killed in the cars by their companions before the train reached St. Paul.

The idea of a trainload of buffalo rocking, roaring, and goring their way across the U. S., not to mention Canada, created a sensation. Crowds turned out to see this train of trains. Many people who had never seen a buffalo except in their imaginations, racing across the plains pursued by Buffalo Bill or Buffalo Jones, now saw the Red Man's Cattle in the flesh.

When the Buffalo Train pulled into Kansas City there was further sensation. Thirteen head got away and stampeded through the streets, finally taking refuge in the lowland along the Missouri bottoms. There had not been such excitement since Jesse James held up the race track. A small army of Missourians and Kansans, led by the great general, finally overpowered the buffalo.

By now the Dominion Government had raised hue and cry over its lost herd. "We wuz robbed!" it said in effect. The U. S. was in a delirium of delight. Kansas City was enjoying a Roman holiday. The railroad was in a state of consternation as to whether this was good advertising or a painful disruption of train schedules. And Jones was thoroughly enjoying himself.

He disposed of part of the herd to a buyer from Salt Lake City (they ended up on an island in Great Salt Lake) and with the remainder moved on to Garden City, using the cash from his Salt Lake sale to pay his bills.

His homecoming was a regular triumph and he found a stack of mail from all over the country and the world.

The Stony Mountain purchase made Jones' buffalo herd by far the largest and most important in existence.[4]

Nor did he neglect the capture of other animals while concentrating on the buffalo. His passion to subdue and preserve all forms of wild life was incorrigible. While waiting for a train, for example, at Emerson, Manitoba, he got into conversation with an Indian who said he knew where there were "several old moose of prodigious size," and several young ones. That to Jones was like the bell to the fire horse.

Within an hour he, the Indian, and a neighboring livery stable owner, were bowling over the prairie in a spring wagon, headed for a nearby tamarack swamp.

There, in a grove of quaking aspens, Jones was confronted by what he felt confident was a grizzly bear. It turned out to be a female moose, her long legs like fenceposts, her face ugly enough to frighten a frontiersman. She passed within a few feet of him and made a bee-line for a grove of trees.

"Now for the fun," he said to himself, watching, lasso in hand, to see if there were a calf following.

Just then the Indian emerged from the brush carrying something that looked like a young colt. It was the baby moose, legs like handspikes four feet long, neck six inches in length.

Jones took the baby to Garden City, turned it loose on the Buffalo Ranch, sold it to the park in Hutchinson, Kansas, where it continued to thrive.[5]

Next he determined to do with the buffalo as he had once done with his father's oxen: make them regular draft animals. This would be the realization of man's divine mission as he saw it: to subdue and utilize nature. It was undoubtedly the central idea of his time and he merely symbolized in high degree that which was everywhere prevalent. But the subduing, in this case, took some doing.

He began with two full-grown young bulls. One of them had killed a man previous to his purchasing it, and he was fully aware of the danger. "The only way to handle buffalo," he said, "is to face them, preferably on foot. They'll run a man on horseback all over the lot. But if you get off, advance, never wavering, never turning your back, they'll back down just before the supreme moment arrives." And, for example, he cites in his autobiography what happened to him when the first buffalo calves grew to maturity: "The master bull in particular became very obstreperous, and often when I would ride into their corral, he would charge me viciously. The only way to save myself and horse was to dismount and with uplifted quirt advance to meet him. Immediately he would slow up while I would advance even against his puffs and snorts, and then just in time to escape contact he would lower his tail and return to the opposite corner."

And further: "If a person feels he cannot face a wild beast and bluff it out and there is no means of escape, he should play dead, as no animal will attack anything dead unless driven to it by hunger. Herbivorous animals will under no circumstances attack anything without life. Before I learned to bluff animals I was attacked by one of my buffalo bulls. He was several hundred yards away and started for me. I knew from his actions he was coming to kill and there was no way to escape, so I fell sprawling on the ground. He was beside me instantly. He smelled of me but I never flinched. Then he turned and walked away. It took far more nerve to lie still than it does to face the most formidable beast."

It was now to be a "High-Noon" situation, face to face, man to man, and see who backs down.

"No man," he said, "had better undertake to control the male bison, unless he is imbued with the belief that he was given power over *all* brute creation."[6]

Here was the spiritual element, the mystique.

He tied the two young bulls together and let them fight. Six months of this kind of gentling and they were ready to hitch to a cart. Though Jones was strong he didn't attempt to control his two two thousand-pound cart horses by force of arms. As mechanical aid he installed a windlass, the sort of thing used for raising and lowering anchors of ships, on the forepart of his cart, and when he wanted the buffalo to turn or stop he simply windlassed them. The reins were stout ropes running to heavy iron bits in the buffaloes' mouths.

He could control each animal individually simply by turning one of two cranks attached to the windlass, and the brakes were adjusted by his feet, so that he could exert more pressure with one hand and one foot than could ten men under ordinary circumstances.

Then the Buffalo King, drawn in his chariot, drove through the streets of Garden City. Horses climbed trees, women screamed, strangers fainted, and there was a sensation generally on a level with the Second Coming.

After he had used the buffalo team to draw a hay-wagon and even to plow, Jones felt confident he could trust his new draft stock. One day he was rolling along with them hitched to the two-wheeled cart. The road led beside a stream. It was a hot Kansas day as only a summer day can be in Kansas. The cool stream below the bank looked especially inviting. . . . Next moment, Jones, buffaloes, cart, windlass and all the rest, were in a sodden heap in the water.

That ended training buffaloes to be draft animals.

All the while he was continuing his efforts at preserving the species. He made additional trips to the Panhandle for calves. He went to Washington and tried to persuade Congress to pass legislation protecting the few survivors. No luck. But Representative Lacey of Iowa introduced a resolution honoring him for his work of preservation and awarding him a pension for life in recognition of his services. Jones refused to allow Congress to consider it.[7]

He realized that if the buffalo were to be preserved, he would have to continue to do it himself, and to pay for it himself. There was justice in this. He had lived by them. Now he would let them live.

CHAPTER EIGHT

The Last Hunt

THE LAST HUNT took on the dimensions of a national event. The Chicago *Times* furnished carrier pigeons to get speedy coverage and the nation held its breath as "the Colonel," at the head of a small army of men, horses, mules, milk cows, bloodhounds and baggage wagons, advanced into the wilds of the Texas Panhandle.

It was in all probability the last caravan to travel the historic Santa Fe Trail. The completion of the railroad to Albuquerque in 1880 and on to Los Angeles in 1885 had rendered freighter transportation all but obsolete, and the ghosts of Kit Carson, Wild Bill Hickok, William Becknell would not hear the sound of wagon wheels again. . . . Nor would the sounds of buffalo hunters' rifles be heard beyond this year, because it was the spring of 1889, and after this, no more buffalo were seen alive outside the national parks and game preserves.[1]

The first carrier-pigeon dispatch, released from thirty miles south of the Canadian River in northwest Texas, told of a three-day pursuit of a herd numbering twelve cows and two bulls. During the chase other buffalo were flushed and three calves caught. "We have seen but twenty-four altogether," Jones reported. "Verily the days of the buffalo are numbered. There cannot be more than one hundred left in the whole United States outside of those in the National Park," (Yellowstone, the one and only national park at this time), "and they will probably be destroyed by the hunters before winter sets in. . . . The pigeon now goes. Each of us will throw one of our old shoes after it for luck. — C. J. J."[2]

Straight to Garden City the pigeon flew. From there telegraph carried the news to the waiting world.

America had a new kind of Western Hero — a humanitarian who was putting as much adventure into creation and preservation as the old-fashioned frontier heroes put into death and destruction.

As the pigeons winged northward, Jones advanced deeper into the wilderness. As usual, he furnished his own dramatics.

As I was turning the team around the head of the gulch, which is about twenty miles above the headwaters of the Beaver River, two large cows with one calf accompanying them suddenly 'winded' me and went scampering over the prairie in a southwest direction. I had no saddle; neither spurs nor revolver. Dick Williams, who was to keep near the wagon, riding the fast running-horse, "Cannon Ball," was fully equipped with all the accoutrements necessary for such an occasion, but he was nowhere in sight. What should I do?

There was a calf worth a thousand dollars, and all that I had to do was to catch it.

In an instant I was out of the wagon, off came the harness from one of the horses, and snatching the rope used to picket the team at night, I mounted the animal bareback, and was away like a flash.

By the time I had finished my crude preparations for

pursuing the animals, they were at least half a mile in advance.

My horse, only a buggy animal, knew nothing whatever of what was expected of him; he was as green as a tenderfoot on his initial tour of the Plains. I made him understand, however, by the application of the rope, that he was to get over the ground as fast as his legs could carry him.

In less than a hundred yards, my hat went flying in the breeze, but right on I flew. . . . Only a short distance more to gain, and then I would be between the calf and its mother. The calf seemed to realize this as well as I, and the last hundred yards were the hardest to gain in the whole race. I laid on more of the rope, came closer to the little brute, which now began to grunt like a pig waiting for swill. Suddenly the old cow stiffened her forelegs, threw her hinder parts around in the air, and using her front legs as a pivot, reversed ends in a second.

I took in the situation at once, having been accustomed to such tactics before, and by a desperate effort, crowded in ahead of the calf, and bore it away to the northwest. The mother looked first at her calf and myself, then at the other cow, fleeing in the opposite direction, when to my surprise and delight, she turned and resumed her flight with her companion.

At the turn things had taken I breathed a sigh of relief, as I had no revolver with which to protect myself in case of emergencies, and muttered, "All I have to do now is to catch the calf," and paraphrasing the celebrated Horace Greeley, "The way to resume is to resume," — "the way to catch a buffalo calf is to catch it."

Making a noose as I sped along, I gathered up the heavy rope and swung it over my head, preparatory to throwing the precious circle around the hoped-for captive's neck; but my broncho was not used to having anything of the kind flying above his head — the only instrument he was accustomed to was the butt end of a whip in the hands of my hostler, who often had knocked him down with it when he balked in harness.

You should have seen that broncho dodge and buck. He was worse scared than the game we were pursuing, and his antics gave the calf an advantage.

The calf soon broadened the distance between us of more than the length of a dozen ropes. Still, "all I had to do was catch the calf.". . . but I was satisfied that without saddle, spurs, or proper lasso, I was not going to succeed, and concluded the best thing was to turn the fleet-footed little rascal down towards the east, where I had last seen Dick.

I swung my rope again, but for a different reason this time, laying it on behind me in such vigorous manner that the broncho quickly appreciated what it meant, and accordingly got down to work without any further misunderstanding between us, and I soon had the calf turned and headed in the right direction . . . .

And he and Dick caught the calf.

As an experiment it was decided to rope a full-grown buffalo cow, for the first time in history.

This was ticklish business. The cow showed a tendency to rip things open, which she was fully capable of doing with her vicious sharp horns and natural quickness, but Jones and his able helpers Lee Howard and H. M. De Cordova devised a plan. First they ran her to a standstill, then Howard lassoed her by one forefoot — this was the delicate part, because it is hard to lasso anything by one forefoot, especially a wildly cavorting buffalo cow — and De Cordova got her by one hind foot, and they stretched her out; while Jones, dismounting, approached with a pair of chain hobbles. This sent the cow into such a frenzy that she came near snapping both lines, so Jones put his own rope on her for good measure,

then hobbled her powerful front feet with the chains. . . .
Overpowered but still resisting, she gave a final spasmodic
jerk, and lay still, "dead of pure mortification," as Jones expressed it.

Finally after many adventures they established camp
at the head of the Palo Duro Canyon in Texas and went to
reconnoiter the whereabouts of the last herd. Jones hoped
to capture the entire herd alive and drive it back to Kansas.

*In the evening DeCordova reported having discovered
twenty cows and one bull about eight miles from camp. The
next morning, after an understanding had been reached on a
code of signals and an order of operations had been written
by me, the signal was given. . . . Howard had the command,
he was to follow the herd, "to the ends of the earth," if necessary . . . never to lose sight of it, day or night. Should the
herd escape, bloodhounds were to be put on the trail until
the buffalo were overtaken; but this method was to be resorted to only as a last resort.*

*Those in camp were always to keep watch from a high
butte by day and by night, and like the devoted Aztecs, who
keep the fire glowing for the return of Montezuma, so the
watchman was to always keep a beaconfire on the summit
and watch for signals.*

*When the drivers of the herd were sighted, the reserve
at camp was to go immediately with fresh men and horses
to relieve those who had been on the drive . . . .*

*Everything ready, Howard with one other man started
twenty-two full-grown buffaloes — twenty-one cows and
heifers, and one bull. The bull had been wounded, and on
the second day became so lame that he dropped out of the
herd.*

*A light rain fell the night before starting them, and the
weather was favorable, the recent rains making it easy to
track the animals . . . .*

The buffalo at first endeavored to shake off their pur-
suers, especially at night, but by ten o'clock the next day
they were sure to be overtaken. They invariably held a
straight general course; therefore the tracks could be easily
followed. . . . When first sighted the herd would go "all to
pieces," but by proper strategy and movements on our part,
would soon come together.

It was the fourth day before the camp was sighted. Men,
team, and saddle-horses were in a deplorable condition. Only
one water hole had been found, and had it not been for the
water carried in a barrel, the pursuit must have been aban-
doned. During the first three days' drive the herd avoided
water altogether, which shows their endurance on the desert
to be equal to that of the camel, and their capacity for rang-
ing a great distance from water to be unprecedented.

The herd being now somewhat tractable, and Jones
having urgent business in Garden City, he took a saddle horse
and rode three hundred miles, concluded his business in one
day, separated twenty-five domesticated buffalo from his
herd, and drove them two hundred miles to the camp in
Texas, with a view to merging them with the wild bunch
and thereby bringing the wild buffalo to civilization in peaceable fashion. Meanwhile Howard and De Cordova kept
coming northward with the wild bunch. The merger took
place peaceably enough and all went well, though strenu-
ously, until they reached the limits of the buffalo range and
got a whiff of civilization.

"We . . . followed them continually day and night for
forty-two days," says Howard, "changing horses about
twenty times. The buffalo became very thin and footsore,
and seemed so lame they could scarcely walk, yet would not
allow us to approach nearer than two hundred feet, when
they would start off and run with as much alacrity as though
nothing was the matter with them. Often we could trail them

for miles by the blood left in their tracks."

At the limit of the buffalo range, the wild ones threw up their heads, took one sniff, and as one animal, departed.

"All the cowboys on earth could not have stopped them or made them turn one hair from their path — which was back to the wilds," said Jones.

He determined to lasso each of them. It was a prodigious feat, never yet tried even by him, to rope a whole herd of grown buffalo. He captured all but four, but half of them died — just as the first cow caught had done — within twenty-four hours after being hobbled.

"They usually took fits, stiffened themselves, then dropped dead, apparently preferring death to captivity. It appeared to me they had the power to abstain from breathing."

Tragedy was stalking his Last Hunt but so was victory. With the remainder of the adult buffaloes he edged along toward Garden City, but they all died before reaching the Ranch. He did succeed, however, in bringing back seven calves.

If the triumph was marred by tragedy, the tragedy was probably unavoidable. Observers generously pointed out that if he hadn't captured the last herd, hunters would have killed it.[3] At least he lost it while trying to save it. Other aspects of the hunt were beyond question: unsparing effort, episodes measured in hundreds of miles, lavish expense, men performing like heroes in legends. . . . A report of it went straight to Capitol Hill, Washington, D.C.

"It was the greatest feat ever accomplished," flatly declared William T. Hornaday, the renowned zoologist and official of the Smithsonian Institute, in his report to the Fiftieth Session of Congress. "The skill and daring displayed in the several expeditions by Colonel Jones . . . far exceeds anything that has ever before been experienced in hunting wild game for the purpose of capturing it. Some of the results of Colonel

Jones' expeditions seem incredible. During the month of May, 1889, he with his party not only captured seven calves, but also eleven full-grown cows, of which latter, many were lassoed while rushing in their maddened speed over the prairie, then thrown and hobbled, and all in a shorter space of time than it requires to tell it. Others were actually 'rounded up', herded, and held in control until a bunch of tame buffalo was driven out to meet them. . . . This was a remarkably brilliant feat, and can be properly appreciated only by those who have themselves endeavored to capture the buffalo, and know by experience how difficult the task, to say nothing of the extreme danger in an undertaking of this character."[4]

Not only was he famous, Congress had a first-hand account of him. The poor boy from Money Creek in backwoods Illinois had come a long way indeed.

CHAPTER NINE

The Buffalo King Abroad

ONE DAY not long after the Last Hunt, Jones was in his barn pitching down hay from the mow into the mangers, when a boy appeared in the doorway with a letter.

"Stick it on the end of the fork," Jones yelled to him, at the same time reaching down as low as he could with the pitchfork. The boy obligingly impaled the letter on one of the tines, and Jones hauled it up and read it.

It was a cablegram from a wealthy Englishman named C. J. Leland, asking if ten full-grown buffalo could be delivered at Liverpool at a price upwards of ten thousand dollars. Jones cabled back in the affirmative and on the 19th of October, 1891, he loaded five pair of adult buffalo into a palace stock car at McCook, Nebraska — then a sub-center for his buffalo activities — and accompanied by his chief hired man, Wayne Boor, departed for the Old World.[1]

New York City of 1891 had seen some sights, Jumbo, the African elephant, for instance, and General Tom Thumb, the amazing midget, Jenny Lind, the Swedish nightingale, but now came Buffalo Jones and a railroad car full of wild-eyed buffalo, straight from the Wild West. The car was shunted onto the docks of the White Star Steamship Company and the next questions were: 1) How to get a buffalo bull up the gangplank of the steamer, *Runic?* 2) How to get the crowd out of the way?

"Gangplanks with sideboards six feet high and two feet thick were what were needed," said Jones, as answer to the first question, "but where on earth was I to find one?"

With the aid of a load of lumber and a carpenter a suitable gangplank was produced, and one by one the buffalo were ushered aboard, to the *ohs* and *ahs* of a crowd that ranged into hundreds. The spectators became a real problem. To avoid them, the main work of transferring buffalo from shore to ship had to be accomplished at 4 a.m. However, the glare of the electric lights—Thomas A. Edison's newly installed invention — at this early hour was such as to excite the Red Man's Cattle and they began playing hide and seek with Jones among the boxes, cotton bales, and other items of cargo lying about the dock. "One huge bull," Jones reported, "apparently concluded he required more music; so he mounted the piano box, and thrust one foot down through it. The keys he struck gave notice to all that he had gotten up to 'G.' The next animal climbed nine points higher in the scale; while the last off the car broke his rope and ran frantically over everything that chanced to be in his course, for fully an hour."[2] At last all were aboard and the gangplank hauled up.

The *Runic* was one of the biggest, fastest freight steamers of her time, and for this trip she carried more than one hundred thousand bushels of wheat, hundreds of bales of cotton, and a couple of hundred head of cattle destined for the British market. All went well for the first few days. But the morning of the twenty-eighth of October, a gale blew out of the north that made even hardened sailors pale, and soon the buffalo were deathly seasick.

Waves came piling over the sheds on the deck which housed them and left them soaking wet and freezing cold. Jones went climbing anxiously around among the sheds and pens, disregarding his personal safety, and nearly getting swept overboard as he administered to his seasick charges. He found them lying prostrate in agony, grating their teeth, rubbing their noses on the deck, rolling their eyes in pitiable fashion. He went to the captain with a protest. "These animals are worth a thousand dollars apiece to me, and they're dying of cold and seasickness!"

"Seasick buffalo? I've heard everything!" the skipper might have retorted, but with true British courtesy he offered the free use of some old tarpaulins, and these were thrown over the sheds to protect the buffalo from spray and rain. Gradually the animals found their sea legs just like the human passengers and by the voyage's end were up and around and rather enjoying themselves.

Meanwhile vast damage and loss of life were caused throughout the British Isles by the same storm. The *London Times* for November 12, 1891 reported: "The barque S. C. *Pflyger* of Bremen went ashore at St. Leonard's yesterday morning. . . . Great damage was done at Brighton. . . . At Eastbourne, great damage to property as well as loss of life was caused by the gale. . . . The crowning tragedy of the storm has been that of the ship *Benvenue* which left London on Tuesday bound for Sydney, and is now lying stranded off Sandgate, a total wreck."

Fighting his way through this wrack and ruin, Jones and his buffalo approached Liverpool, Jones quoting from Scripture (Matt. 8:24-26):

"And behold, there arose a great tempest in the sea, insomuch that the ship was covered with the waves: but he was asleep. And his disciples came to him, and awoke him, saying Lord, save us: we perish. And he saith unto them: Why are ye fearful, Oh ye of little faith? Then he arose, and rebuked the winds and the sea; and there was a great calm."

It was not always clear whether these quotations sprang from bona fide religious impulse or from a man acting the part of Bible-quoting, grass-roots, keep-your-powder-dry, Christian pioneer; perhaps the truth lay somewhere between.

Landing at Liverpool, he was met by half a dozen reporters and staff artists from London and Liverpool papers. "Tell us about catching the buffalo. Tell us about fighting Indians. Tell us your experiences in the storm." It was the sort of a situation Jones was made for. Next day the journals of the United Kingdom headlined stories and pen-pictures featuring "The Buffalo King and Some of His Subjects" who had weathered every obstacle to reach the Old World.

After delivering his animals to the purchaser in Liverpool, Jones toured Europe briefly, came back to Scotland and conferred with the Scottish cattle breeder's association — it was the Scottish Galloway strain that he was producing his cattalo from — and returned to London in time to receive an invitation to call at Buckingham Palace and meet the Prince of Wales. But affairs were pressing and he replied to the Prince that unfortunately business required his leaving immediately for New York. In token of regret he sent His Royal Highness a beautifully woven buffalo's hair rug — and a picture of C. J. Jones.

Although it was against all etiquette for a Prince of the Blood to accept such gifts, the king-to-be not only accepted

but wrote a note of thanks, which Jones received after his return to Garden City.

> Sandringham,
>
> Norfolk, 30 Dec. '91

My Dear Sir:

I am directed by the Prince of Wales to thank you for your letter of the 8th instant . . . for the handsome rug which you sent for his Royal Highness's acceptance, and which the Prince accepts with much pleasure.

The Prince has always taken the greatest interest in the American buffalo, and agrees with you in regretting the wantonness of the slayers of such a noble race.

His Royal Highness wishes you every success in the efforts you are making to reproduce this almost extinct race of animals.

I am also directed to thank you for the photograph which you have sent to his Royal Highness.

> I remain, my dear sir,
> Truly yours,
>
> (signed) D. M. Probyn
>
> General Comptroller
> and Treasurer[3]

CHAPTER TEN

Cherokee Strip

AFFAIRS were truly pressing. His creditors were demanding payment. His successes had been partly based on borrowed money — the money borrowed by a creative spender who needs more to make more to pay off more to keep growing bigger and bigger. He had gone into debt to promote Garden City and Jones, to build the Buffalo Block, stage the Great Southwest Fair, build the railroad to Dighton, develop irrigation, catch buffalo, become Colonel Jones. As long as things were booming he was solvent. But when the recession of the early nineties came along he had to pay, and he couldn't.

He was rich in possibilities, short on cash. . . . True he had lived flamboyantly beyond his means, taking risks, betting on the future. True his enemies had fed his appetite with ready cash. They were waiting for the day he would be overextended and would fall. They understood the money market and the new commercial ethic that was replacing the code of the frontier. They also sensed his contempt for them, the money men, who were taking control now that the danger was over and the battle won, and the day of the plainsmen at an end.

Martha knew too that he could not pay. Sitting in the house on Ninth Street, watching the afternoon breeze in the trees along Jones Avenue — trees he had planted — American elms — she thought of those faroff days in Troy when he had come courting her, driving out to the house with a high-wheeled buggy and highstepping black horse to take her riding on Sunday afternoon. Her hair was white now, but then the future had been bright and the air full of expectancy, she sitting in the parlor, waiting for her sweetheart, and she could hear the rattle of the buggy spokes half a mile away, and dashed upstairs to put finishing touches to her already much-finished hairdo and blue taffeta. And when he arrived she had come downstairs cool, serene, and *so* surprised to see him.

At the height of his fame he crashed. They took house, land, buffalo, even his rifle. He left town bankrupt, not a penny to his name.

"Manfully he worked," writes a neighbor, "trying to save something from the wreck for himself and his family, but finally went down to defeat as many another pioneer had done..."[1]

As many another pioneer had done, he had to hit bottom. He didn't take his licking easily. Yet there was that in him which probably would have made him leave Garden City in any case. His chief work there was done. The creation had taken place. Not much more remained but consolidation of the victory, and consolidation was not his natural role.

In middle age he would have the privilege of starting over again from scratch.

He sent Martha and the girls to Troy and struck out alone for the Gulf Coast to take advantage of certain opportunities he heard were opening. But while still in transit, word came that the "Cherokee Strip" of Oklahoma was about to be opened for settlement. He decided his chances were as good as the next man's. This was old buffalo land, his stamping ground. He would find himself a place there. It would be his first step on the Road Back.

In the never-say-die rococo prose of the period, he wrote:

Many, many years ago, I read in a newspaper: "There is a tract of country about as large as the state of Massachusetts, lying south of Kansas in the Indian Territory called in the Indian language, 'Oklahoma,' " which by interpretation means 'The Beautiful Land.' Little did I at the time think that I should be the first paleface to enter that picturesque spot for a home. A third of a century rolled on; then the newspapers announced that a portion of "the beautiful land" would be thrown open to settlement on September 16, 1893; that it was unlawful for any person to enter upon that land or even pass over it prior to that date. . . .

It was known as the "Cherokee Outlet," from the fact that it was many years ago set apart by Congress as an outlet for the Cherokee Indians to the Great Plains, where roamed millions of buffalo upon which the red men depended for food. The Government finally bought this tract of land from the rightful owners, the Cherokee Indians, and organized a "free-for-all" race to citizens of the United States, to determine who should win the prizes to be given away. . . .

There were fully eight thousand horsemen who awaited the signal at the starting-point. As the noon hour approached, they became more and more anxious; even the horses realized that a great race was in prospect, as they pawed the earth, reared and snorted in their eagerness to go. The horsemen were lined up twenty deep, one behind the other, standing side by side for a mile along the line.

I was waiting on the extreme left of the assembled throng, with two horses — my old buffalo-horse "Jubar" and the strongest and best racehorse to be had in the state of Nebraska — each one rigged with the lightest saddle possible, weighing only eight pounds each, while a strong rope about

*three feet long, attached to the ring of the cinch of each sad-
dle, held the horses together.*

Jones would change from one horse to the other without
stopping.

*The soldiers rode back and forth in front of the vast array,
to see that no one entered before the proper time. When 'high
noon' arrived, one of the soldiers discharged his gun, which all
understood to be the signal to start, and the great race was on.
It was one of the most exciting and desperate struggles ever
recorded.*

*Being on the extreme left, I started straight north for
Perry* [Perry was the village already existing in the strip which
everyone knew would develop into its metropolis.] *Having
been in so many exciting races on the Plains, and in lassoing
and driving buffalo bulls in chariot-races, I was not disturbed
in the least, consequently noticed many things which no doubt
others failed to recognize.*

*The first thing that attracted my attention after starting
was the mighty buzz and roar of the horses striking the weeds
and grass with their feet, and the rattle of their hoofs on the
hard, dry earth. It brought back most vividly the olden days,
as it was a duplicate of the sensation when in close proximity
to a buffalo stampede.*

*When about a mile out, and just after changing from my
racehorse to Jubar, I heard someone in the rear shout in
thundering tones, "Get out of the road! Get out of the road!"
I was just slacking up a little in order to cross an old trail which
had been partly grown over with grass, and fearing a deep
gutter was hidden beneath it. . . . I knew it would be dangerous to go at full speed across it.*

*When safely over, I looked back and saw a magnificent
team of horses hitched to a buckboard, and a man standing
thereon, his coat off, while he was laying on the lash unmerci-
fully. On the seat sat a young woman, with hair as red as red*

could be. Just then the horses leaped the old trail, the wheels
went deep into the gutter, then flew high in the air, which
sent the man and the woman fully four feet upward. As they
came down, both grabbed the seat, holding on for their lives.
The horses circled to the left, and it was the last I saw of the
"jehu" and his red-haired darling.

Just as I was making my second change of horses, about
two miles out, a horse ridden by the man ahead of me fell
dead. The animal I was mounting gave a tremendous leap to
clear the feet of the fallen beast, which precipitated my right
foot to the ground between my two horses. Having a good grip
on the horn of each saddle, and my left foot across the rope
which held them together, I gave a spring from the ground
while the horse was high in the air, and with a mighty pull
with my arms as he came down, I went safely into the saddle.
On looking back I shouted to the unfortunate man, "Stick
your stake and claim the land!" It was a beautiful tract, but I
afterward learned that the man's leg was broken in the fall,
and that he was sent to his Eastern home.

I learned also that the soldier who gave the signal had
his horse knocked down, and both horse and rider were tram-
pled to death by the resistless avalanche.

When within three miles of Perry, two men and a lady,
"sooners" (who had sneaked in before the gun), came dashing
up out of a ravine just to my right.

Having fresh horses they had advantage of all others. The
lady rode a jet-black charger, and was one of the most reckless
horsewomen I ever saw, and would have done credit to the
"Rough Riders." I whipped my horses severely, but could not
pass her. It was humiliating to go into Perry with a lady
leading.

I jumped to my old favorite buffalo-horse, Jubar, cut the
rope that held the horses together, and dashed past the mys-

terious equestrienne. On looking ahead, I saw the two houses which composed the city of Perry.

The trail made a detour to the left in order to descend a steep bluff, which dropped off into a deep valley. . . . Seeing nearly a mile could be saved by making straight for the houses, I left the trail and went thundering down the bluff for fear the lady would again pass me.

The grass was high on the side-hills and hid innumerable flat rocks, and Jubar was right among them before I knew of their presence. . . . About halfway down I saw he was going to land on a large flat stone which was tilted up at an angle of about forty degrees. I felt certain his feet would go from under him and he would land on his left side.

I quickly jerked my left leg up high, that I might not be caught as many are who fail to keep their legs in an advantageous position when on a falling horse; but contrary to my expectation, he appeared merely to touch the stone, just enough to send him to a good footing, and I breathed much easier when we reached the trees and brush.

In the descent I passed eight or ten horsemen, and continued the wild ride until reaching the ravine, which was about eight feet across, with a high bank close beyond. I reined the horse a little diagonally, and he made one of his famous leaps and passed along without checking.

I then crossed the main stream and ascended an almost perpendicular bank about forty feet high, which was accomplished by the horse running up obliquely while I ran at his side until reaching the level, when I was again on his back.

In ascending I passed the last two competitors, and it appears to me the fastest race I ever made was the last mile to the claim adjoining Perry on the south where I stuck my flag and claimed the land as a homestead. I then proceeded to the "city" arriving there before all others except "sooners."[2]

He had won. He was on the Road Back.

CHAPTER ELEVEN

Arctic Adventure

HE DID NOT BRING Martha and the girls to Oklahoma. This venture was too raw for them. Besides, he was ready for new steps on the comeback trail. And he was by nature the man without women, adventuring on frontiers alone. Not that he wasn't happily married. By all accounts the union was extremely happy. But it just wasn't the Age of Togetherness.

He went to Texas and sold a group of Beaumont business men on the idea of building a railroad to Port Bolivar at the mouth of Galveston Bay. Somehow he acquired a right-of-way for construction of this road; perhaps it was through charm, through being the "Colonel," because the fame of his buffalo-saving exploits had by no means died, and Texas favors flamboyant men. Whatever the reason, they threw in with him, and construction of the line started. For a time all went well and to hear Jones tell it, they would all be millionaires in a few months, but the rains came, the right-of-way got water-logged, the scheme bogged down, and The Populist Railway Company — named after the popular political party of the time — went bankrupt after seventy-five miles of line had been constructed and sold out to the Santa Fe.[1]

Colonel Jones moved on to greener pastures. As a bread-and-butter job he took a position as sergeant-at-arms to the Oklahoma Territorial Legislature, a semi-honorary position that did not pay much but enabled him to meet the right people. However, he was hungry for greater glory.

On the twelfth of June, 1897, he left for the Arctic Circle to capture a wild musk ox. Fantastic? Yes, quite.

If asked to explain, he might have said something like this: "I'd made a little out of my Oklahoma property, lost most of it in Texas, dickered around on Omaha, sold some buffalo in McCook, Nebraska, and with what was left to finance me, I saw how at one step I might redeem myself in my own eyes and the eyes of the world, for my failure in Garden City, my failure in Texas, my comparatively insignificant showing in Oklahoma, and become once again Buffalo Jones, the nationally famous, the champion. Because, you see, the eyes of the world were on the North. This was the great age of arctic exploration, the Pole not yet attained, Amundsen, Peary, Nansen active. . . . And the musk ox, the mysterious Northern animal, as yet uncaptured. The musk ox represented in the popular mind the life of an unknown region which repelled human exploration. Some people even thought that like the unicorn it did not exist. . . . And through my friends and acquaintances, Hornaday, Grinnell, and others, I hoped to bring back remunerative specimens for museums and zoos. I also wanted to investigate the possibility of establishing a silver fox farm on an island in the Bering Sea if circumstances permitted."

He went by rail to Winnipeg, Canada, and then to Edmonton. There he bought seven shepherd dogs, fifteen-hundred pounds of flour, four-hundred pounds of bacon, beans, oatmeal, coffee, tea, sugar, and a rubber life preserver for strapping around himself while he floated northward down the rivers that led to Great Slave Lake and the musk ox range. He planned to travel by boat to the edge of the Arctic Circle, and from there on foot and with dog sled to his destination.

"When I loaded a lumber wagon at Edmonton," he wrote, "I found it would carry but little more than half my outfit. Another team was secured and I climbed upon one of the wagons with a dog-whistle in my mouth, as it took continual calling to keep the little dogs together."[2]

Edmonton residents thought this man crazy, whistling to his little dogs, going into the Far North by himself, utterly ignorant, they thought, of what lay ahead of him.

The fourth day, through mud, rain, mosquitoes, and large horseflies (known in that country as 'bulldogs' on account of their propensity for blood), he reached Athabasca landing, on the Athabasca River, one hundred miles to the north.

Now he had a mere six hundred miles by river and lake to his destination. He built his own boat out of lumber obtained at Athabasca Landing. It was twenty-five feet long, nine feet in the beam, with a capacity of five thousand pounds.

"At sunrise the dogs and I weighed anchor and started off. The day was an ideal one, and I flattered myself I should find easy sailing, but before going five miles discovered that my craft was entirely too large to be successfully managed by one man, and that it was drifting dangerously near the shore; while immediately ahead was a treacherous shoal. The Athabasca River is noted for the number of these shoals and rapids, and to steer clear of them requires constant vigilance and good seamanship. I managed, with the aid of a large oar, working it first on one side and then on the other, to pass safely over.

"About three o'clock in the afternoon a terrific rainstorm overtook me, and I was thoroughly drenched. I protected my supplies by covering them with a tarpaulin, but did not dare to crawl under it myself, as the wind was constantly drifting the boat out of its course. As soon as one of these peculiar tempests cleared away, another would follow in quick succession, and they continued until sundown, when I pulled to the shore for the purpose of camping. Just as I was going to land I cast my eyes toward the bank, and saw a group of forty squaws and children intently gazing at me.

"I immediately turned into the current again, upon which the Indians set up a lamentation. They had expected I would certainly land, and it would be a grand opportunity for them to beg supplies.

"After passing a bend of the stream, and now being out of sight of the beggarly savages, I turned to the shore and tied up for the night. The first act after fastening my boat securely was to loose seven shepherd dogs and one bloodhound, that I had kept chained for over a week to prevent the Indians from stealing them; consequently they were very savage. One of them I had purchased from a half-breed boy, who informed me that the animal was a mixture of collie and spaniel; that he was a 'scrapper' from 'way back.'

"The moment I turned him loose he stationed himself on the bank of the river, and as fast as the other dogs landed he 'went for' them individually, and gave them such a shaking that their howling soon informed the Indians in the whole region where I had camped.

"Another storm was brewing, and I hastily set fire to a pine log, made a cup of tea, spread my robes under a clump of trees, and after partaking of the frugal meal, was soon wrapped in my blanket, listening to the pattering of the rain that had commenced to fall on my rubber tarpaulin.

"The Indians, very shortly after I had retired, found their way to my camp, but 'Scrapper,' as I called him, led the whole pack of dogs in a break for the intruders, which I encouraged by 'sicking' them on, and in a few minutes the redskins incontinently dashed away through the brush and left me to sleep peacefully."

Jones floated down the Athabasca, shooting rapids, dodging rocks and Indians, guiding the boat as he felt a boat ought to be guided. He was not an experienced boatman but he had boated on the Illinois streams when a boy and had the general know-how of the frontiersman who is at home on land or water. Will power did the rest. He forged ahead through rapids, rainy weather, and inexperience, till he met an obstacle of a new sort.

Crossing Lake Athabasca he reached Fort Smith, a Hudson Bay Company post on the Slave River between Athabasca and Great Slave Lakes, and there he was invited by the Indians to a council of "great chiefs." The council turned out to be a collection of disreputable-looking characters in castoff clothes, sitting crosslegged in a circle under the trees, and not very glad to see him. They solemnly informed him by means of an interpreter that they opposed his entrance into the North.

"If you take out animals alive, it will offend the Great Spirit," they said. "All our game will leave. The musk ox is sacred to us," they added, "if it leaves, other game will follow."[3]

Jones listened politely till the interpreters finished, then told the assemblage that he had come three thousand miles not to destroy but to preserve the very animals that they were engaged in killing, that they should learn to domesticate and propagate them in the manner ordained by the Great Spirit in the White Man's Bible, and then they would not be in danger of starving. He failed to convince the Indians. They failed to convince him. Thereby developed much trouble. The meeting broke up in complete misunderstanding, and the Chippewas, Crees, and Slaves who comprised the council went away shaking their heads and planning in secret how to stop Jones.

CHAPTER TWELVE

White Wolves

THEIR FIRST MEASURE against him was the boycott. At the Fort Smith portage, where for sixteen miles he must rely on Indians to carry his outfit around rapids, he was informed there was no one to help him. He was taboo. His cargo was hot. He was further informed that he ought to go home.

He replied that he would go where he pleased, a statement that took some nerve, seeing it was made in the face of three hostile Indian tribes; and perhaps feeling a bit lonely on the strength of it, he teamed up with a fighting Scotsman, a "bra chappie" named John R. Rea. Rea, an independent trader-trapper, was bucking the Hudson's Bay Company's monopoly as well as the elements and Indians. He was the kind of man Jones was looking for, built like a bulldozer, handlebar mustaches down to his shoulders, and the nerve that went with that kind of hair.

"I want to do some trapping up toward the head of Great Slave Lake," he said quietly, "I'll throw in with you."

They had a partnership.

On August seventeenth they got their first view of Great

Slave Lake, an inland sea, stretching beyond the horizon between rocky shores on which grew short trees.

There I met an old half-breed, from whom I learned that many years ago the Cree Indians of the south had come to this far-away country, Jones wrote, *captured the natives, and carried them back to their own villages, where they were doomed to a hopeless bondage of slavery. The raids of the southern tribes were of such frequent occurrence and so successful in results, that the name "Slaves" became the appellation of the northern tribes, and from them the lake and the river were given their names by the first white men who entered the region.*[1]

Jones also found trouble brewing on the shores of Great Slave Lake. The Indians had sent messengers ahead of him, commanding their people not to assist him in any way.

I was compelled to build a boat suitable for traversing the dangerous and turbulent waters of the lake, and had only the assistance of my friend, Mr. Rea, and of a half-breed Indian who bade defiance of the traditions of his tribe and the dictation of the headmen. There was no large timber in the vicinity, and the only resource was the driftwood. We were obliged to follow the shore for many miles before any logs were found suitable for our purpose. Then we had to raft them to our camp and saw them up by hand, to get lumber to construct the boat. All this took valuable time, and before the boat was ready for launching, the weather was growing colder and more disagreeable.[2]

He had planned to reach the head of the lake by September tenth and to start home by the first of October. If unable to locate the musk ox in that period, he would remain in the North and send word to Ft. Resolution, a Hudson's Bay post in Slave Lake, by shepherd dog, to be forwarded to Edmonton and the outside world by dog-train. Meanwhile his human problems increased.

What surprised me more than anything else was that some of the Hudson Bay Company's officials prompted the savages to take the action which they did, particularly Dr. McKey, of Chippewayan. He came out boldly, and advised the Indians in my presence not to give me assistance in any form; and when he saw they could not turn me back, he took it upon himself to read me, from a volume of statutes, the law in relation to killing game in the Northwest Territory, notifying me that if I violated it he would "prosecute me to the bitter end."[3]

To Jones this was a challenge.

On the sixth of September my boat was completed. The little yacht was a "daisy"; twenty-two feet long and six feet in the beam. The wind and rain were strong from the east. Northeast was our course, yet we were obliged to go five miles westward to round a point that encloses a bay. What an experience we had after leaving Fort Resolution on the sixth! I had often been told of the perils and hazards of the "Great Spirit lake"; that it was the most treacherous of all waters; that the storms rose when least expected; the waves so short and choppy that no boat could be constructed that would withstand the tempests, and many were the bones of human skeletons that strewed the bottom, where bottom was to be found; that in numerous places no bottom had ever been discovered. . . .

Guided by friendly Indians who defied the ban against them, Jones and Rea pushed ahead.

On the eighth of September came a howling blizzard from the north. . . . The wind was blowing a perfect gale, but the Indians who accompanied us agreed to make the venture, and at four o'clock we set sail. After going about five miles the wind shifted due east, which was almost a headwind. . . . Then the heavens began to roll and tumble; the waves commenced to emulate them, while the gale increased in fierceness, piling the billows up in great black masses. Then came a tempest of wind with increased velocity, heaping them higher and higher, until they seemed to reach the low, black clouds above them. What a night it was! In the stern sat 'Old Siena' (the Indian had passed the allotted three score and ten), guiding our frail bark, as the mighty waves tossed us about like a straw. The old fellow would occasionally emit a groan, which seemed as if it might be his last; at times I could not see his form, crouched down under the inky blackness surrounding us. All the others could do was to bail water as rapidly as possible, and by herculean exertions we managed to keep our craft afloat on the angry surf.[4]

Threading their way through a maze of islands, some no more than rocks, some extending for miles, some six feet above the water, some a thousand, they traversed Great Slave Lake for three hundred miles, and stumbled onto the ruins of cabins built by Captain Black of the Royal British Navy, sixty-five years before while in search of the lost explorer Sir John Franklin. Apparently no one had visited the spot for sixty-five years. Not far from this rather ghostly site and near the head of the lake, they selected a location on rising ground close to shore and made camp. They scouted the country but found no sign of musk ox and realized they would have to spend the winter if they were to accomplish their mission; so they got out saws, cut timber, built a cabin sixteen by twenty, while curious half-starved Indians gathered and begged for food.

They employed some of them to build the cabin, rafting logs five miles on the lake, and carrying them the hundred yards from the beach to the building site. They worked hard and fast to make a shelter before the first storm.

On the second of October they moved in, and that night a blizzard swept down while they snuggled comfortably by the fire.

"Jones," said Rea, "I don't reckon you figured on this

when you left sunny Oklahoma. It may snow from now till May. You prepared to be patient?"

"Rea, I'd like to get you out on the plains some time. I was caught out in that blizzard of '86 while hunting antelope, and I firmly believe that though the storms may start up here, they don't *really get rolling* till they get down to us."

Rea said, "I'd feel better if we had a door on this cabin but blankets will do."

"Especially buffalo robes," said Jones, "warmest thing this side of hell, Rea."

"Next to the snowshoe rabbit, I'd bet."

They argued while the snow fell.

It snowed for a week. They had as Rea said no lumber for doors or glass for windows, so they used blankets, which made things a bit drafty inside, but for the Far North it was comfort. And Jones had his buffalo robes and Rea his rabbit blanket.

Inspired by the shining sun after a week's storm, they fitted the window with a white shirt, which let in a maximum of light and added a gayer touch. Rea took canvas they'd been using as a tent and made a harness for the four big sled-dogs they'd procured. He also built a sled and soon was hauling plenty of good dry wood.

Storms continued throughout October. The lake froze. The fish left. The poor starving Indians begged for food. The seasonal caribou migration had not taken place and they were in desperate plight.

"Look what happens when people refuse to make a partnership with nature and domesticate animals," Jones said.

"These are the Yellow Knives," Rea replied, "worst off of all the tribes. They inhabit the farthest-north fringes of Indian civilization, pushed up here by their stronger relatives, I reckon."

The Yellow Knives were extraordinarily inept at getting a living and totally lacking in the charm and dignity which often characterized the Plains Indians Jones knew.

One of them, however, touched his heart. She was a girl named Emma, twelve years old, who became their interpreter. Once during a blizzard Jones went to the lake for water. As he reached the bank, he saw Emma, dressed in a one-piece garment, step from the lake with a birch-bark pail of water. The load was too much and she slipped, spilling water all over herself. It instantly froze. There she stood, sheathed in ice, arms reaching for help, head bare, without shoes or stockings, just a ragged frock of caribou skins to cover her nakedness.

Jones picked up her pail and by signs told her he would get the water and carry it to the top of the bank.

What really infuriated him was when he got to the girl's tent and found her father and two grown brothers, strapping fellows, lounging in the tepee on caribou rugs, by the fire, wood for which had been chopped and hauled over the ice a mile or two by Emma's sister, aged fourteen.

"An Indian of the Far North treats his woman worse than his dog," Jones declared. "A woman can work both summer and winter, while the dog works only in winter. I've seen women, half sick, barely able to stand, out stretching a tepee in temperatures of 50 and 70 below, while the men sat idling in our cabin from morning till night, only getting out when we kicked them out. . . . If we sent a bowl of hot gruel to a squaw we knew to be sick, a buck would nine times out of ten intervene and eat the food himself."

These were the people who told him he must not hunt the sacred musk ox for fear of offending the divine spirit. It just didn't make sense.

One morning he opened the cabin door to see thirty boys and girls staring at him. They ran away when he appeared. They had never seen a white man before, nor had Jones seen their like. A whole new tribe had moved in during the night.

When one brave youngster dared look back in midflight, Jones beckoned. The boy stopped. A few other brave ones stopped too. The rest scampered on toward the tepees. Jones stepped inside the cabin, came out with two handfuls of sugar. Putting a lump in his mouth he said,

"Nazou! Nazou!" (Good! Good!)

The boy came near and shyly held out a hand. These Indians had never eaten sugar although they were familiar with salt, which was abundant in some of the marshes roundabout. The child put the sugar in his mouth. His eyes popped. Turning to the others he proclaimed,

"Sweet salt! Sweet salt!"

From then on Jones was pestered by youngsters asking for sweet salt, and ingratiated himself with the younger generation by doling out an occasional ration, but it was his standing with the adults that was worrying him. Much of his plan depended on the good will and cooperation of the Indians. So far, these tribes appeared not to have heard the bad word concerning him. He hoped his luck would hold.

By the twentieth of October the outlook was not good. Meat was almost gone. Hundreds of Indians were camped roundabout begging for food. They would have stolen everything they could lay hands on if it hadn't been for Rea. Jones tended to be trusting and sympathetic at first. But Rea, who had wintered in the Arctic before, was not so friendly.

One day a big Indian got uppity. He came into the cabin

and kicked over the bread pan. Rea hit him under the right ear and laid him cold. Then, to revive him, Rea choked him till his eyes bulged like peeled onions — while the other Indians looked on respectfully.

A couple of days later another visitor arrived with fifteen or twenty braves to back him. Jones and Rea were eating dinner — watched by a room full of hungry savages. The newcomer stamped in as if he owned the place and, without so much as a how-de-do, grabbed a cup of tea and drank it.

To condone such behaviour was to invite disaster. Rea and Jones exchanged glances. The arrogant newcomer then stuck his dirty hand into the pot and pulled out a hunk of meat. Jones jumped on him, wrung his neck, yanked the meat out of his mouth, sent him spinning for the door, and took the meat-pot into the corner, though still hesitating to clear the room of Indian spectators and declare war.

Turning to Rea, Jones demanded: "Are you going to stand for that?"

"No," laughed Rea, "but I wanted to see if *you* would."

They were sizing each other up, partners under pressure.

"Okay," said Jones, "let's go to work."

They used their fists, knocking Indians right and left. United, the Indians could have wiped them out. But they never got organized. Jones and Rea soon had the cabin to themselves.

Before starting the hunt it was necessary to wait till the dead of winter when the musk ox would be at the southern-most limit of their range, which was several hundred miles north of the cabin.

In November Rea made a scouting trip accompanied by one Indian — twenty-three days and he came upon the track

of a musk ox bull, so fresh it sent the shepherd dogs into a
spasm of barking, but he lost it in an oncoming blizzard.

Out of food, half-frozen, he returned to find Jones sitting
before a roaring fire, dressed carcasses of twenty-five caribou
stowed away in the roof, plus fifty or sixty huge whitefish,
plenty of hot biscuits baked and a large pot of beans smoking.
Jones' prowess with the rifle had secured meat for the starving
Indians, too, and his mercy had been such that when a tribe,
during the height of the hunger period, moved off in search
of game and abandoned an old sick squaw, he took the squaw
on his own sled and traveled sixty miles through storms to
return her to her people, only to find them gone.   So he
brought her back and gave her a home in the cabin until he
could build her a tepee nearby. She made moccasins and
snowshoes for him and for Rea and they fed her all that
winter.

The Indians had never met with this kind of compassion.
It did not fit the ruthless pattern of survival that characterized the North. Jones the preserver was at work again, in
the snow of the Arctic as in the nursery at Troy and in the
arid Panhandle, making things grow and encouraging life.

Late February came. Now the musk ox would surely be
at the southern limit of their range, and there was bustle of
preparation in the Indian camp. The men were busy making
sleds and snowshoes, collecting meat and fish and running
races to harden their muscles, because to drop out of a hunt
was a disgrace. The women were tanning skins, making moccasins, chopping and hauling wood, feeling strong, thanks to
the meat Jones killed for them. The bucks tinkered with sleds
and made the frames of snowshoes, and talked of the meat
they would bring home.

Jones and Rea said nothing about capturing a musk ox alive. As far as these Indians knew, it was just a hunt.

The partners also realized that if they left their cabin and supplies to the tender mercies of the Indians remaining while they were gone, they wouldn't have a scrap of food — and probably not a cabin — left when they got back. So Jones rigged up a burglar-proof device. He fastened his Colt revolver to a post in the middle of the cabin floor, breast high, and aimed it straight at the door, tied a cord to its trigger, ran the cord through a pulley attached to the door casing, and fastened the cord to the doorlatch and — having called the Indians to witness — pulled the cord.

The bullet struck the door casing breast high and made splinters fly. The spectators got the point.

Toward the end of February they called for the Indians planning to accompany them to assemble at the cabin.[5] They expected a dozen or two of the best braves complete with sleds. Instead two appeared. One of these backed out and only Sousie Barromie, a small wiry fellow of thirty-five, remained.

With Sousie, they left early on the morning of February 28, 1898, the sun rising clear over Great Slave Lake, coming from behind mountain ranges where they intended to go.

They had two sleds, four dogs to each sled, and the seven shepherd dogs running loose. Mushing easily on their snowshoes over the firm-packed snow, they went across a corner of the frozen lake and struck into the northeast. All day they broke trail through small birch groves, across many small lakes. It was extremely cold. At sunset they made camp in a clump of timber, next day pushing on again, cutting tepee poles from the last trees, and in the afternoon emerged into the "land of little sticks" — the end of timber — where the trees twisted and stunted by the winds from the barrens, are no bigger than sticks.

A blizzard caught them. For two days they lay in the tepee while the wind howled. At midnight of the second night, the storm having subsided, Jones heard the dogs whining. He thought Indian dogs from some nearby camp were on the prowl.

Don, his pet shepherd, screamed suddenly. Jones jumped up. It was still so stormy that he hesitated to go out, knowing that as soon as he did his bed would be filled with snow that sifted through the tent. But outside the dog was crying pitifully. Grabbing the axe, he stepped out. As he did so, Don ran against him, and cowered between his legs. He realized that all the dogs were circling the tent at terrific speed.

Behind them raced a white creature — *a whole series of white creatures — wolves — white Arctic wolves.*

CHAPTER THIRTEEN

Nazzula! Nazzula!

"REA, HAND ME THE GUN!" he shouted.

A white wolf lunged at the dog between his knees and he struck at it with the axe but missed.

Don bravely seized the huge beast by the hind leg. With a snap the wolf had the dog in its jaws and started off into the storm. Jones felt the gun thrust into his hands by Rea.

He ran, staggering in the fresh snow and half-blinded by the flying flakes, following the disappearing shape of the white wolf. The wolf was slowed by the weight of Don in its jaws, and Jones got almost close enough to touch him with the rifle, then fired. The animal dropped Don and sprang at him. He threw up the rifle just in time. The teeth grated on the barrel, locked tight, then slowly relaxed.

Jones knew he'd had a close one but not till long after did he know how close.

They took the dogs into the tepee, watched till day-break, then struck out for the north. No wolves were in sight but Sousie Barromie said the pack would follow.

All day they mushed through soft snow. The storm had

not completely subsided, and they must keep moving or perish. They passed a vast herd of caribou and killed three. The wolves were howling on their trail. They left two caribou for the wolves, hoping to rid themselves of their pursuers, and pushed on, again taking the dogs into the tent at night. At daybreak the wolves were snapping outside the canvas. They drove them off with gunfire, killing two.

The wind was blowing a gale from the northeast as they started. All day they kept watching for signs of musk ox, the wolves hovering near. The wind grew colder and colder. They had reached the southern limit of the musk ox range, and about noon of the fourth of March, in the teeth of the gale, they discovered their first track. It was cloven-footed and looked like the track of a domestic bull.

Sousie Barromie scouted ahead and found a herd of six musk ox bulls and hurried back to report. Jones went with him and saw six black hairy creatures moving away over the white landscape. They looked like full-grown cattle with very long hair, and curly down-drooping horns, flattened at the base.

Sousie began talking to them in a loud voice, and they ran into a compact group, looking in all directions for the source of the sound. Sousie kept talking.[1]

Jones and Rea joined Sousie in hiding behind a large rock. Sousie continued to talk to the musk ox. He told them in a clear voice to keep quiet, because they were going to be killed. "It's a lot better to be killed this way than to be dragged down by a pack of wolves and painfully torn to pieces," he pointed out, easing the victims' final moments. And he added that the Great Spirit wished them to die, and that no more of them would die than the Great Spirit determined; and having so informed the musk ox, he motioned to Jones to shoot.

The three men fired almost at the same time. Three musk

ox fell; two more fell as Rea and Jones fired again.

Then they inspected the kill. The musk ox bulls were nearly as big as cattle. Big-boned. Chests were wide as Percheron horses'. Hindquarters resembled those of buffaloes. The tails were short but the horns were massive, expanding out across the forehead at the base, then curving downward outward, and up, with a spread of twenty-five to thirty inches. The meat on the hams came well down, and the fat was white as marble. The fur was long, compact, and fine as silk, and so tough Jones could hardly break it when he twisted it around his finger. On neck and sides it hung so low it had swept the ground when the musk ox walked. Underneath the outer hair and close to the skin was the wooly coat of very fine soft light brown hair, so dense that neither cold nor moisture could penetrate it.

Dissecting the stomach, Jones found grass and moss. But nowhere did he find a musk gland. The musky odor they had all smelled at the first excited run-together of the musk ox had now disappeared, nor did any seem to cling to the carcasses.

A secondary reason for the hunt was to collect museum specimens, so Jones skinned out the heads and carcasses and boned out the flesh of one animal. He found the anatomy more like a goat's than a cow's, and gave up the idea he'd been cherishing of crossing the musk ox with domestic cattle or buffalo. But he continued steadfast in his determination to bring a musk ox back alive — a calf, if he could find one.

That night it sounded as if all the wolves in the Arctic had congregated outside the tent. At daylight he looked out and saw the ground practically covered with them. Some were as near as seventy-five feet. With the exception of a few blacks and greys, all were white. They sat on their haunches in ranks and groups, waiting. He reached back inside the tent, got his Winchester, and slipped it through the opening in the canvas, and selecting a huge white wolf, fired. The wolf hobbled off, then fell. The others drew back.

Going out to examine what he supposed was his kill, Jones was amazed to see the wolf spring up and hobble off on three legs, one forefoot hanging limp. He fired again. The wolf fell, this time dead. He set about skinning. Then he saw to his horror that the wolf's right forefoot, the one he had wounded and which had hung limp, was gone. The hunger-crazed brute had chewed it clean off.

His astonishment was even greater when he found that the five musk ox carcasses had not been touched by the starved wolf pack. Why? Why should the wolves pass up the dead musk ox and wait for the living men? An eerie sense that the Great Spirit did, as Sousie Barromie said, play a part in their affairs, entered Jones' mind.

With sunrise the wolves dispersed. Rea announced it was time for breakfast, and they sat down to musk ox steak. There was no taint of musk. It was just like delicious T-bone cut from good wild beef.

Guided by Sousie they traveled north-northeast for four days, crossing the Great Fish River, a tributary of Eliott Bay and the Arctic Ocean, and reaching a latitude of approximately sixty-six degrees, but saw no more oxen. On the return trip, Sousie got lost, but Jones' sense of direction held true, and he led them back to the fringes of timber. The wolves did not follow them there.

Now they relaxed and built a heaping fire, cooked their meat, then Jones faced up to the hardest task he'd met yet: telling Sousie they weren't going home, they were going back for more musk ox. Even so, he couldn't bring himself to say they were going back to capture calves. He knew the reaction such an announcement would bring.

"Sousie," he said, "we want you to guide us again. We want more *ageter.*"[2]

The Indian's eyes rolled white, and he exclaimed angrily: "Why can you be so mad as to wish to go again and freeze and be eaten by white wolves? Haven't you killed already enough musk ox? I told the oxen when they stood still for me that we would kill only what we needed." He looked sternly on Jones and Rea and they could not meet his eyes. "I have told the Great Spirit a lie!"

Say what he might, Jones couldn't persuade Sousie to change his mind.

"Well there's an Injun for you," said Rea, tossing another chunk on the fire, as Sousie, still shaking his head, cracked the whip over his dog team and started home.

Jones shrugged. He wasn't happy. But he couldn't turn back now.

"At least he's taking our musk ox heads and skins home with him. That will save our dogs the burden."

"And he's got his share of the meat. That will keep the hungry mob quiet."

They heard Sousie's muttering dwindling off into the darkness: "Nazzula! Nazzula!" (No good! No good!)[3]

CHAPTER FOURTEEN

Musk Ox Calves

WITH SOME MISGIVINGS, which neither of them put into words, Jones and Rea struck off alone.

For two days they traveled east-northeast through a blinding snowstorm. On the third day they reached a tributary of the Dubawnt River, the weather cleared and they followed the stream in a northeasterly direction until night and, as Jones recorded in his journal, ... *camped in a large cañon at the mouth of the Doobaunt [sic] proper, just north of the lake of the same name. Here were dead spruce trees, some a foot in diameter. Next day we found the river trending to the east, and abandoned it where it empties into Chesterfield inlet, taking a northerly direction.*

Just before leaving the river we came to a camp of Eskimos containing twenty men and three women. They were dressed entirely in furs, and looked robust and healthy. I supposed they were Indians, until I came in close proximity to them; but when I saw holes in the under lips of the men, with ivory buttons inserted, I knew they were not Indians, but Eskimos. I attempted to pass around them, at which one

*of the old men struck himself on the breast and uttered
some words which I interpreted to be, "Me good Indian!" He
had evidently been among the whalers of the Arctic ocean.
I stopped, and repeating the signal, turned toward the little
fire they surrounded.*

*As soon as Mr. Rea arrived he remarked, "Well, I guess
we have run into a hornet's nest." I answered, "Yes, no
doubt." We had a pot of tea made, and invited them to drink,
and to eat meat. They certainly drank tea, but touched the
meat lightly, as they had an abundance of their own.*

*Apparently, they seemed determined to drink tea all
the afternoon; so, to rid ourselves of them, we gave them
about a pound of it and a sheet-iron bucket to boil water in.
This seemingly satisfied them, and we hastily drove away.
They ran after us, but we paid no attention to their chatter,
not stopping until late at night. While among them I noticed
shotguns and a few small breech-loading English rifles. That
evening we found where they had made walls of blocks of
snow to shelter them from the piercing storm that held us
so close to the tepee.*

*On the 16th and 17th we passed through some of the
most rugged and God-forsaken country that I have ever seen.
The caribou were abundant, and we never lacked for meat. We
saw a few jack-rabbits, and numberless wolves; several black
wolves were also seen, and many tracks of the Arctic fox,
but the animal is so shy we never saw one.*[1]

On the eighteenth they saw droppings of the musk ox,
and late in the evening spotted three old bulls but did not
disturb them. The next day was clear and warm and before
they had gone far they crossed tracks of a dozen musk oxen,
made that morning. They stopped and Rea scouted the tracks,
soon returning and reporting the herd just ahead. They
slipped forward, got behind some rocks and counted six
cows, five or six young animals, but only one yearling. As

yearlings were what they wanted, they decided to make this
herd a test case in terms of behaviour, rather than a serious
objective, so stood up and walked directly toward the oxen,
who promptly came to meet them, coming so close "we could
see their eyes bulging out." Finally one of the cows gave a
snort and away they all went, running southward against
the wind.

Jones and Rea went back to their sleds and drove to the
shelter of a high ridge of stone a mile to the east and pitched
camp, determining to circle around for game. While they were
pitching the tent their shepherd dogs kept barking and trying to get loose — they usually kept them chained to the
sled — and Jones climbed to the crest of the nearby ridge, and,
looking over, saw a herd of musk ox just beyond.

In it were animals of all sizes. Just what they wanted.
Heart beating hard, he slipped back to the tepee where Rea
was boiling tea. They ate and drank quickly, then opened the
bag of ropes, swivels, hobbles, etc., and got them ready, sling-
ing their lassos around their necks, also a long half-inch-thick
rope intended for an anchor line, and carrying their guns.

By the time they reached the crest of the ridge, under
this heavy load, Jones was out of breath and for one of the
few times in his life had to call a halt and rest. He glanced over
to see how Rea was taking it. The Scot was cool as cool.

I had supposed he would get very much excited, Jones
wrote in his account of the trip, *not having had the experience
of myself in catching buffalo and other wild animals, but I
could not detect in him a motion that evinced the least nerv-
ousness. Long before leaving our cabin on the Great Slave
Lake we had our plans well matured as to the manner in
which we were to capture the animals we were after. We were
to run up to within a hundred yards of them, under cover if
possible, and shoot down all but two cows and the yearlings.
We were then to break the hind legs of those cows, so they*

could not run, but stay and fight. We expected the yearlings would keep close to their mothers until we could lasso and tie every one.

It went very much as they had planned, except that at the last minute, just as they were creeping into position behind some rocks, five dogs came tearing by, headed straight for the musk ox. They had left the shepherds tied to the sled believing the sled dogs would stay as usual, but Scrapper, most energetic of the shepherds, had slipped his collar and now led the pack full-tilt toward the quarry. This added a complicating factor. Jones swore in the strongest language he ever used, "hell and damnation," but it had no effect. The musk ox crowded together, then split into two groups, under the dogs' attack, and ran off in opposite directions.

But luck was not totally against the hunters: with one group ran all five of the calves, and only three adult animals — two cows and a two-year-old.

Two shots sounded and one cow and the two-year-old sank to the snow.

"Break the legs of that last cow!" Jones yelled. "Shoot, Rea." Jones had had a touch of snowblindness and was wearing "smoked" glasses and felt that under these circumstances Rea was the better shot.

Rea did not disappoint him. The second shot dropped the running cow to her hock joints. "Cruel," Jones records, "true, but such acts are always pardonable in the interests of science."

The five calves milled in bewilderment about the crippled cow, and Jones unslung his lasso. These would be the first musk oxen ever brought into captivity.[2]

The pretty, black, glossy creatures were terribly excited, and hovered around the old cow like a brood of goslings around a fighting gander when danger surrounds them.

When I arrived at throwing distance one yearling stood alongside the cow, his head close to hers. I whirled the noose in the air till it fairly hissed, and let it fly for the prize. The rope went fairly well to the mark, but a little too far, and hooked over the point of the old cow's right horn, where it hung up. The little dog (Scrapper) was biting at the heels of the animals, which kept them twisting around in all directions, while our sled-dogs stood in front of the old cow, keeping up such a continual barking that it held her steadfast facing them.

I paused a moment; just then Scrapper nipped the heels of the yearling I was after, which caused it to make a bound forward right into the loop, knocking it from the cow's horn, when with a quick jerk I fastened it safely around its neck.

So they got the first one and the others were treated similarly, hog-tied and left on the snow, till only one remained to be caught. By this time Jones was so nearly exhausted he could hardly stand, and the dogs were making things hot for the last yearling. Sometimes it would be fighting them, sometimes running around the old cow, Jones throwing and missing, until finally Scrapper nipped it so sharply it ran to Jones for protection. "I was sure it had selected me to take vengeance on, and made ready to jump aside to let it pass, but it ran to my left side, and as it did so I whirled around and laid the noose over its head without throwing it at all."

Afterward he was so tired that for one of the few times in his life he had to stop and ask for help. Rea went to camp to fetch him some tea. Maybe the reason for his exhaustion was the northern latitude, maybe it was his fifty-five years, or maybe it was the unspoken misgiving that had been troubling him perhaps more than he knew. In any event, while Rea was gone to prepare the tea he had time to size up the catch, "and it was a very interesting hour of my life, when I could quietly stand and see every twinkle of their eyes. The long shaggy fleece that covered the little creatures was of a browner color than that on the old bulls. They looked more like doll animals than real live musk oxen. Their short legs made me liken them to a little Shetland pony colt, as compared with a race-horse. They had a tuft of long hair on the shoulders and also on their necks. The males had small sharp horns that pointed straight out from the side of the head and protruded about an inch through the thick mat of hair; while the females' horns were not visible at all, yet could be felt beneath the clump of hair. Though they seemed diminutive, they were deceiving in size and weight of their bodies."

After the refreshing drink of tea, he and Rea began to gather up the captives. They took a long rope and tied five loops in it about twelve feet apart and fastened each end to large rocks and pulled it tight. From each of the five loops a short rope was attached, at the end of which was a swivel, which in turn was fastened to the small rope around the animal's neck, so that it could be tied without tangling or choking.

Jones had handled buffalo calves so often that these were comparatively easy. They pitched camp nearby and watched the calves frisking on the line until the sun went down. With sunset, their pleasant interlude came to an end.

Rea swore softly as he heard it: the first baying of the wolf pack, just over the ridge.

"No sleep for us tonight," Jones said grimly, bracing himself to face still one more crisis. The tea had hardly cured the weariness which attended his protracted exertion in the northern climate and was coupled with the uneasy feeling of having, perhaps, done not quite the right thing by Sousie Barromie and the Indians' religious beliefs. On the plains, where he had more than once violated the customs and mores of the natives, his guiding spirit had been that of necessity. But now he had come north for purposes of glory and profit, not survival, and come into the musk ox range under false pretenses, and could not rid his mind of the figure of Sousie

Barromie disappearing into the dusk uttering the ominous words, "Nazzula, nazzula!" However, certain necessities demanded action.

"Rea, we'll have to watch these calves all night if need be."

"Let's set the dogs lose. It might keep the wolves off as long as daylight holds, and give us a chance to rest a little more."

"All right. We're going to need all our strength before morning, that's sure!"

The wolves were drifting over the ridges into the hollow where they stood. In the dusk they looked like the scouts of an invading army. The dogs, tied to the sled, bristled and whined. The musk ox calves stopped their frisking and looked sober.

The dogs were set lose. But instead of staying on patrol near the camp, Scrapper, true to his name, dashed off over the ridge in pursuit of what appeared to be a retreating wolf, and that was the last they saw of him. They called the others back and chained them up, and then all night long — through nine hours of darkness — they stood guard over the picket line of calves, Rea at one end, Jones at the other, rifles in hand.

"We never pretended to shoot when a wolf was more than forty yards away," Jones wrote later. "Sometimes they would come singly, some times in howling groups, two to a dozen at a time."

The wounded dragged themselves away and were instantly devoured by the pack, but when morning came, the sleepless and red-eyed men, almost tottering with fatigue, saw with dismay that there were apparently just as many wolves as before. The sun was high before the survivors slunk off. Light did what the men and rifles had been unable to do. The partners lay down and slept, grateful for the respite, and for the light.

Toward noon they woke and broke camp as fast as possible, eager to be gone from this place of death and to put as many miles between them and the wolf pack as they could. Adding to their uncanny feeling was the fact that the carcasses of the grown musk ox had not been touched by the wolves.

Breaking the calves to trail was something outside even Jones' experience. He wrote:

We tied the one end of our anchor-line to the carryall, I walking behind, holding the other. We set the shepherd dogs at heeling the yearlings up, as they were very stubborn at first, refusing to be led; but within an hour we succeeded in cooling them down somewhat. We fixed hackamores in the mouths of our animals, so they could not pull very hard on the line, which saved me many upsets.

The day was warm, the snow melting rapidly, with the thermometer registering forty-eight degrees above zero at noon. We set our compass, marked our line of retreat, and started off, desiring to get along as fast as possible, as it was four o'clock in the afternoon before we got fairly under way.

When the start was made, some of the animals pulled back on their haunches and stopped the whole train. At this juncture all I had to do was to point my finger at the refractory animals, when Don would fly at them, nipping their heels, at which they would take a spurt forward and I be pitched headlong on the sloppy snow; then they would change ends in order to fight the dog. Sometimes the animals would become tangled in the line; the hind one in front and the front one behind. It was certainly discouraging. If we undertook to untangle them we were sure to receive a butt or two that would send us rolling over and over. My shins that night were "as black as the ace of spades."

Musk ox were, he found, unlike the buffalo in one respect: they kicked harder and oftener. They were if anything harder to handle, and only three miles were covered that first day.

Again the wolves appeared, as numerous as the night before, and more than ever determined to have dog, musk ox, or human flesh for supper. Sometimes it seemed they would get all three. Ammunition was running low. They did not dare waste a single shot. They were obliged to use the dogs to help run the wolves off, but the dogs had no stomach for it and skulked back to the tent. "We threw stones, and even resorted to clubs as weapons, taken from our wood supply. We shot only the foremost one of the pack, which was always an old white male. If we drew blood on one, it retreated to the main pack in the rear, where it was instantly devoured without ceremony — every morsel eaten excepting the skull and skin."

When morning came they started on again. All that they had taught their musk ox the day before had been forgotten, they discovered, and they struggled along till ten o'clock, made camp, slept, with no wolves to bother them in broad daylight, woke and hit the trail. The calves traveled better and by the time darkness fell they had covered ten miles. The night was a repetition of the two previous.

They were off early and traveled till near midday, stopped and slept two or three hours, then pushed on. They were swinging south toward the divide that separates the Dubawnt River from the Great Slave Lake watershed, and were looking for timber because their stock of firewood was very low. Likewise their cartridges. That night they fought the wolves off by using some of the last sticks of firewood, and they used the dogs too, and by morning only Don, of the shepherds, remained. They were down to their last few cartridges. Their meat was almost gone and they were feeling weak from hunger. However, as compensation, the calves had begun to paw through the snow and find moss to eat, and were so well broken to the trail that they could cover eighteen miles a day.

Again they started early and pushed hard, knowing they must find timber within forty-eight hours, or have no way to build a fire to cook meat and melt snow for water. They stopped at midday as usual and pitched the tent. Timber could not be far away and they felt that another day, even this one, might see them out of danger.

After a cup of the cold tea which Jones carried in his rubber life preserver, they rolled up in their blankets for a sleep. About mid-afternoon Rea woke and went out to look at the calves. His angry yell waked Jones.

"Jones, Jones — we're ruined — somebody has killed the calves!"

Jones was so stunned that he merely lifted the edge of the tent and looked out. There lay the bodies . . . five black mounds in the snow, Rea bending over them, uttering savage imprecations. Jones let the tent back down, relapsed into his blankets, rolled over and fell asleep utterly exhausted, his firm control broken for once.

A few minutes later Rea came rampaging into the tent and shook him awake. Rea's lips were blue with anger. "They cut their throats, Jones, and let them lie!" Still half-dazed, Jones went out with him to the scene of the crime.

A raiding party of twelve or fifteen men on snowshoes — so said the tracks — had been following them, evidently observing their movements, and during the rest hour had slipped forward and cut the throats of the five calves, and had then retreated the way they had come, leaving the carcasses untouched. The ropes were around the calves' necks. The bodies were still warm. "How can it be?" asked Jones, "it happened within sixty feet of the tent — in broad daylight!"

"There was only one dog left that might have given warning," Rea replied, "Don, and he was in the tent with us, so bad hurt he was sleeping as soundly as we were."

Don had been badly cut up in the wolf fights, and they had given him a place of comfort indoors. The native sled dogs had apparently not stirred at the approach of intruders.

"It was an act of execution, a religious act," cried Jones, kneeling, "see, each throat is cut in similar fashion. Do you think Barromie had something to do with it?"

"He might have. He was dead set against us after he found we were turning back for more oxen."

"Do you suppose he sicked them onto us? Look, Rea."

Jones held up a peculiar knife that had been lying partially buried in the snow. Its blade was four inches long, riveted to an eighteen-inch handle, made of a caribou rib. It had been used in the ritual and deliberately left behind.

"I hope their *Great Spirit* is satisfied," said Jones somberly, as he stared at the remains of the sacrifice, knife in hand, "Do you suppose Sousie did it himself?" And then after a moment, he added, "Well, we can't bring 'em back to life, that's sure, but maybe we can find out who did it and make them pay."

They backtracked the raiding party for four miles and found where the trail branched off to the east.

"They could be either Eskimos or Indians," Rea said. "We're right where their hunting grounds join. And we've got just cartridges enough to settle their hash, Jones, come on!" But Jones had been thinking. "No, we'd better not. I wouldn't want to find Sousie in that bunch, Rea, and I'm afraid I might." But Rea wanted to go on. Jones argued further: "After you've used up your cartridges on them, what will you have left to use on the wolves?"

"This," said Rea, holding up his fist. Jones shook his head.

They were too tired and depressed to make an outdoor stand that night so they called the dogs inside and sat guard while the wolves howled and snapped around the edges of the tent. In the morning they discarded all but their essential equipment and prepared to head south fast. With a shock, Jones noticed something truly uncanny. "By God, Rea, look!" For the first time the wolves had broken their taboo against carrion; they had eaten the musk ox calves. It threw a still more eerie light on an already weird situation. The wolves had not touched dead meat before. But after the sacrificial offering of the calves, they had done so. "They must be really hungry," muttered Rea, "or they wouldn't have touched 'em." But it wasn't what he was thinking. Both men felt a supernatural power had intervened. As fast as they could, they finished loading the sled and headed south.

The day was warm and the snow melted rapidly. Ridges and rocky points were bare, and the sled was forced into valleys and lake basins. However, that evening they reached a river canyon where there was wood and supplied themselves with fuel for what they estimated would be a week's run to Great Slave Lake. The wolves had disappeared.

"It's just as though they know the show's over," said Jones moodily, as he and Rea sat by the fire that night with nothing for supper but hot tea, "as though they'd come just far enough to see the babies slaughtered and then turned back." He was depressed and could not rid himself of the bad-luck feeling. Nor did their luck get better.

Before reaching home they were out of meat and down to their last cartridge. It was up to Jones to kill one of two caribou that had run out of a draw and stood half facing them, four hundred yards away. Once again he was reduced to the first principle: survival. To eat, they had to have that caribou. It was a fantastically long shot but he bent to it coolly. There was the telltale spat as the bullet struck.

On the strength of that caribou they reached the cabin. They had been gone forty-five days and had covered about a thousand miles.[3]

CHAPTER FIFTEEN

Presidents and Grizzly Bears

DESPITE THE LOSS of the calves, the Arctic Expedition turned out to be something of a triumph. In fact, the loss, and the manner in which it occurred, added to the romance and mystery of the North, the musk ox, and Jones. He continued home by way of the Yukon and Bering Sea, encountering further adventures, but not before he and Rea added one last chapter to the sequence on Great Slave Lake.

Shortly after they returned to the cabin from the musk ox hunt, an old sled dog named General, a faithful defender of the camp during the wolf fights, his head scarred by wolf fangs, began trying to bite the other dogs. Rea tied him with a chain. General mashed the chain links flat with his teeth, broke the chain by throwing his weight against it, and attacked Rea. Only thick mittens saved the Scot from being bitten. Jones shot General.

Then little Don, Jones' faithful shepherd, began foaming at the mouth. One by one the dogs went mad and were shot. The white wolves had had hydrophobia, and the dogs had caught it from them. During all those night-long fights with the wolf pack, the men had been within arm's length of rabies — and terrible death. Then as now there was no cure for rabies, and indeed the Pasteur treatment for prevention was only recently developed and certainly not available in the far North. Backwoodsmen had a primitive method of treating the rabies' victim. They tied a stick in his mouth, tied his hands and feet, and let him chew the stick until he died foaming and raving.[1]

Jones and Rea went homeward by way of the Mackenzie River, the Arctic Ocean, and the Yukon. They had heard about the Klondike gold strike and wanted to see it for themselves, but at Fort Yukon they separated, Rea going upstream to Dawson, Jones deciding to head for home via Bering Sea and the Aleutians — and on the way he spotted an island that looked like a promising place for propagating fur-bearing animals. His optimism was incorrigible.

When he reached Troy laden with silver fox skins, walrus ivory and other mementos of the North, he was given a hero's reception. As he walked onto the stage of the opera house the audience rose and sang *Home, Sweet Home!* It was sweet music indeed to the man who had left another Kansas town bankrupt and in disgrace a few years before.

Martha and the girls were well, though they had worried when they had not heard from him for six months. He admitted that if the white wolf's fangs had closed on him instead of on the rifle barrel the night he saved Don, they might not have heard from him at all.

As for Sousie Barromie, he did not enter the picture again, but he remained perhaps the most significant figure of all those Jones met in the Arctic.

As for the men at home, Ernest Thompson Seton, Theodore Roosevelt, and William T. Hornaday recognized his achievement, and Seton went so far as to retrace much of Jones' route a year or two later, and saw the cabin and the skeletons of the wolves, thus refuting certain critics who doubted the old plainsman's account.[2] Altogether, the trip was attracting so much attention that Jones decided to write a book. It seemed time to capitalize on his adventures if he could, and the exchequer, which had never been very full since Garden City days, was running low again. In collaboration with Colonel Henry Inman, author of *The Old Santa Fe Trail,* and other authentic volumes on the West (Inman was a former assistant quartermaster general of the U. S. Army and friend of General Phil Sheridan in buffalo-hunting days at Dodge, and had just done a book with Buffalo Bill Cody called *The Great Salt Lake Trail*) Jones produced a rambling readable account of his adventures, including the Arctic trip, and called it *Buffalo Jones' Forty Years of Adventure.* It was published in Topeka in 1899. It wasn't a money maker, but it was and is a solid source book of Indian and Plains lore and an indispensable record of Jones.

For its author, it marked a psychological, if not a financial milestone. He was known again, but he was in the position of the celebrity who finds himself in need of a job. He went to Washington and got an assignment from the Smithsonian Institute to catch Rocky Mountain Sheep for the National Zoological Park, went back to Colorado, and lowered his eighteen-year-old daughter, Olive, down an eighty-five foot precipice in the Colorado Rockies and hauled her up with a baby bighorn in her arms. He wrote an account of it in *Harper's* magazine for January, 1901. On the cover of that issue was a portrait of the children of Theodore Roosevelt, then vice-president of the United States.

In September of the same year, fate brought President Roosevelt and Jones closer together. An assassin stepped up to President McKinley at the Pan-American Exposion in Buffalo, and Roosevelt went to the White House, at forty-two, the youngest President in U. S. history.

Jones lost no time in getting to Washington too. Just what transpired between the Colonel of Rough Riders, former Dakota rancher, deputy sheriff, author-President, and the Colonel of Buffalo Hunters, plainsman, author-explorer, has not been set down but it is not hard to imagine. Conservation was the burning issue of the day: conservation of animals, men, natural resources, land, water, human dignity. Years of uncontrolled exploitation had laid waste forests, not to mention human beings. Animals like the buffalo had been all but exterminated. People had been mistreated too. Roosevelt wanted to put a stop to this.

One popular measure he took was to appoint Jones game warden at the national park.[3]

By reason of the fact that it was called *the* national park and was for many years the only one, Yellowstone was famous. It stood in the public eye as a kind of symbol: a fortress against exploitation and selfish interest. Defender of the fortress — at least of its wild life — was to be Jones, a field commander, you might say, in the new President's popular campaign against anti-social forces. So Jones remained nationally prominent by means of a job that today sounds quite commonplace, warden of Yellowstone.

Before he ever took office the battle was joined. Poachers, symbolic of the predatory interests, had decimated the wild buffalo herd that for years — since the last open-range killings of the eighties — had roamed Yellowstone. One New York millionaire paid fifteen hundred dollars for a black market head.[4] Poaching was encouraged by such prices. Buffalo continued to be killed. People were furious. Jones was looked upon as the champion who would put a stop to poaching, the white knight who would slay the dragon.

He arrived at the Park July 16, 1902, and found it being operated by the U. S. Cavalry on behalf of the Department of Interior. Yellowstone was regarded as a military preserve, though tourists were admitted and a concessionaire operated camps and hotels. Soldiers acted as police patrols but now Jones was to have charge of the game warden duties.

He made a tour of inspection with the commander of the Park, Major John Pitcher, selected the site for an enclosure for a buffalo herd (the establishment of such a herd had apparently been a project discussed between him and Roosevelt) in a grassy valley near Mammoth Hot Springs, a site since familiar to many, set about constructing fences and then prepared to spend the fifteen thousand dollars Congress had appropriated for the purchase of a herd. The public backing which he had asked for and been denied in the eighties was now granted him, and he moved to represent the American people in the preservation of the buffalo.

He went to Texas and bought three bulls from Colonel Charles Goodnight, and while there met Goodnight's foreman, a Texan named Jim Owens, who was to play a significant part in his life and in the life of the West in the years to come, and then went to North Dakota and purchased fourteen cows from the Allard Herd, which had existed since his own buffalo-saving days.[5] And he apparently sold the government several animals from a herd he himself was re-establishing in Kansas and Nebraska. There is a story, now taking on the proportions of legend in Kansas-Nebraska-Wyoming, that he drove a band of buffalo overland to Yellowstone Park. Imagine it. Dust rising from the shaggy brown mass of bodies as they trail up the long aprons of the Rockies, into the pines and glacial valleys, to the basin of the big lake and the hot springs, the men on the bright-colored ponies, ropes whirling. Let us say that he called out his old gang, DeCordova, Howard, and John E. Biggs to do the job once more, as he had done in the days of the last hunt, and up they went with him across the Smoky Hill Country, past Russell Springs, Goodland and St. Francis, the Republican, and Robb and Ovid, and into the barrens beyond Cheyenne, north from Casper, into the Wind River country, past Thermopolis and Cody into the rocky gateway of the Shoshone, to the pines at last. If it didn't happen it should have. Jones' daughter Jessie says it did. So does J. N. Hulpieu, who is still living at Dodge City and remembers the night when he was a boy on his father's ranch north of Garden City and Buffalo Jones and the buffalo herd stopped on their way to Yellowstone.[6]

In any event the nucleus of a domestic herd was established in the Park and the animals were branded with a "U.S." on the horn and on the hip, to show that they belonged to the people of the United States.

Since poaching was not at the moment a problem, thanks perhaps to the publicity given his arrival and the general new attitude of the nation toward such things, Jones decided that in order to add primitive strength to this domestic herd he would take time to capture some calves from the wild herd that roamed the farthest recesses of the Park. Their number had steadily decreased until only about thirty head remained. To catch them would be to preserve them from slow extinction.

He left Mammoth on skis on the sixth of April, 1903, on a mid-winter buffalo hunt. He'd caught buffalo every other way — why not on skis?

As he tells it in his own words:

The first day we made only eleven miles, and camped that night in an old abandoned cabin, without bedding, and as the thermometer was probably about ten above zero we suffered from cold. . . . The next day we made nine miles, and put up at the Norris Station where soldiers stay during the winter. The third day we came to the Grand Canyon of the Yellowstone through a blinding snow storm, where we found the soldier boys delighted to see us. The fourth day we reached the habitat of the buffalo, thirteen miles away, on the Pelican River.

The snow was about three feet deep . . . and the ther-mometer registered about twelve above zero when we left the soldiers' quarters. The worst feature about the journey that day was to cross the Pelican River. . . . There were several wide places where it was swift, but only about two feet deep, so we concluded to divest ourselves of our shoes and stock-ings, roll our trousers up, as little boys do, and plunge into the icy cold water, where the floating slush ice came thick and fast. . . .

Carrying our skees [sic], shoes and other paraphernalia we managed to wade through, and that night we reached a hut which had been built for just such emergencies as this. A few quilts and plenty of straw had been provided, also crackers, canned pork and beans, so we felt quite elated to be able to take a good rest. The next morning by using our field glasses, we discovered a herd of buffalo, fifteen cows and two bulls, about three miles to the eastward. By making a long circuit we came within a quarter of a mile of them, and endeavored to see if there were any calves with them. They were so on the alert, however, that our presence was dis-covered and they dashed away at full speed. . . . They finally halted in a deep valley . . . and we saw that there were three calves with them.

The day was warm, and traveling on the skees was ex-ceedingly arduous, (so much so as to make the chase out of the question) so we slipped around them and reached our quarters without again disturbing them. The next morning we were up and out at four o'clock. . . .

At daylight we looked into the valley, but the herd had fled. Their tracks indicated that they had gone toward the neighborhood where we had first located them. I stationed one scout half way up the mountain just above their trail, and instructed him, if the herd came up again, to descend with all speed and place himself between the herd and the calves, which would be sure to be behind. I knew that the calves could not break a trail for themselves, and, by standing in the trail of the old ones, he would cut the little fellows from the herd.

I had not expected that the little rascals would attempt to "butt" the scout out of the trail, which was about three feet deep and two feet wide, or I would have told him not to attempt to lay hands on them, but just to keep them back until the old ones were out of hearing distance, or their bleating would bring an avalanche of horns upon him.

I went a mile northward, and stationed myself so as not to allow them to go up the river, as I knew they would do so to avoid the deep snow. I felt sure that by firing a revolver it would turn them down the river and send them near Scout Holt. The other scout, Morrison, was sent on their tracks to start them going. It was perhaps an hour after we had parted that I heard a revolver report in the direction taken by Scout Morrison, and presently down came the herd, with four calves tagging along behind. When they saw me they shied off, and took the trail down the river, as desired, and as they passed the base of the steep mountain, Scout Holt went down upon the herd like a bald eagle after a rabbit. He was an expert on skees, and soon landed in front of the calves. But the little brutes plunged right at him, and, unfortunately, he grabbed them both as expected, they bawled right lustily, and back came their mothers in a great fury.

There was only one thing to do, and that was to get out of the trail with all expediency, which Holt immediately did, and as soon as the old ones saw that their little ones were free they wheeled and followed the herd, with the calves at their heels. But Holt was game, and the gait he took up over the hills and down the valleys was one not known to even the Norwegians themselves, who are the most expert snowshoers in the world. He soon headed off a calf which had *dropped so far behind that its bleating could not be heard, and quickly had it tied and was off after another one, which he overtook after a long chase. The next consideration was how to get them to some place where they could be cared for.*

It was impossible to carry them, so I ripped up some "gunny" sacks and made a harness for the three lion hounds which I had allowed to follow me on the trip. The dogs had never been in harness before, and were much surprised at such an innovation, but being intelligent and obedient creatures they soon trotted off like well-broken horses. We were off the next morning at break of day, so as to take advantage of the crusted snow. As the night had been severely cold crossing the river again was terrible work, as it required several trips across, as we had to carry the calves and the sled in our arms.

By eleven o'clock, the day after the calves were captured, we had them at the Lake Station, where there were some domestic calves and their mothers. Here the little fellows were given their first lesson in domestication. One of them was very greedy and gorged himself until he came near dying, but they both pulled through and are now fine specimens.

During the trip I became totally blind from the snow, and for six days was obliged to employ one of the soldiers to care for me, as I was unable even to feed myself.

We read of the shepherd who was not content with the ninety and nine, but went on the mountains through rain and snow to find the sheep which was lost, but I dare say he did not travel so far as did our little party to rescue the last calves, and thus rekindle the last spark of a dying race. . . .[7]

President Roosevelt came along later that spring and inspected his work at the buffalo enclosure, and toured the Park in company with Jones and John Burroughs, the renowned author and naturalist.[8]

All was not sweetness and light, however. Jones antagonized the Park concessionaires, the Wylies, from the start.[9] They thought him pompous, opinionated, a thoroughgoing fourflusher and poseur. Mrs. Wylie chased him "and his infernal hounds" — he usually traveled with a pack of hounds because his duties included hunting mountain lions — out of her camp kitchen with a broom. But by and large the visiting royalty, as well as humbler members of the tourist public, were charmed by him.

Victor Sandek, who was a musician at Mammoth Springs Hotel in these days, recalls that Jones occasionally thrilled people by appearing on the hotel porch in the fringed buckskin clothing of the Wild West, and when Mr. Vanderbilt of New York was stopping at Mammoth, Jones worked up a deal with him for the purchase of a buffalo robe, a rare and costly item. Jones brought the robe and laid it, folded, on the porch and went to find Vanderbilt. In the meantime Mrs. Vanderbilt came out and stumbled over the robe and ejaculated in most unladylike fashion: "Get that damned thing out of here!" It queered the deal.[10]

C. J. (White Mountain) Smith, a stage driver in the Park then, later its superintendent, recalls that Jones was a law unto himself, flocking alone at the Buffalo Enclosure up the valley, appearing suddenly now and then like a vision from some bygone age, and disappearing as suddenly. Smith recalls his aloofness, his stern independence. Jack Haynes, now and for many years Park photographer, remembers him in the same way. "He had a little museum out there next to the Buffalo Enclosure," Haynes says, "but he didn't seem to care whether you looked at it or not."[11]

However, Major Pitcher of the Sixth Cavalry, acting Park superintendent, accused him of selling mementoes to tourists and generally prostituting himself for commercial gain and against Park regulations.

The Wylie company continued to claim that he terrified tourists with tall tales of bears and cougars, and cost them business.

Relations between Jones, the Army and the Wylies worsened to the point where he and Major Pitcher were writing letters to each other, though separated by only a statute mile or so.

Maj. Pitcher to Jones:

You will in the future devote your whole time and attention to the care of the new buffalo herd now located near the Mammoth Hot Springs. If by your undivided attention to this herd, you make a success, and perpetuate the species, you will have done a good work, and will have accomplished the purpose for which you were sent to the Park. . . .

You will also assume direct charge of the pack of hounds which were purchased for the purpose of killing mountain lions in the Park, see that they are properly trained and cared for in every way, and that whenever they are used for the purpose intended, they are returned to their kennels and not permitted to run at large in the Park.

Whenever I desire or need your advice or assistance concerning other matters pertaining to the Park, I will inform you of the fact.[12]

Jones to Maj. Pitcher (Aug. 7, 1904):

About ten days ago you ordered me to proceed to the Canyon and Lake Stations to look after some unruly bears and to cut tin cans off some grizzly bears' feet. I found at the Canyon four or five bears which paid but little respect to anyone. . . . I found at the Lake Hotel about four bears very much like those at the Canyon. They had broken down a door and smashed a window at the Wylie camp, also had broken in to outhouses at the Lake Hotel. They on several occasions drove the driver of the garbage wagon, Mr. Bert Gleason, off his cart and took possession of the garbage, and only with difficulty could he regain possession. I caught three of the worst of these bears in a rope snare and hauled them up with a block and tackle.[13] *I then gave them as big a scare as possible and switched them besides. I also prodded them in a humane manner with a pole and prod, but so short as not to reach through fur and skin. These animals now believe everybody has a snare and a prod for them and they will not stand for a person to come within fifty feet of them.*

These bears have been fed and petted by people, and have become insensible to fear. This must be counteracted by punishment in order to drive them wild again, or they become dangerous.

But they are good bears now; for reference ask Mr. Gleason.

I could not punish the bears at the Canyon, for the lack of rope, block and tackle, and had no team to get any, but gave them a good scare which will no doubt do them for a time. . . .

You sent Scout Wagner with me to assist in the work, but he saddled his horse and left me without even notifying me of his intentions. . . . I caught one of the grizzlies which had a tin can on its foot. His leg was swollen twice its natural size, but being alone I was unable to pull his foot high enough to prevent him from cutting the rope with his teeth, and he escaped. . . .

As you gave me orders not to 'even suggest' anything to the soldiers at the different stations, I could not demand their services, so gave up and came to the Post, leaving two bears in deplorable condition. . . .

I have several times asked you to select someone who is an expert with a rope and all around good western man . . . who would be in accord with me and not always finding fault, hoping thereby to have me discharged that they could get appointed game warden, but as yet I am obliged often to go alone or take men who have never been fitted or trained to such peculiar work. Furthermore you have forbidden the game warden from firing even blank cartridges at bears, you have also given him instructions not to even 'punish a bear' no difference how great the offense, but you have often given the scouts orders to kill bears for what I should term frivolous offenses.

Now as Game Warden of the Park I feel it my duty to protest against any more killing of bears, when I will guarantee, if permitted, to make as good a bear of the most vicious brute, as there is in the Park, and that, too, without inhuman methods, not even drawing blood or maiming them in the least. . . .

Jones went on to say that if the Game Warden must abdicate his power of decision over animal affairs in the Park, it was time to appeal to the American people to dispense with military administration of Yellowstone and place it under civilian control.

You can imagine how this sat with Major Pitcher. He saw red, white, and blue — and whipped out a boiling nine-page typewritten letter to the Secretary of Interior, Jones' immediate superior, accusing the ex-plainsman of everything from four-flushing to embezzlement.

Among such negative items as absenteeism, charlatanism, and laziness, Pitcher cited a letter from a man claiming Jones had hornswoggled him out of one hundred dollars for the promotion of a flying machine to be used in the navigable balloon contest at the World's Fair at St. Louis in 1904. To support Pitcher, the record shows that Jones did in fact attend the Fair, but whether he did so for fraudulent purposes or not is another matter. Pitcher's letter closed with: "Mr. Jones is now absent in Arizona, where he has gone for the purpose of making arrangements to establish a cattalo ranch. It is to be hoped that he will be successful in his efforts and that they will result in his speedy removal to a scene and work which will be much more agreeable to him than his present position."

Jones nevertheless had the last word, and he resorted to the nation's press to get it in: The *New Haven Evening Register* for November 15, 1906 reported:

BUFFALO JONES SAYS
SOLDIERS LACK BACKBONE

Famous Hunter Makes Caustic Comment in Lecture

In his address delivered in the public lecture course at College Street last night, Col. C. J. Jones, better known as "Buffalo" Jones, whose prowess as a hunter of wild animals and whose experiments in crossing ordinary domestic cattle with the buffalo have made him known nationally, made some caustic comments about the lack of bravery among the United States soldiers stationed at the forts in the West and speaking generally, he classed them as being utterly useless in the work of protecting game in Yellowstone Park. . . .

"Not a very long time ago," Mr. Jones said in speaking of this matter, "I went to one of the Army posts and asked for a man to help me in a lion hunt. The commander of the post gave me a soldier who, he said, would no doubt fill the bill. With this man I went on a lion hunt with a friend. We struck the tracks of three mountain lions and that soldier, as soon as he saw the tracks broke from the party and beat the trail back to his post. I supposed he had slipped off the side of a mountain somewhere and giving up the lion hunt I went looking for the missing soldier. When I returned to the post later I found this fellow there. . . ." [Taking it easy.]

Jones concluded his New Haven comments with a few well-chosen disparagements of the Army, ending with the suggestion that soldiers "ought not to be allowed in the Park at all."

The *Evening Register* commented on his talk: "Colonel Jones' lecture was one of the most interesting ever given in this course. By means of moving pictures he showed some of his actual experiences in hunting big game. The lecture was largely attended."[14]

It may have been coincidence but about this time commanders at the Park were changed, and it was not long till the Army left Yellowstone for good, as the outspoken game warden had suggested.

Jones' resignation as Yellowstone Park Game Warden had become effective September 15, 1905.

CHAPTER SIXTEEN

Arizona Wilderness

HE HAD NEVER given up his dream of the cattalo, the new hybrid that would be a practical as well as a dramatic success and would make his fortune.

There is a story by Eugene Manlove Rhodes which tells how a cowman in his later years tired of wandering about New Mexico and Arizona and decided to settle down if he could find the right spot. This spot he found near the Tonto Basin — one of those idyllic canyons and meadows with its own stream and high forest and lush lowlands that every cowman dreams about. By great good fortune he was able to file on the land in the nick of time, and prove up his claim. Finally, after many tribulations and some bad and mostly good luck, he had all his buildings and fences and water works and stock, just as he had dreamed they should be. And there was a sweet young girl who was not too happy with her parents and used to ride out from the only crossroads in that wild basin, and see him on weekends. She fell in love with him, and there he had all the ingredients of a perfect home and a

happy life. The point of the story is that, just as he is ready
to settle down and make a home, he can't do it. He tries to
explain it to himself, but it is the girl from the crossroads who
understands him. In an unforgettable dialogue, she says, in
effect, "There are two kinds of people in this world. Most of
them are 'stayers,' and only want their home and their secu-
rity. The other kind are the 'movers.' And you've been trying
to kid yourself that you're not the other kind. But I know
you. No matter where you go or what you find, after you've
been there a bit, the ground you stand on will start to burn
your feet, and you'll move along. I'd like to marry you, but
we could never make a go of it because if we did, you'd just
move along." And the story ends as the cowman gives away
his claim, then heads eastward again, to see what's on the
other side of a fascinating mountain range.[1]

That was Jones.

On his trip to Colonel Goodnight's ranch at Palo Duro,
he had met Goodnight's foreman — one day to be famous in
Arizona lore as "Uncle Jimmy Owens" — and the foreman had
come to Yellowstone to be his assistant. Owens was a quiet
sort but a real western man after Jones' heart — Indian fighter,
roper of wild longhorn steers, and of buffalo. They talked
about starting a ranch together sometime, where they could
be free of the Army and bureaucrats, and their minds turned
naturally to one last realm of the unspoiled free West — in
northern Arizona and southern Utah, a place beyond the north
rim of the Grand Canyon. Jones went once again to the President. He soon had authorization from the U. S. Park Service
to survey the Kaibab Plateau as a possible game preserve. In
July 1905, Jones went down to Kanab, Utah, just across the
line from the Arizona Territory. There he met Edwin D.
Wooley, a prominent Mormon cattleman, who was builder
of the first suspension cable across the bottom of the Grand

Canyon, and Ernest Pratt, son of the U. S. Forest Supervisor for the area. When Jones explained the purpose of his visit, the men agreed to guide him through the Kaibab. At Fredonia, a few miles to the south, they obtained a wagon, horses, and supplies and set out for the Plateau.[2]

The old buffalo hunter had heard praises of this wild expanse but still he was not prepared for the breathtaking vistas, the endless forests, the countless herds of deer that streamed across every slope of the lush mountain meadows. His enthusiasm was contagious and soon his companions were themselves enthralled with his accounts of the fortunes to be made by breeding buffalo bulls to Scottish Galloway cows and turning them out on the Kaibab range.

Jones pointed out that the hybrid would inherit the buffalo's ability to face out the coldest winter blizzard instead of drifting to disaster before the flying snow. The hides and meat would be in great demand. By the time they returned to Fredonia, the three had agreed to form a development company to put Jones' scheme into effect. Jones himself was to be president, and Pratt was to serve as vice-president but the "company" was never legally incorporated for reasons which will become apparent.[3]

Three problems now faced "President" Jones: A land permit; money to finance the venture; and the breeding stock, including Persian sheep which he had decided should also be introduced because of the profits to be made on the Karakul wool hides.

To solve the land problem, Jones combed Buckskin Mountain from the far breaks of the Siwash, on the northwest, to the dizzy precipices of the north wall of the Grand Canyon on the southeast.[4] He was unable to choose the best spot for his buffalo, for every vista encompassed a paradise for game and stock. Finally, the thought struck him: "Why not the whole of the mountain?" If his friend, Teddy Roosevelt, could be persuaded to set it all aside, the future of the buffalo could be assured. Man, in his greed, could never search out and destroy life in this fortress in the sky — a land which needed few fences because of the vast canyons which hemmed it in on three sides and the waterless deserts which barred the northeast. Once again Jones found the same silences he had known in the far north and in the open prairie before the buffalo hunters came. Here were both challenge and refuge. Here was a place where trains and cities could never intrude. Here a man could always discover his own soul, uncontaminated by the works of man. And at the same time, Jones could not help looking for each meadow and glade to which he might introduce the works of man in the form of the domesticated buffalo and cattalo.

Jones did not know then what has since been discovered: that, although the American bison did not in modern times extend into Arizona, the species was once part of the fauna of the Grand Canyon Region. Hair found in the caves occupied by prehistoric man has now been identified by the National Museum at Washington, D. C., as belonging to the species that Jones had hoped to introduce.

On January eighth, 1906, Jones received a federal permit to fence a large area on the Kaibab for buffalo and other big game animals. Later, in that same year, President Theodore Roosevelt established the Grand Canyon National Game Preserve covering the entire Kaibab Plateau.[5] Jones' visions bore fruit, and the results stand to this day.

His arrangement with Washington took the form of a partnership whereby he furnished the care and know-how and the bulk of the livestock, and the government furnished the land and, on loan, some of the animals. Both partners would share in the increase. The Secretary of Agriculture immortalized this arrangement in a letter to the Secretary of the Interior. He wrote:[6]

Sir:

A special concession has been granted Col. Chas. J. Jones in the Grand Canyon Forest Reservation in Arizona for the purpose of experimenting in the hybridizing of buffalo and cattle, the Government to retain a certain percentage of the produce. I am informed by Col. Jones that there are two buffalo bulls in the Yellowstone Park which the park authorities would be glad to have removed and which he could use to the advantage of the Government, and, himself, in the breeding of hybrids. If there is no objection to turning these two animals over to the jurisdiction of this Department, to be removed to the Grand Canyon Reserve, and loaned to Col. Jones, I recommend that it be done.

I have the honor to be Sir,
Very respectfully
Your obedient servant
(signed) James Wilson
Secretary of Agriculture

Jones helped solve his financial problem by issuing stock certificates for the proposed company. Edwin Wooley agreed to accept a large number of shares in return for heifers from his own herds, the latter to be used to obtain black Galloway cows in Kansas at an exchange rate of three heifers to one cow. One hundred Galloways were thus obtained. Jones sold enough company stock to buy the buffalo he needed, as well as sixty-seven black Karakul sheep in Montana. Many of the buffalo came from the Goodnight ranch in Texas. There Frank Anscott caught the cattalo fever, sold his home, accompanied the buffalo west, and settled down in the Kaibab as manager of the new project which he had helped finance.

The problem of breeding stock was not to be solved just by purchasing animals. They had to be gotten somehow onto the new range. And that story is a chapter in itself.

CHAPTER SEVENTEEN

The Cattalo Ranch

ONE FIERCELY HOT June afternoon a strange scene was enacted
at the little desert station of Lund, in southwest Utah, a whistle
stop on the Union Pacific railroad. Cowboys from ranches a
hundred miles distant, grizzled prospectors, gathered to see
Jones, Owens, Anscott, and a ranger named T. C. Hoyt take
charge of the strange cargo of massive, wooly animals descending the ramps of the cattle cars into trackside pens.

A mythology has grown up around this event. Some say
Jones went to the Grand Canyon driving his buffalo with
Jimmy Owens all the way from Texas. Some report, with Zane
Grey, that he trailed them from Salt Lake City, three hundred
seventy-five miles.[1] Others say that the buffalo were driven
in from the east and made to swim the river at Lee's Ferry.
This apocryphal version states that a time of low water was
chosen; otherwise they never would have made it. Lee's
Ferry is a treacherous ford. The water there is silt-saturated
and a man in clothes, for instance, would soon be sucked
under, and sheep don't do well either, because the silt settles
in their wool and weights them down. Cattle, however, could

go right on across, and also buffalo. The buffalo allegedly were buoyant because they had a lot of grease in their hair.

Lon Garrison, superintendent at Yellowstone Park, and himself a student of Jones and Jimmy Owens and Western lore, says that two carloads of buffalo arrived at Lund, Utah, on the Union Pacific in June of 1906. One load of fifty-seven was in fairly good condition and made the trip over to the Kaibab, one hundred seventy-five miles by trail. But the other group of thirty was in poor condition and Jones and Owens "tolled" them along — induced them to proceed — by buying wheat for them from the Mormon farmers. Garrison's account is now so well authenticated not only by his own records but by the testimony of men like Pratt and Wooley that it must be accepted as the correct version.[2]

The carload of thirty buffalo had come from the ranch of a Californian named Molera — Señor E. J. Molera — at Monterey. They were part of Jones' original herd that had passed through various hands after the sheriff's sale and finally ended up on the rolling Santa Lucia hills of Point Sur Rancho overlooking the Pacific Ocean.[3] The journey across the hot Nevada deserts had nearly finished the poor creatures, who reminded Jones of the pathetic specimens in the traveling circuses. Still, after a day's rest with feed and water, they might be able to endure the long trip south to the Kaibab.

But it soon became clear that the buffalo would not drive. As soon as the coolness of early morning gave way to the stifling heat of the Utah summer, the exhausted lead bulls simply lay down and refused to budge, despite all the prodding and salty language that Jones and his hands could produce. By the end of the day they were less than a mile from the Lund station.

Owens and Hoyt were disconsolate. "These here critters," commented Owens pithily, "are too dead beat to do anything but bury. They should never have left Monterey and they know it, and the quicker we sell them for steaks to the Mormons the better." But Jones was stubborn. He said, "I'm going to get these buffalo to Buckskin if it takes all summer, and I'm not leaving any behind. There are bulls in here I lassoed in the Panhandle and I can still feel how much work it was! . . . We've got to find some way to lick this heat. They're used to the ocean breezes of the California Coast and they're still in some of their winter coat. They can't stand this Utah sun yet! If only . . . I've got it!" he shouted. "The bulls have got more sense than we have. They want to sleep. We'll sleep them by day, and drive them by night." Anscott shook his head. Owens too was doubtful, but they agreed to give it a try. Jones had one more trick up his sleeve. He purchased two wagons and loaded them with sheaves of wheat.

As soon as the sun lowered that afternoon, Jones hitched the horses to the wagons, and he and Owens started the teams just ahead of the buffalo who had had little feed for the day. Throwing sheaves of wheat behind the wagons to the famished bulls, he persuaded them to follow sheaf by sheaf along the road to the south. And, where the bulls went, the cows and calves followed without protest. By this strange procession the herd was led through the red sands of the Escalante Desert, past Cedar City, Rattlesnake Gap, across the Virgin River and down to Short Creek and Pipe Springs. Sleeping in midday, moving in the cool of the evening, they crawled across the plain to the western slopes of Buckskin Mountain. At last they felt the ground rising again to the high plateau of the Kaibab. Some animals had sickened and died in the desert sands, but most of the original herd survived.

One which did not survive was a fierce, old monarch who met his fate, not because of illness or starvation, but because he got plain "homesick" and would have nothing of the new range that was planned for him. Not long after the herd had made crossing of the Virgin, this gigantic bull took it into his head to return to Lund. He broke loose one evening from the guards and headed back northwest. Nothing could stop him. Shouts, whippings with the lariat, gunshots — all were of no avail. They only succeeded in spurring the bull to a gallop until he shook off his pursuers in the dusk.

The next day Jones took up the pursuit and found that, true to instinct, the buffalo, with his keen scent, was back-tracking the path of the herd from Lund. Jones caught up with his charge just as the bull approached the rushing waters of the Virgin, swollen from a previous night's rain. On the opposite bank, shaded by the bright green foliage of cotton-wood clumps, a Mormon freight wagon, pulled by a pair of bay mares, rolled slowly into the current and headed for the inclined trailway which led up the steep bank by Jones and the buffalo.

The old bull hesitated for a few moments as the wagon forded the stream. But, just as the horses began to heave the creaking burden up the slope, Jones rushed up with whirling lariat unable to see the wagon which, by this time, was hidden from him by the steep fall of the bank. The bison, sensing himself trapped, took, for him, the quickest way out. With a sprint which made the earth tremble to his weight, he lowered his massive head and drove straight into the team and wagon. The team shied, the Mormon driver whipped and shouted, the body of the wagon executed a graceful arc over into the current, spilling the three women passengers like pinwheels into the wet foam. The mares broke from the fractured wagon tongue. Barrels and pots and sacks burst out on all sides. But the bull drove on and trotted out on the far bank with his black heaving sides streaming water. Lodged between his hooked horns was a smashed flour barrel from which a cloud of flour poured down and back over his head and mane and shoulders, giving him a grizzly appearance which contrasted ludicrously with his gleaming black sides. Jones eyed the old rascal disgustedly as he plowed his way past the cottonwoods and was lost to view.

The plainsman helped round up the mares, repair the wagon tongue, and re-harness the team. The women, except for their pathetic appearance in their long, heavy, dripping skirts, were unhurt in the upset and soon had the righted wagon loaded again with the salvaged cargo. The Mormon, red-faced and outraged at first, came at last to the humor of the incident and laughed with Jones at the ridiculous. He even refused an offer of compensation for the barrel of flour.

And the buffalo? He made it. Yes, all the way to Lund, where the station agent, instead of giving him return passage to Monterey, felt obliged to shoot him and distribute the meat to the local citizenry.[4]

A second shipment of buffalo was sent to Lund from Montana. Like the Monterey buffalo, these had come from Jones' original Garden City herd, had been sold to Charles Allard, and shipped to Montana. The new group was also trail-herded from Lund and added to the transplanted stock on the Kaibab Plateau.[5] Later, most of these were moved to the grasslands of House Rock Valley to the east.

There, in a basin of empire proportions, sloping up toward Buckskin Mountain on the Grand Canyon's north rim, Jones established his cattalo ranch, some of his own original buffalo on it, the last American bison propagated in a last bit of undisturbed West. The buffalo were saved. And along with their brethren in the north, remained to perpetuate the species. That was success.

But the cattalo were another story. Not only did the buffalo and Galloways breed reluctantly, but the results produced unforeseen problems. The major cause of the trouble has been reported to be the persistence of the buffalo hump in the foetus, which made delivery difficult or impossible without human assistance. But Charles Goodnight, reporting on his Texas experience in crossbreeding buffalo with polled Angus cows states "There is no trouble whatever in giving birth."[6] However, male calves from the first crossbreeding were either aborted or caused the death of the cow. The heifer calves would breed readily, but when bred to buffalo bulls, produced sterile male calves because the thick coats of the latter kept the reproductive organs at too high a temperature. Only by breeding back again to domestic cattle could fertile males be obtained. Apparently these rigid and complicated breeding requirements could not be met successfully in time to meet the needs of the "company." It fell apart and the scheme collapsed with but minor breeding successes and no substantial financial return. The advantages which were later confirmed by Canadian and Texas breeders were not realized in the Kaibab: the cattalo's immunity to diseases, his resistance to cold, and the rich, tender meat produced from a minimum of feed.

The different investors attempted to recoup their losses by claiming the stock. Anscott took and sold the Galloways. Wooley got the sheep. Owens and Wooley and a B. F. Saunders got the buffalo and Uncle Jimmy later bought out the other two. Eventually, he sold the herd to Arizona to establish the present state-owned herd. Jones himself never quite lost faith in the cattalo. And indeed his vision and enthusiasm may yet some day result in the successful utilization of the vast sub-Arctic regions for meat production by cattalo types — at least if Canadian government hybrid efforts continue to show results. But that too is another story.

The old plainsman had other strings for his bow. He could hunt lions and the Kaibab had them. He stayed on at the "ranch," still engrossed in his hybrid breeding experiments — and Zane Grey found him there.

CHAPTER EIGHTEEN

Wild Stallion

In 1907 Zane Grey was a thirty-five-year-old dentist who had been overcome by an urge to write and had shut himself up in a furnished room in New York City. He was not having much success when friends suggested he go West and take a hunting trip in Arizona with Buffalo Jones.

Grey was introduced to Jones who was then on a lecture tour in the East. They went West together, and Grey wrote:

One afternoon, far out on the sun-baked waste of sage, we made camp near a clump of withered piñon trees. The cold desert wind came down upon us with the sudden darkness. Even the Mormons, who were finding the trail for us across the drifting sands, forgot to sing and pray at sundown. We huddled round the campfire, a tired and silent little group. When out of the lonely, melancholy night some wandering Navajos stole like shadows to our fire, we hailed their advent with delight . . .

Jones, erect, rugged, brawny, stood in the full light of the campfire. He had a dark, bronzed, inscrutable face; a stern mouth and square jaw, keen eyes, half-closed from years of

*searching the wide plains, and deep furrows wrinkling his
cheeks. A strange stillness enfolded his features — the tran-
quility earned from a long life of adventure.*

*He held up both muscular hands to the Navajo, and
spread out his fingers.*

"*Rope buffalo—heap big buffalo—heap many—one sun.*"

The Indian straightened up, but kept his friendly smile.

"*Me big chief,*" *went on Jones,* "*me go far north — Land
of Little Sticks — Naza! Naza! — rope musk ox; rope White
Manitou of Great Slaves — Naza! Naza!*"

"*Naza!*" *replied the Navajo, pointing to the North Star;*
"*no — no.*"

"*Yes — me big paleface — me come long way toward set-
ting sun — go cross Big Water — go Buckskin — Siwash —
chase cougar.*"

*The cougar, or mountain lion, is a Navajo god and the
Navajos hold him in as much fear and reverence as do the
Great Slave Indians the musk-ox.*

"*No kill cougar,*" *continued Jones, as the Indian's bold
features hardened.* "*Run cougar horseback — run long way —
dogs chase cougar long time — chase cougar up tree! Me big
chief — me climb tree — climb high up — lasso cougar — rope
cougar — tie cougar all tight.*"

"*White man heap fun. No.*"

"*Yes,*" *cried Jones, extending his great arms.* "*Me strong;
me rope cougar — me tie cougar; ride off wigwam, keep cougar
alive.*"

"*No,*" *replied the savage vehemently.*

"*Yes,*" *protested Jones, nodding earnestly.*

"*No,*" *answered the Navajo louder, raising his dark head.*

"*Yes!*" *shouted Jones.*

"*BIG LIE!*" *the Indian thundered.*

*Jones joined good-naturedly in the laugh at his expense.
The Indian had crudely voiced a skepticism I had heard more*

delicately hinted in New York, and singularly enough, which had strengthened on our way West, as we met ranchers, prospectors and cowboys. But those few men I had fortunately met, who really knew Jones, more than overbalanced the doubt and ridicule cast upon him. I recalled a scarred old veteran of the plains, who had talked to me in true Western bluntness:

"Say, young feller, I heerd yer couldn't git acrost the cañon fer the deep snow on the north rim. Wal, ye're lucky. Now, yer hit the trail fer New York, an' keep goin'! Don't ever tackle the desert, 'specially with them Mormons. They've got water on the brain, wusser 'n religion. It's two hundred an' fifty miles from Flagstaff to Jones' range, an' only two drinks on the trail. I know this hyar Buffalo Jones. I knowed him way back in the seventies, when he was doin' them ropin' stunts thet made him famous as the preserver of the American bison. I know about that crazy trip of his'n to the Barren Lands, after musk-ox. An' I reckon I kin guess what he'll do over there in the Siwash. He'll rope cougars — sure he will — an' watch 'em jump. Jones would rope the devil, an' tie him down if the lasso didn't burn. Oh! he's hell on ropin' things. An' he's wusser 'n hell on men, an' hosses, an' dogs."[1]

The trip West was the turning point of Grey's life and Jones was the hinge of the turning.

All that my well-meaning friend suggested made me, of course, only the more eager to go with Jones. Where I had once been interested in the old buffalo hunter, I was now fascinated. And now I was with him in the desert and seeing him as he was, a simple, quiet man, who fitted the mountains and the silences, and the long reaches of distance.[2]

They rode on toward House Rock Valley. As they entered the great basin:

"All of a sudden Jones stood up, and let out a wild Comanche yell. I was more startled by the yell than by the great

*hand he smashed down on my shoulder, and for the moment
I was dazed.*

"There! look! look! the buffalo! Hi! Hi! Hi!"

*Below us, a few miles on a rising knoll, a big herd of
buffalo shone black in the gold of the evening sun. I had not
Jones' incentive, but I felt enthusiasm born of the wild and
beautiful picture, and added my yell to his. The huge, burly
leader of the herd lifted his head, and after regarding us for
a few moments calmly went on browsing.*

*The desert had fringed away into a grand rolling pasture-
land, walled in by the red cliffs, the slopes of Buckskin, and
further isolated by the cañon. Here was a range of twenty-four
hundred square miles without a foot of barb-wire, a pasture
fenced in by natural forces, with the splendid feature that the
buffalo could browse on the plain in winter, and go up into
the cool foothills of Buckskin in summer.[3]*

They rode on toward the cabin and shook hands with Jim
and Frank, Jones' cowboys.

*The cabin was the rudest kind of log affair, with a huge
stone fireplace in one end, deer antlers and coyote skins on
the wall, saddles and cowboys' traps in a corner, a nice large
promising cupboard, and a table and chairs. Jim threw wood
on a smoldering fire that soon blazed and crackled cheerily.*

*I sank down into a chair with a feeling of blessed relief.
Ten days of desert ride behind me! Promise of wonderful days
before me, with the last of the old plainsmen! No wonder a
sweet sense of ease stole over me, or that the fire seemed a
live and joyously welcoming thing, or that Jim's deft
maneuvers in preparation of supper roused in me a rapt
admiration.[4]*

By the fire Grey heard of Old Tom, the biggest cougar in
those parts, whose tracks were big around as a horse's, and
Jones told him of his cattalo breeding experiments, revived
here in House Rock.

"Twenty cattalo calves this spring," said Jones rubbing his hands. "Ten thousand dollars worth!"

He told how the cattalo had the hardiness of the buffalo, faced storms, could be easily handled, had stomachs so tough they could digest almost anything that grew, had fourteen ribs instead of thirteen like domestic cattle. "Enables 'em to endure rougher work and to go longer without water," he explained.

Then they talked of remarkable dogs, of heroic hunts, of Mormons, of sandstorms, of Indians, of snow and ice, of hidden canyons, and Grey fell asleep with his head whirling.

Next morning they rode out to see the buffalo. Jones and Grey took up position on a knoll, and Jim and Frank drove the herd by them. Grey estimated there were seventy-five. He was so engrossed in snapping photographs with his Kodak, that when a buffalo bull charged him only clever footwork on his horse's part saved him.

"Shouldn't have put you on a white horse," apologized Jones. "If there's anything buffalo hate it's a white horse."

A sandstorm blew down and chased them to the cabin. There Jones told of his experiences.

A tame wild animal is the most dangerous of beasts. My old friend, Dick Rock, a great hunter and guide out of Idaho, laughed at my advice, and got killed by one of his three-year-old bulls. I told him they knew him just well enough to kill him, and they did. My friend, A. H. Cole, of Oxford, Nebraska, tried to rope a Weetah that was too tame to be safe, and the bull killed him. Same with General Bull, a member of the Kansas Legislature, and two cowboys who went into a corral to tie up a tame elk at the wrong time. I pleaded with them not to undertake it. They had not studied animals as I had. That tame elk killed all of them. He had to be shot in order to get General Bull off his great antlers. You see, a wild animal must learn to respect a man. The way I used to teach the

*Yellowstone Park bears to be respectful and safe neighbors was
to rope them around the front paw, swing them up on a tree
clear of the ground, and whip them with a long pole. It was a
dangerous business, and looks cruel, but it is the only way I
could find to make the bears good. You see, they eat scraps
around the hotels and get so tame they will steal everything but
redhot stoves, and will cuff the life out of those who try to shoo
them off. But after a bear mother has had a licking, she not only
becomes a good bear for the rest of her life, but she tells all her
cubs about it with a good smack of her paw, for emphasis, and
teaches them to respect peaceable citizens generation after
generation . . .* [5]

Jones took Grey into his confidence and told him about his
life, a bit here, a bit there, by campfires, under the pines and
bright stars. By day they went hunting wild horses.

They found a secret passage running between two bare-
rock canyons. It was scarcely six feet wide. The mustangs'
hoofprints led along it. "Those are the tracks of the White
King," said Jones, "last of the wild stallions in Northern Arizona and he's got his band with him." The passageway was
so narrow in places Grey had to pull his legs out of the stirrup
as they rode on the trail of the White King.

"I used to catch a good many wild horses in early days in
Kansas," Jones confided. "When the buffalo played out, we
had to make a living somehow so we took to wild-horse hunting. Our method was to tire the herd with relays of fresh
horses, keeping them moving for weeks if necessary, till they
became so footsore they could be handled.

"We'd have to be careful not to crowd 'em too close or
the stallion would turn on us and we'd have to kill him. If we
did, it ruined our chances. With the leader gone, the herd
scattered.

"But if you kept the stallion alive, you could guide the
herd toward a corral. We didn't have fence-wings running

out into the prairie — there wasn't much fencing available — but we found that a wild horse won't cross a freshly plowed furrow — he thinks it's a snare so we'd plow furrows, v-shape, away out into the prairie, and between those wings we'd drive the horses; until we got close to the corral and inside the wings of *real* fences, and then we'd crowd 'em in, with shots, yells, everything."

The passageway they were traveling through opened onto a canyon floor, between sheer walls.

"I know this canyon," said Jones. "There's water toward the head of it. The mustangs have gone there. But the walls are sheer all the way. If Frank and Jim can get around to the head of it, they can run the herd back down to you and me."

He sent Jim and Frank by a roundabout route that would require two days' travel. Meanwhile he and Grey would wait.

Jones tied their horses to a scrub cedar that grew on a neck of level ground between the canyon's central wash and its rocky hillside. He explained that when the mustangs, on their flight down the canyon, came in sight of the tied horses, the White Stallion would at first mistake them for wild horses, would stop, snort, paw earth, anticipating a fight, sending out a challenge, giving Grey a wonderful opportunity to take photographs. Grey had brought his Kodak along.

Then Jones made a hiding place in the brush beside a huge rock a few yards up the hillside from the tied horses.

They watched all day, sitting with their backs against the rock in the broiling heat, and Grey found that like an animal Jones could sit perfectly still for hours, never moving a muscle. He marvelled at the power in this sixty-three-year-old man. During the night they took turns watching.

Late in the afternoon of the second day Jones said:

"Put your ear to the ground."

Grey did. He heard the drumming of faroff feet.

"They're coming," Jones said. "Look. There's the dust."

Coming toward them around a bend of the canyon was a dust cloud. Out of it shot a white streak. It was the White King. Behind him ran a line of black mares. Manes and tails tossing, hoofs thundering, the band swept down. Grey and Jones stayed hidden.

All of a sudden there was a whistling snort. The stallion came to a sliding stop. "He's winded the tied saddle horses," Jones whispered. The stallion planted his hoofs, reared, and then, snorting, advanced one proud step, and then blew another challenge.

"He's daring our horses to come and fight." There was admiration in Jones' whisper. "Isn't he magnificent? Watch now!"

The old plainsman leaped to his feet yelling and firing his pistol. The stallion wheeled and raced back up the canyon, his band following. Grey snapped pictures.

"Come on!" yelled Jones. He ran for his horse. "Jump in the saddle," he called, "they'll be back in a minute. Keep close to the base of the cliff. When they come, we'll try and part out the stallion and lasso him."

Grey swallowed hard. He thought that parting out and lassoing the stallion would be like parting out and lassoing a whirlwind. He watched Jones on his bay gelding take up position behind a large boulder on the canyon floor, throwing his lasso rope out behind him in the dust as he rode and recoiling it so that no kinks were in it, and hanging it loosely on his saddlehorn.

In a moment down came the herd, frightened by the shots and shouts of Frank and Jim up-canyon.

Jones had his lariat in hand.

"Get ready," he yelled.

Grey began to sweat. Jones rode out from behind his boulder directly into the path of the oncoming mustangs, loop singing, and yelled: "Turn 'em, Grey."

Grey fired his pistol and spurred gamely out from the canyon wall. He had the sensation of being inundated by a flood of tossing manes, flashing eyes, thudding hoofs. They would have run him down if his horse had not jumped back out of the way. They passed within arm's length of him and went down the canyon, and when the dust cleared, Grey saw that by some miracle Jones had separated the stallion from the rest of the herd and was chasing him back up-canyon along the rim of the dry wash that split the canyon floor. The wash was fifteen feet wide and no horse could cross it.

Jones' powerful bay ran as Kentuck had run after the buffalo twenty years before. By sheer will power, it seemed to Grey, Jones overhauled the stallion. It was impossible. Yet it was happening. Jones leaned forward, chin stuck out, beard thrust forward, the very picture of old Uncle Sam horseback, his lariat loop singing.

The stallion raced along the edge of the dry wash. Jones forced him closer and closer to the edge, getting into position for the throw. The stallion dodged, feinted, whirled. Jones matched him turn for turn, whirl for whirl, feint for feint, rising to a height of performance that was superhuman in Grey's estimation . . . while Jim and Frank closed in from above.

Jones' Comanche yell rose in the still hot air: "We've got him, boys!"

The stallion broke away in desperation toward the canyon wall. Jones matched him stride for stride, turned with him and back they came, toward the gulch, and Grey realized he didn't want the stallion to be caught but wanted it to be free and victorious, and then his breath almost stopped as he saw what the stallion was going to do — it was racing straight for the brink of the uncrossable gulch and it was going to jump, and it was jumping, and Jones' rope was shooting out, and such was the perspective from where Grey looked that the stallion appeared to pass directly through Jones' loop and vanish into thin air. Grey blinked his eyes.

When he opened them the White King was disappearing down the canyon on the other side of the gulch and Jones was recoiling his rope with a peculiar expression on his face.

"He deserved to be free," Jones said at last, with a chuckle.

Caught in the end of his rope where the noose had closed tight were four long white hairs from the stallion's tail.

They spoofed Grey that night, telling him the cave they slept in was full of scorpions and spiders, and Grey woke in the night and the cave *was* full of spiders and scorpions, and tarantulas — so he let out a war whoop and submerged himself deep in his sleeping bag, while the others exploded into wakefulness, slap-banging at the multi-legged life in the cave while Grey chuckled to himself deep in his bag. Grey gave as good as he took.

Then they went after Old Tom, the big cougar. They cornered him in a cave on the north rim of the Grand Canyon and Jones, rope in hand, turned to Grey:

"Are you to be depended on here?"

"I? What do you want me to do?" I demanded, and my whole breast seemed to sink in.

"You cut across the head of this slope and take up your position in the slide below the cave, say just by that big stone. From there you can command the cave, our position and your own. Now, if it is necessary to kill this lion to save me or Frank, or, of course, yourself, can you be depended upon to kill him?"

I felt a queer sensation around my heart and a strange tightening of the skin upon my face! What a position for me to be placed in! For one instant I shook like a quivering aspen leaf. Then because of the pride of a man, or perhaps inherited

*instincts cropping out at this perilous moment, I looked up
and answered quietly:*

"Yes. I will kill him!"

*"Old Tom is cornered, and he'll come out. He can run
only two ways: along this trail, or down that slide. I'll take
my stand by the scrub piñon there so I can get a hitch if I
rope him. Frank, when I give the word, let the dogs go. Grey,
you block the slide. If he makes at us, even if I do get my rope
on him, kill him! Most likely he'll jump down hill — then
you'll have to kill him! Be quick. Now loose the hounds. Hi!
Hi! Hi! Hi!"*

*I jumped into the narrow slide of weathered stone and
looked up. Jones' stentorian yell rose high above the clamor
of the hounds. He whirled his lasso.*

*A huge yellow form shot over the trail and hit the top of
the slide with a crash. The lasso streaked out with arrowy
swiftness, circled, and snapped viciously close to Old Tom's
head. "Kill him! Kill him!" roared Jones. Then the lion leaped,
seemingly into the air above me. Instinctively I raised my
little automatic rifle. I seemed to hear a million bellowing
reports. The tawny body, with its grim, snarling face, blurred
in my sight. I heard a roar of sliding stones at my feet. I felt
a rush of wind. I caught a confused glimpse of a whirling
wheel of fur, rolling down the slide.*

*Then Jones and Frank were pounding me, and yelling
I know not what. . . . I felt the hot barrel of my rifle, and
shuddered at the bloody stones below me — then, and then
only, did I realize, with weakening legs, that Old Tom had
jumped at me, and had jumped to his death.*[6]

Grey was blooded now; he was sealed into the tribe.

CHAPTER NINETEEN

Zane Grey Gets an Eye-Full

GREY STUDIED this extraordinary man, last of a breed that was vanishing as the buffalo had vanished. "No doubt something of Buffalo Jones crept unconsciously into all the great fiction characters I have created," he said later.[1]

He heard Jones' reply to a man who had questioned the validity of capturing wild animals:

And God said, "Let us make man in our image, and give him dominion over the fish of the sea, the fowls of the air, over all the cattle, and over every creeping thing that creepeth upon the earth." "Dominion over all the beasts of the field!" repeated Jones, his big voice rolling out. He clenched his huge fists and spread wide his long arms. "Dominion! That was God's word!" The power and intensity of him could be felt. Then he relaxed, dropped his arms, and once more grew calm. But he had shown a glimpse of the great, strange and absorbing passion of his life.[2]

Grey watched Jones rope a vicious female mountain lion alone and unarmed. The old man climbed into a tree after her and threw the rope over her head.

We heralded this achievement with yells of triumph that made the forest ring.

Our triumph was short-lived. Jones had hardly moved when the cougar shot straight out into the air. The lasso caught on a branch, hauling her up short, and there she hung in midair, writhing, struggling and giving utterance to sounds terribly human. For several seconds she swung, slowly descending, in which frenzied time I, with ruling passion uppermost, endeavored to snap a picture of her.

The unintelligible commands Jones was yelling to Frank and me ceased suddenly with a sharp crack of breaking wood. Then crash! Jones fell out of the tree. The lasso streaked up, ran over the limb, while the cougar dropped pell-mell into the bunch of waiting, howling dogs.

The next few moments it was impossible for me to distinguish what actually transpired. A great flutter of leaves whirled round a swiftly changing ball of brown and black and yellow, from which came a fiendish clamor.

Then I saw Jones plunge down the ravine and bounce here and there in mad efforts to catch the whipping lasso. He was roaring in a way that made all his former yells merely whispers. Starting to run, I tripped on a root, fell prone on my face into the ravine, and rolled over and over until I brought up with a bump against a rock.

What a tableau riveted my gaze! It staggered me so I did not think of my camera. I stood transfixed not fifteen feet from the cougar. She sat on her haunches with body well drawn back by the taut lasso to which Jones held tightly. Don was standing up with her, upheld by the hooked claws in his head. The cougar had her paws outstretched; her mouth open wide, showing long, cruel, white fangs; she was trying to pull the head of the dog to her. Don held back with all his power, and so did Jones. Moze and Sounder were tussling round her body. Suddenly both ears of the dog pulled out, slit into ribbons.

Don had never uttered a sound, and once free, he made at her again with open jaws. One blow sent him reeling and stunned. Then began again that wrestling whirl.

"Beat off the dogs! Beat off the dogs!" roared Jones. "She'll kill them! She'll kill them!"

Frank and I seized clubs and ran in upon the confused and furry mass, forgetful of peril to ourselves. In the wild contagion of such a savage moment the minds of men revert wholly to primitive instincts. We swung our clubs and yelled; we fought all over the bottom of the ravine, crashing through the bushes, over logs and stones. I actually felt that soft fur of the cougar at one fleeting instant. The dogs had the strength born of insane fighting spirit. At last we pulled them to where Don lay, half-stunned, and with an arm tight round each, I held them while Frank turned to help Jones.

The disheveled Jones, bloody, grim as death, his heavy jaw locked, stood holding to the lasso. The cougar, her sides shaking with short, quick pants, crouched low on the ground with eyes of purple fire.

"For God's sake, get a half-hitch on the saplin'!" called the cowboy.

His quick grasp of the situation averted a tragedy. Jones was nearly exhausted, even as he was beyond thinking for himself or giving up. The cougar sprang, a yellow, frightful flash. Even as she was in the air, Jones took a quick step on one side and dodged as he threw his lasso round the sapling. She missed him, but one alarmingly outstretched paw grazed his shoulder.[3]

They quickly spread her out between three lassoes, one to her neck, one to each pair of feet. Jones calmly drew from his pocket the clippers and taking each paw in turn he gave the lady lion a manicure.

"Get me the collar and chain," he called, and these items, regularly carried on his saddle, were brought to him.

He collared and chained and muzzled the lion. She was harmless now. He took off the lassoes and patted her head and ran his hand over her sleek fur, while he kept up the strange, low undertone of Jones-talk, the peculiar language he used toward animals he caught.

There was something between him and them, some understanding that was beyond ordinary comprehension. And Kitty calmed to his soft, guttural talking. Yet the wildfire smouldered in her eyes.[4]

"She'll never give up," Jones said. "They never do. That's lion."

He said he considered lions the kings of the wilderness. "Why, even the grizzlies of Yellowstone will make way when a cougar comes. A cougar will just as soon eat a wolf or a bear or a coyote. A cougar is a killer. But there's a difference among 'em. I knew one old Tom up in Yellowstone that was the killingest of 'em all. In his den I found a pile of twenty elk and only five or six of them eaten. I hunted him months and found that he'd killed three animals a week on the average, and when the hounds and I chased him to the Yellowstone River, he swam it at a point impassable for horse or man."

During his comparatively short tour of duty at the Park, Jones had killed seventy-two cougars and captured a number alive.

"It's all nonsense about a cougar not screaming," he said. "Ever since I was a boy in Illinois, I've heard cougars scream. It's always the same. Always the same weird wild sound. Like a hysterical woman. I don't know what it means unless it's the hunger cry, or maybe the mourning of a female for her cubs. The Toms are great cannibals, you know. They'll eat the cubs at every chance they get. So the females will come in heat again."

While at House Rock Valley beyond the Grand Canyon's north rim, Jones was lassoing lions for public zoos and, occasionally, helping to support himself by sending in lion pelts for the state bounty.[5] He went on lecture tours. He visited Washington, promoted a tree-planting project for the treeless plains (some trees were actually planted under government auspices), helped stage a rodeo at Garden City, and wrote Colonel S. B. M. Young, the *new* commandant at Yellowstone Park:[6]

Dear Sir:

President Roosevelt and his Secretary of the Interior, Mr. Garfield, have kindly consented to let me have a buffalo bull and a mountain sheep ram from the Park, as a loan, to assist me in my hybridizing experiments in connection with the Agricultural Department at Washington. I have sent my brother, N. C. Jones[7] in the Park a description of the animals I need. Should he be absent from the Park it might be well to delay capturing the ram till he returns or I can come out and assist in doing it. It will require an expert to care for the ram after he is corralled. Also the corralling must be done with care to insure safety to the animal and only those who have had experience with wild animals should undertake it.

Very respectfully yours,
C. J. Jones

The letter was signed in bold flowing hand, written in ink by the great man personally, and spoke confidently of his intimacy with the President and Garfield.

He had secured some Persian sheep and was hoping to cross them with wild Rocky Mountain bighorns to produce a strain, durable and mighty, that would serve the future of mankind along with the cattalo. With his sheep and cattle hybrids he would dominate the meat market of the future. He

would be the benefactor of man's new state, in the New World
— in the Far West — where all things were possible — new
ideas, new animals, new men.

The sheep hybrid did not succeed. Jones did produce a
creature called the "Perserino," a cross between the Persian
sheep and the common Merino strain — but that is all that
is left of his fantastic idea: a fantastic word. As related earlier,
it was much the same with the cattalo: the male calves proved
sterile because of a modified form of cryptorchidism — which
in ordinary language means that the scrotal sack inherited
from the buffalo maintained the testes at too high a temperature for spermatogenesis. But the main drawback was: times
were changing, the West was taming. Instead of vast wild areas
where a hardy breed of cattle was needed that could roam
weeks and months alone, and fend for itself, there were fenced
farms where a man could feed his cattle by hand if need be,
and see personally that they stayed fat and got shelter. New
and heftier meat-producing breeds like the Hereford were
becoming popular. It was not till mid-century that the Government of Canada began to capitalize on Jones' work — to
conquer the wastes of Northern Canada with this same hybrid.
But meanwhile there was no demand for a bony cattalo. Robes,
too, were a thing of the past. As man developed artificial means
of heat and mechanical devices like trains and automobiles,
he needed less clothing, less blanketing. Changing times had
caught Jones. And he was thinking of changing too. . . .

There came a night: "The red glow of the burning logs
lighted up Jones' calm, cold face," wrote Grey. "Tranquil, un-
alterable and peaceful it seemed; yet beneath the peace I
thought I saw a suggestion of wild restraint, of mystery, of
unslaked life.

"Strangely enough, his next words confirmed my last thought.

"'For forty years I've had an ambition. It's to get possession of an island in the Pacific, somewhere between Vancouver and Alaska, and then go to Siberia and capture a lot of Russian sables. I'd put them on the island and cross them with our silver foxes. I'm going to try it next year if I can find the time.' "[8]

He didn't find time. Something bigger in its way than an island intervened. And it was through Grey that it came. Grey went home and wrote books about Jones and the West — began the series of Western novels that made him famous and in which he featured Jones as his hero, but he could not stay away from Buckskin.

He returned the next year and the next — with friends — and through one of these friends, Jones was led to perhaps the greatest adventure of his career.

CHAPTER TWENTY

The Greatest Challenge

MEANWHILE Martha had died at Topeka. Characteristically, he did not hear the news of her illness until almost the end. He was driving a band of Persian sheep across the waste stretches from the ranch to the railroad and did not know she was ill until he stepped off the train at Garden City.[1] She died October 27, 1907, at the home of their daughter, Olive, in Topeka, and he buried her in Valley View Cemetery, Garden City, on a knoll overlooking the river and the old Santa Fe Trail and the place where he and the Fultons and Stevens had come together so long ago to make a town, and where so much of him was invested — where he had achieved victory, where he had suffered disgrace, and where his sons were buried. After all, and in terms of final definitions, it was home, and there he would be buried too; and no doubt standing there beside her grave, he thought of the frontier that had been, with the two of them, young and full of anticipation, and of how he and she had followed that frontier as men follow stars, west and south and north; and how he had at last come to the end of it on the slopes of Buckskin Mountain, where he would return.

On Buckskin, fate came for him in strange guise. It took the shape of a Massachusetts business man named Charles S. Bird, a well-to-do industrialist and a friend of Zane Grey's, who had come west to hunt lions.

After a successful chase, Bird and Jones were sitting under a piñon tree on the north rim of the Grand Canyon opposite El Tovar Hotel, looking down into the rugged gorge and the river far below, when Jones suddenly turned to him and said:

"Bird, let's you and me go to Africa and lasso wild animals!"

Bird looked at him in astonishment. "Are you out of your mind? I'll admit you can handle these Arizona cougars, but there's one place this game won't work. The African lion is beyond any man's power to handle unless he's got modern weapons. You'd be torn to pieces in two minutes."

Jones replied, "I can handle any animal in Africa with nothing but my lasso and a good Arizona cowpony!"

"Any animal in Africa? . . . I'll bet you you can't."

"I'll bet you my life that I can."

The Buffalo Jones African Expedition took shape then and there. Who knows but that Martha's death helped prepare him for it psychologically by severing him from old ties, battle-grounds, goals that had lost their validity?

And in Jones' own words we have this: "After having captured and conquered every species of animal on the North American continent, like Alexander the Great except as to the greatness, I longed for other worlds to conquer. Having had so much experience with wild creatures I could read their very thoughts, I thought no more of roping a grizzly than of going into my corral and roping a domestic steer. I would just as soon crawl into the den or climb fifty feet into a tree and rope a two-hundred pound panther and pull him out and bind his legs, as to go into a corral and tie down a butting billy goat. I felt perfectly confident I could rope and tie down the African lion, cheetah, rhinoceros, and all of those far-away dangerous beasts, but no one else believed it except those who had seen me master American wild animals.

"Such sport had become stale to me, so one day I sat on a log on my ranch and wrote these lines:

"I've heard of a country far away. . . . "

And there follows one of the poems, of his original composition, which he was beginning to write, purely and simply to express himself.[2]

Anyway, Bird financed the African expedition. It would do what no human being had yet tried to do and would be termed — beforehand — an absolutely crazy undertaking.

Afterward, the President, stepping out of the White House, would say that no more memorable African hunting trip ever took place.[3]

Preparations went forward smoothly. Guy H. Scull, Harvard man, member of Roosevelt's regiment in the Spanish-American War and veteran of the charge up San Juan Hill, became field manager. W. G. Sewall of the Boma Trading Company in Nairobi made preliminary arrangements for safari. At a farewell dinner in New York the night before he sailed, Jones was honored by Zane Grey, Ernest Thompson Seton, Captain Jack Crawford, the famous Indian scout, and other admirers. Grey had brought along a copy of his new book, *The Last of the Plainsmen,* all about Jones and himself and their hunting trips on the Grand Canyon's north rim, and he presented it to the Colonel with best wishes for the coming trip, and Jones laughingly autographed other copies for those present, signing them with a flourish, *C. J. Jones, Last of the Plainsmen.*

Someone ventured to raise the question of how he was going to hold a two-and-a-half-ton rhinoceros with a finger-thick rope and a thousand-pound Arizona cowpony, and Jones replied simply, "We'll do it." He apparently made it a practice never to let shadow of doubt intervene, once he had decided on a course of action, and he never bothered too much about the "how" once he had decided on the "why." The "how" seemed to take care of itself.

"What are you going to do when the lion charges?" they asked.

He shrugged and indicated by his manner that he would do whatever was necessary.

He managed to impart to those present, sophisticated men of adult mind, that he would be equal to any occasion.

Reaching London and having ordered the handcuffs that might be necessary for lions, he went to the offices of the Boma Trading Company to make arrangements for a photographer to accompany the expedition. There he was introduced to a husky Yorkshireman named Cherry Kearton. Kearton was one of the best-known photographers in England. He had been to Africa and knew the country and its game, and he was skeptical of Jones' scheme and had not yet agreed to go along with him. However, the necessary documents lay open on the table when Jones walked into the room.

He and Kearton talked for a minute or two, and Kearton finally exploded, "How on earth are you going to do such a thing?"

Jones said calmly, "We'll do it."

Kearton signed the papers.

At Aden near the mouth of the Red Sea they joined forces with the main body of the expedition which had come direct from the States. This consisted of two Arizona-New Mexico cowboys, Marshall Loveless and Ambrose Means, twelve cow-ponies and four hound-dogs from Jones' Grand Canyon pack (to which he now added seventeen brought from England),

and the bulk of the gear and supplies. The ponies were ordinary ranch stock, distinguished only by capability and durability, and designed to prove Jones' thesis that ordinary Western horses and Western men could do just about anything that was required of them. It might be well to say that the world's preoccupation with animals probably reached a height in these days following the settlement of the last frontiers — and the opening of Africa, in reality a vast new frontier — and people doubtless saw in the King of Beasts much more of a wild natural symbol — and recent enemy — than we do now, when acquaintance with him is often by way of the Metro-Goldwyn-Mayer movie screen.

As for Loveless and Means, they were two as characteristic cowboys as ever rolled a five-cent smoke from a pack of Bull Durham. Loveless, short, quick-stepping, energetic, from the Portales-Las Vegas district, had been known to Jones for some time. Means, taller, easy-going, laconic, had been a champion roper in the Wild West show, and had come recommended by Bill Cody as the best of the best. Men, horses, and dogs had that intangible something that advertised them as Outdoor Western American, and they looked odd indeed against the Oriental backgrounds of Aden.

"The horses came through in fine shape," Loveless imparted to the Colonel, "but the dogs have a little distemper."

"We'll cure that," said Jones, "as soon as we hit open country. What kind of a voyage did you have?"

"Oh, it was a little rough," drawled Loveless, "we left New York on December 30 on the *Prince Adelbert* as you know, got to Hamburg without losing anything much besides our lunch, took a layover at Rotterdam, Naples, Italy, and Port Said, and other than that we ain't had any complaints till we got here. This here is the hottest hole this side of hell."

Jones allowed himself a laugh. "Mombasa is our next stop," he said, "and that's quite a way from Albuquerque."

"Say, they're ridin' us pretty hard about these lions," put in Means. "You got your vocabulary sharpened up, Colonel?"

"Leave 'em to me," Jones grinned.

On the boat to Mombasa was a British sportsman who had spent a considerable amount of time hunting African lions with dogs, then a not-too-unheard-of pastime among the sporting gentry, and he asked Jones seriously if he could throw a lasso three hundred feet.

"My ropes are forty feet long," replied Jones just as seriously.

The Englishman laughed. "How do you expect to arrive within forty feet of a lion, may I ask?"

"On my horse," said Jones, even more seriously.

At Mombasa, East Africa, they boarded railroad cars that were screened to protect passengers from tsetse flies, and rolled inland, reaching Nairobi on the third of March, 1910. At Nairobi they found that Theodore Roosevelt, now out of the White House and engaged in his famous African hunting trip, had passed through the district a few weeks before, bagging — in the very region into which they were going — a record rhinoceros. Newsmen had asked Roosevelt if he thought Jones and his party would be able to lasso wild animals such as rhinos and lions and the ex-President had replied: "I wouldn't be surprised if they do. Those cowboys are a reckless care-for-nothing bunch."

Was it coincidence that put the two expeditions in the field at practically the same time? Some say the apparent coincidence was deliberately brought about. They say that Bird financed the Jones Expedition in order to discredit Roosevelt by showing that unarmed men with lassos could do what the heavily armed Roosevelt party was doing with guns and bullets. Here is what Ambrose Means says:

"Our job was to rope and tie up every species of animal that Roosevelt had shot with his big high power rifle. I might be wrong, but I think that Theodore Roosevelt had the very definite idea that by hunting big game in Africa he could stay in the limelight, and remain a popular hero with a mighty good chance of being returned to the White House if he could swing the Republican nomination at the end of Taft's first term. Whether I am right in that guess or not, Charles S. Bird, big Democratic politician of Willapah, Mass., was of the same opinion, and set about a plan to dampen the fame that Roosevelt might win in Africa . . . "[4]

As if to bear Means out — Roosevelt *did* run for the presidency at the end of Taft's first term, split the Republican party, and insured the election of Democrat Woodrow Wilson.

Whatever the truth — and Bird and Jones both declared otherwise than Means[5] — Jones set about making arrangements in Nairobi for a safari to carry their baggage into the interior, while Means and Loveless knocked around town in high-heeled boots and attracting widespread attention.

Whatever Nairobi thought of Means and Loveless, it thought Jones a fool. "Wait till he ties onto a rhinoceros with that spotted horse," the sportsmen on the veranda of the Colonists' Association said, "He'll find out what it is to meddle with African wild life."

Despite this antipathy he found a white hunter, Ray Ulyate, who was willing to go along with him as a guide, and arrangements were concluded at the Boma Trading Company for porters to carry baggage and supplies.

And pretty soon it wasn't all antipathy, either, and the ice began to melt.

As Jones describes it:

From all sides of the streets as I rode along I could see the mockery that came from white persons who nudged their companions and uttered a hushed sentence. I could see it on their countenance, and feel it in the electrical air. It was repeated to me from every quarter by friends that the incredulous were invariably saying, "There is the damn fool who thinks he can lasso a lion and rhino." We frequently went to the city to exercise our horses and get such things as we needed. One day in Nairobi, we saw a circle of men. It appeared a pony had thrown his rider and his bridle was gone. He was about as wild as a Texas broncho, and ran round and round, no one daring to touch him. Loveless happened to have his rope on the horn of his saddle and was soon inside the ring and as the horse came around, the rope twirled in the air and gracefully fell over Mr. Horse's head, and such a yell as went up from the natives' throats can only be imagined. They had never seen such a sight before and in fact had never heard of the American cowboy until we came among them. The English Lords hired the natives to run one block, giving him a rupee, and if one of us failed to catch him with the rope, he received two rupees. It was great exercise for our horses but only a few received rupees.[6]

When the expedition marched down the main street of Nairobi — the customary procedure for safaris leaving town — it presented by all odds the strangest sight seen in those parts in many a day. At the head of the procession came Jones, dressed in buckskin-trimmed garments of the wild west, crowned with white pith helmet. His v-shaped white beard gleamed in the sun and he was riding a rawboned skate of a brown-and-white spotted Arizona cowpony that looked, even to generous eyes, about ready for the glue factory. Trotting at his heels were twenty-one assorted hound-dogs, and then came Loveless and Means sloping in their saddles with that deceiving cowpunchers' slouch, and then came the somewhat pompous Kearton and his assistant, Gobbet, both a bit embarrassed at being seen with this motley crew but still under the spell of Jones; and finally there were one hundred thirty native porters on foot, carrying everything from movie cameras to the branding irons that were intended to brand "B. J." (Buffalo

Jones) on the rumps of African lions. Over the long line of porters flew the Stars and Stripes and the house-flag of the Boma Trading Company, which — by uncanny coincidence — was a white buffalo skull.

Underneath the skull in Latin was this motto: "A wise man is vigilant."

It was as if providence had provided symbolic meanings for the occasion.

Ulyate, their guide, had gone ahead into the interior to make arrangements for ox wagons to transport heavy baggage and equipment, and within three days they were lining out across the plains in a manner familiar to Jones from his earliest prairie days.

The scenery was different but the principle was much the same. The Kedong and Rift valleys have two extinct volcanoes that rise black against the sky, and the valley floors are covered by volcanic dust that stings your throat and eyes and makes you sneeze. Hot and thirsty, the safari had trudged four miles that first morning, when Ulyate reined in and pointed to three dark objects on the plain half a mile away.

"Wart hogs," he said. "Do you want to rope 'em, Colonel?"

"They're just what we need to practice on," said Jones, "they'll take the kinks out of us. Come on, boys!"

Now, the wart hog is a mean customer. He stands between three and four feet high at the shoulder and has tusks that can rip a man or a horse open. Here would be the first test of Jones' idea: that men and horses and ropes would perform just as well in Kenya as in Arizona; and perhaps a little better.

He, Loveless, and Means got leisurely down and tightened their cinches, then swung to their saddles and cantered off westward, under a hot sun, to get around the three wart hogs and start them back toward the cameras. Jones was on his favorite mount, the baldfaced pinto, a leggy unprepossessing brute tough as Kaibab cedar, that he had had at the ranch on Buckskin when Grey was there, and Loveless rode a black, and Means a big bay gelding, cowponies all.

The line of native porters was by this time arriving at the spot where Kearton and Gobbet had set up their tripods and cameras to photograph the coming action.

As each porter arrived, he set down his load and sat on it, and stared at the cameras and photographic gear. Movie cameras had hardly been seen in the United States then, let alone Africa.

Kearton called out a warning. With a swirl of dust, the riders were coming. They had parted out one big hog and all three were after him, hell for leather, and he was just about the fastest moving pig they had ever got behind. He ran easily, snout low, tusks flashing. Loveless' pony was nearest, its head low too, and its nose out, racing over the foreign ground and watching the hog, and Loveless' reins were relaxed, giving the horse head enough but not too much. Loveless had taken down his lariat from his horn and now began to build his loop as the horse gained. The rope was made of Russian hemp, hard twist, made especially to order for the Jones Expedition by the American Cordage Company of Brooklyn. It was the thickness of your little finger, and as it whirled it made the same song it had made for Loveless in the Sandia Mountains and on the slopes west of Roswell.

The hog headed straight for Kearton's camera. Kearton, crouched behind his tripod, snatched off his pith hat and waved it excitedly. He didn't want the hog to run over him. But the hog continued straight at him.

Kearton stepped back, undecided whether to run or hold his ground. At the last instant the hog swerved, and passed so close he could have touched it with his hat. And just at that moment Loveless made his throw. He was a "hard-and-fast" man of course, that is, his rope's end was lashed tight to his saddle bow, and he let the whole rope go when he threw, instead of taking turns around the horn as a California roper might have done. He caught one hind leg and the black New Mexico cowpony dug his feet in the African dust, a cloud of the volcanic ash shot up, and when it settled, the hog was lying on its side blowing like a bellows, and the rope was running from its leg to Loveless' saddle, and Loveless was laughing. "Got us a piece of pork, boys."

"Say, that hog really can cut the wind!" ejaculated Means, riding up.

"Travelingest hog I ever see!" Loveless agreed.

But Kearton was angry. "Next time don't run them *at* me. Run them to *one side* of me!" he growled.

"Lucky he didn't run over you," Loveless rejoined.

The porters were nodding and smiling with delight. Here was a new way of doing things and one they clearly approved.

Means roped the hog's head and Jones got down and took the rope off the one hind foot and looped it over the two, then released the hog's head and moved without delay for his horse while Loveless held the two hind feet of the struggling hog tight a moment or two, until Jones was mounted, and then he slacked up and the hog's kicking feet opened the loop and it struggled upright and was free. For a moment it wanted to fight them all but thought better of the idea and trotted off, humped up.

Their first test had proved a success and they were heartened. There was a fair chance that up the valley they would flush larger game and Jones rode ahead, elated, with his two cowboys. Hour after hour they led the way, and the safari plodded behind. At noon the oxen were outspanned and they all rested. The sun was glaring hot. The thorn trees cast little shade. They rested in the shadow of the wagons, and then as they plodded on, it was Jones who first noticed the lion tracks.

"Look here," he said coolly to Ulyate, pointing to the pug marks in the dust. They were essentially no different from those he had seen in Arizona — the rounded marks, the slightly beveled edges where the sheathed claws of the toes were indicated.

They got down and examined them. Ulyate said they were four hours old. There was no use to put dogs on four-hour-old tracks, but Jones suggested following them. There was a chance the lion might be lying up in the shade of a thorn tree, so they fanned out and moved slowly over the plain five or six miles in a great sweeping semicircle. Toward mid-afternoon they reached a crest and looked into a valley that was greener than the rest of the veldt, and saw a herd of antelope grazing in it.

"There is no lion near," commented Jones, "because the game is grazing peacefully. But look yonder. Isn't that a bunch of eland, Ulyate? We might as well try our ropes on them."

No sooner said than done. The eland is a kind of ox-like antelope and though fast, it was not fast enough. Loveless lassoed one by forelegs and neck, in the classic figure eight, and threw it down unaided. The horses, Jones saw with satisfaction, were proving fast enough to bring them alongside the game. He had never had doubts about the men's abilities as ropers.

Meanwhile Loveless had jumped from his black horse and was running forward to make the tie on the eland when the pony took alarm at the proximity of this strange-looking, strange-smelling creature and started bucking, still tied to the prostrate eland.

Loveless, on foot, could not control it, and Means and Jones were laughing fit to burst, while Loveless dodged around and at last "walked up his rope" hand over hand until he caught and quieted his horse.

That night in camp Jones said: "Well, we've found out two things. Our horses are fast enough, but we've got to familiarize them with the smells, sights, sounds of this country or we're going to find ourselves in a jam. Suppose that eland had been a lion, Loveless, and your horse had gone to pitching with you when you were on foot like that?"

"Have I got to get on foot with that lion?" Loveless inquired, in his mild drawl.

They came upon the lions early next morning close to the base of one of the extinct volcanoes that dominated the valley. There was a male and a female, and they did not wait for the horsemen to come close, but departed at a canter for the protection of the nearby mountain. Jones, Ulyate, and the cowboys galloped after them but the headstart was too great and the lions disappeared into the gullies and rocks of the volcano's side.

Jones, in a high pitch of excitement, was prowling the mountainside in search of them when a large cat-like creature shot from almost under his pony's feet. It turned out to be a cheetah, or hunting leopard, the fastest animal on earth for a short distance. Baldy soon began to gain, however, and the cheetah took refuge in a gully. The party gathered at the gully's brink. The porters assembled. It was decided to make a drive and shoo the leopard out. But while the consultation was taking place, an intuition came to Jones, that sixth sense that almost always gave him power in critical situations, and he simply turned his horse and without a word rode into the gully, alone, came close to the cheetah, and, when it failed to spring, dropped a loop over its head and dragged it out into open ground. The cheetah was duly photographed and set free.

"Now some big sportsman can come along and shoot him," commented Jones wryly.[7]

CHAPTER TWENTY-ONE

Rhino

SHOULD THEY STAY a few days longer in the valley and gain experience, and let the horses, dogs, and men acclimatize, or should they push on over the Mau, the hill country, with a chance for giraffe on the way, and on into the Sotik plain, with the promise of both rhino and lion?

Back in Nairobi the sporting crowd was betting five to one against Jones lassoing a rhino, seven to one against his catching a lion. One famous lord expressed the general attitude by wagering five-thousand pounds (twenty-five thousand dollars) against Jones.

As if in answer to these challenges, it was decided to push on over the Mau escarpment. A feeling of expectancy was in the air as the party broke camp next morning. Handcuffs, chains, screws, tongs, muzzles, and branding irons were stowed in the first wagon. The route of march led through barren broken country rising gradually to the Mau rim, but no game was seen until just before noon, when Ulyate pointed out something moving among the treetops. It was the head and neck of a giraffe. "Get him!" ordered Jones. As they began to fan out and slip forward, the giraffe took alarm and started off at a stiff-legged gallop that looked deceivingly slow, but soon proved almost faster than their horses could run.

During the next four hours the caravan lay and baked in the heat, no sight or sound of the four riders, and then there was a drumming of hoofbeats and the dozing porters and Kearton and Gobbet looked up and saw Ulyate reining in his pony.

"Jones wants you — quick," he said to Kearton. "And bring your photographic gear. They've cornered the giraffe."

There was reason for speed. The giraffe might not stand still and the day was growing late.

It was a three-mile ride and when they reached the clearing they saw a long neck outlined against the sky. The giraffe was standing with feet spread apart looking down in a curious, befuddled way at the little creatures running around its feet.

As soon as Kearton set up the camera, Jones gave a high-pitched yell and the giraffe started moving, long neck working up and down like an oil well's pump arm, body rocking stiff-leggedly below.

Loveless' horse was the fastest of the group but it had hard work to gain. The throw would be downhill, at full speed, at a bobbing giraffe's head, more or less in the treetops, forty feet away. But Loveless threw true at the first try and reined in gently so as not to fell the huge creature. Horse and rider acted as brake until the giraffe gradually stopped and the whir of camera shutters ended in the special flapping noise that meant Kearton had used up his film. Loveless and giraffe looked at each other. "Well?" said Loveless after a minute.

Jones rode up laughing. "You caught him. What are you going to do with him?"

"Bring me a stepladder and I'll take that rope off his neck," offered Means.

Then Jones said seriously, "We'll have to throw him to

get that rope off. Can you boys set him down easy?"

Means roped the giraffe by one hind leg and pulled the leg gently out from under. The mass of flesh sank to the veldt. Then they loosened the loops and set him free.

The giraffe rocked off, composure badly shaken but otherwise undamaged, and the party returned to camp in fine spirits. Next day they roped a zebra, and just for the hell of it Means rode it, bareback, and though the zebra humped and pitched a bit, Means said it wasn't nearly so rough as some of those mustangs he'd straddled. Next they caught a hartebeest and tried out their branding irons on it and turned it loose with a "B. J." on its hip.

So they continued, over the Mau, and reached Webb's farm in the Guaso Nyiro Valley on March 16. There they called a halt to rest their horses before tackling the big game — rhino, lion — that the region afforded, and during the twenty-four hour lay-over, their good luck changed. It began to rain. For two days it rained steadily. Jones in disgust put aside his African pith helmet and put on his broad-brimmed Western hat, and the rain stopped, apparently impressed by his change of headgear, and he announced:

"We've got to move fast. When the rainy season really begins it'll soften the ground so that a horse can't run faster than a snail. There's water twelve miles from here, they tell me, at a place called Soda Swamp. We'll start for there in the morning and hunt as we go."

At sunrise they started. There was no road. The wagons rocked across the open plains. The riders fanned out to look for game. The morning passed without incident. Gobbet grumbled, as he and Kearton poked along with the wagons: "I thought this country was so full of big game you couldn't sleep at night for lions roaring!"

"They've heard we were coming and don't want their pictures taken," replied Kearton sourly.

A discussion followed as to the uniqueness of their expedition so far as motion pictures were concerned. The art was in its infancy and certainly no pictures of horsemen lassoing wild African animals had been taken before. They had high hopes for the outcome, financial and professional, of their scheme, and this helped keep their spirits up, till Kearton, glancing down the road, said, "Look, Means is coming."

"He probably forgot his tobacco."

True, Means was always chewing, and he kept true to form by spitting, before he spoke.

"Found us a rhino," he said laconically, getting off and squatting down beside them.

"A rhino?"

Gobbet and Kearton were instantly on their feet, which merely seemed to increase Means' relaxation.

"Yeah, a rhino, sure enough. The Colonel said to tell you to bring your cameras. And the heavy rope."

They searched the wagons for the heavy rope but it wasn't there. Ulyate had gone off on a foraging expedition to a neighboring farm and had taken the wagon that held the rope. They would have to lasso the twenty-five-hundred-pound rhino with their light ropes if they lassoed him at all.

"The Colonel really wants to tackle him, eh?" said Kearton. Though they had discussed the possibility a dozen times, now that the moment had arrived he could not quite believe it.

"Sure, why not?" said Means. "That is — if you want to."

Means sat his pony easily as the three of them galloped back toward Jones, and Kearton noticed that his hands were perfectly steady.

Kearton thought about the rhino. In a way this was more fantastic than roping a lion — to lasso a thing like this.

At the end of half an hour they met Loveless who had unsaddled and turned his pony loose to rest and eat in preparation for the coming exertions, and was himself taking it easy under a tree. He gave them a wave and resaddled. Kearton and Gobbet adjusted their cameras and tripods and they rode on. All at once Jones emerged from a bush in front of them, finger on his lips.

"The rhino's asleep just over there!" he whispered, pointing to a clump of scrub a hundred yards away. He, too, appeared perfectly calm. "Kearton, we want you to catch this show from the start. You can move through this bush and set up, there in the open, and signal when you're ready."

Kearton got down and tied his horse and began slipping forward through the undergrowth with camera and tripod. Now the chips were down and he too was cool. And what was more, he was going into this without his usual protection. Ulyate, whose job it was to stand guard over him with a rifle, was absent. Gobbet followed Kearton. Gobbet was young, thin, active, with sharp black eyes. He had never been on a hunt like this before and was excited.

After tightening their cinches the three horsemen mounted and began to swing out to the right. Kearton had stopped in open ground and placed his camera on top of its tripod, sighted it, and now took out his handkerchief and wiped the lens. The handkerchief flashed white in the sun. Things appeared to grow still, and time to run down. Kearton waved his hand.

Jones' Comanche yell broke the morning wide open, and Jones could really yell — he yelled in the tradition of the Western Men, of the Mountain Men, of the Plains Men, of the Americans generally, and on a good day you probably could have heard him from Kenya to Madagascar.

A vast object that had been lying peacefully in the grass heaved itself up. It was a twenty-five-hundred-pound rhino, and to all of them it looked pretty large. To tie to a thing like that would be a little like tying to an earthquake. However, they did not give themselves over to contemplation.

They rode full tilt at the rhino, hoping it would break

and run and give them a chance for a throw. It did break away but with greater speed than they had foreseen. It went so fast they could not get close enough for a throw. For three miles it ran straight ahead, the horses not gaining, its tonnage rolling along with astounding ease, and then it came to an open country dotted here and there with small thorn trees, found a pool of water left from the previous days' rains, splashed to its center and there turned and faced them. A lull followed while all concerned caught breath.

"We've got to move him out of there," Jones said, when both horses and rhino had had a good blow. "When I induce him to charge me, you fellows move in for a throw."

As he spoke he rode Baldy into the water. For fifteen yards the rhino watched the horse come slowly forward. Then with a furious snort he charged, shooting up water in geysers. Jones whirled Baldy and raced away, but he had to ride his hardest to keep ahead of the menacing horn.

Means fell in behind the rhino and his rope flew. It fell true and Means was tied to a rhinoceros. He set back his big bay on its haunches — and dug up dirt for about forty yards, and then the rope snapped.

"We sure needed that heavy rope!" he commented, slowly reeling in the broken strands as the rhinoceros raced off. The rhino kept after Jones for about a quarter of a mile, then gave up and came to bay, Means' broken rope dangling from its throat like a necktie.

"Never mind," Jones said, riding back. "We'll catch him with what rope we've got. We'll make him charge us one after the other, so that he runs three times to our horses' once. That will wear him down. Then we'll get him."

They proceeded to apply this strategy. Time after time the rhino charged. The cowponies proved just a step faster than the African juggernaut, though each time he came very close to them. They seemed to have just enough speed to do the job they had to do. Of course a misstep or stumble might have meant death. But they did not stumble and they did not misstep.

Little by little the continual charging wore the rhino down. Kearton arrived on his big chestnut, heavy camera under his arm, tripod over his shoulder, reins hanging loosely from the saddlehorn, heels drumming the horse's side, the picture of wild enthusiasm. He was followed by Gobbet on his gray. "What pictures!" Kearton kept saying.

Kearton's number-two assistant, Mac, the Mohammedan, and his number-three assistant, Aro, the Masai warrior, had joined the party on foot, and took the apparatus from him and set it up. Gobbet was standing near a small thorn tree. The rhino caught sight of him — the least offensive member of the party — and charged. Gobbet's porter saw the rhino coming and was up the tree in a flash, but Gobbet was bent over the camera, looking into the view-finder, and did not realize what was happening until almost too late.

"Look out!" Jones yelled.

Gobbet glanced up — and jumped for the tree. But the porter was ahead of him and there wasn't room for two, so Gobbet had to run for it. His chances didn't look very good. The rhino hit the tripod and sent it and the camera flying and bore down on Gobbet, but Means intervened and attracted its attention and Gobbet got away.

Then with sudden surprising courage, Gobbet reversed his field, came back and picked up the wreck of the camera and tripod, found the tripod-head split in two as cleanly as if an axe had struck it, but there was enough left to support a camera, so he quickly mounted it and got into action in time to catch the end of the rhino's charge after Means.

All the while Kearton's camera was clicking. "I hope I got that, all right," he said to Gobbet, as if he were considering asking Gobbet to do it again.

They fought the rhino through the long hot afternoon. Ropes were thrown and caught and broken, mended and thrown again. Rolls of film were exposed and new ones inserted. The rhino alternately sulked and stormed.

After four hours, Loveless' rope was reduced to a piece not much longer than a horse's tie rope. The lariats of the others were dangling as souvenirs around the rhino's neck and legs, and the rhino stood at bay on the ruins of an ant hill, glaring at them, sides heaving, but horn still up. Only an hour of daylight remained. How to get hold of the ropes on neck and legs? How to wear him down in that last hour? If darkness came, they would lose him for sure.

Lying loose in the grass nearby was the stump of a dead tree, with roots sticking out around its bottom. Noticing it, Jones said, "Loveless, fasten that stump to your last piece of rope."

This done, Loveless rode toward Kearton's camera, past the rhino, dragging the stump behind him. The rhino charged the stump. Away went Loveless at a run, followed by the stump, which bounced crazily over the ground, then by the rhino, which charged madly against the bouncing stump, trying again and again to hook it, as Loveless rode straight toward Kearton's camera. There Aro, the Masai warrior, substituting as guard, stood by the tripod with his long spear poised high, while Kearton cranked the camera, shouting at Loveless:

"Damn it, how many times I got to tell you not to bring 'em *directly* at the lens?"

Luckily the rhino was too engrossed in the stump to see Kearton. He roared by the tripod like a fast freight by a signpost at a railway crossing and then, as Jones had guessed, the loose ropes that were hanging from the rhino became entangled in the stump, and the rhino was bound to the stump.

By hauling at the stump gently, Loveless succeeded in recovering two of the ropes and they were pieced together and thrown again, catching the rhino by one hind leg. Now both Loveless and Means put spurs to their horses, pulling forward on the one rope, and they lifted that hind leg — drawn by two horses — ahead. The weary beast let his body follow. Step by step they dragged him toward a tree. There Loveless got down, passed the end of the rope twice around the trunk, and tied it tight.

The rhino charged but Loveless went up the tree as if the thorns in it did not exist. From up there he looked down and kidded the rhino. The rhino next tried to escape by charging in the other direction, but the rope held him — he was weak now — and he tripped, got up unsteadily and then stood quietly, spirit broken, caught. Loveless came down the tree. Kearton snapped pictures.

When the news reached Nairobi the few who had bet on Jones collected their money, at five to one.

When the news of the capture of the rhino reached New York the anti-Roosevelt *Globe* headlined:

JONES ROPES
RHINOS ALIVE

*Famous Western Cowboy
"Makes Good" With
Lariat in Africa*

ROOSEVELT OUTDONE

And there were two columns and a photograph of Jones, lending weight to the thesis that there was a party who wished to discredit Roosevelt and was using Jones' exploits as their instrument, though it did not prove that Jones was their conscious instrument.[1]

The pro-Roosevelt New York *Times*, however, allowed

Jones three inches of type at the bottom of an inside page, following a long column on Roosevelt.[2]

The article in the New York *Globe* went on to say:

An old-time cowboy, still youthful at sixty-five, has gone Col. Roosevelt one better in the African jungles. While the former president, who delights to be called "a great faunal naturalist" has been slaying wild beasts, 'Buffalo Jones' has been roping the critters in true wild western style, and he will bring the animals alive to this country. . . .

For years Jones was government game warden of Yellowstone Park, and while there he made numerous captures of full-grown mountain lions by roping them. Also his feat of manicuring the grizzly bears of the Park made him known all over the country. One of the exciting incidents of his career was the whipping of the bad bears of the Yellowstone Park "to put the fear of man into their hearts."

'Buffalo' Jones guided President Roosevelt on his famous hunting trip through the Yellowstone while President, and they have been firm friends ever since.

"Some of his exploits with wild animals are hazardous to the point of astonishment," Colonel Roosevelt once said.

Roosevelt had gone up into Egypt and then to see the Kaiser in Germany and was not available for comment.

Jones had a broken finger — the index finger of his right hand — as a result of the encounter with the rhino — the damage being suffered in one of the flurries of roping the huge beast — and his comments were unprintable.

CHAPTER TWENTY-TWO

Hound-Dog

DID JONES go to Africa to discredit Roosevelt? The answer is yes and no — yes, in that he truly believed it better, fairer, and in every ethical sense more creditable for a man to capture an animal alive than to shoot it — no, in that he did not primarily go to Africa to discredit a friend. To this day they say in Garden City that Teddy Roosevelt asked Buffalo Jones to accompany him to Africa, and Jones said, "Not if you are going to kill the animals you find there."

The fact remains that when Jones' expedition was over, Roosevelt wrote a glowing introduction to a book about it.[1]

In the meantime the lions had left the Sotik country and it was "lion" they wanted.

Time was growing short. Every day might bring the rains. On the evening of March 25, they faced a dilemma: go or stay. Darkness had fallen and when supper was finished they gathered by the fire that was burning close to where the horses were tethered.

All of them knew the Sotik had proved a failure. They'd

swept and reswept the region without finding a sign of a
lion, and without a lion the expedition was a failure. It was
time for the Colonel to speak.

"We've got to go back," he said, looking into the fire
while he talked, "We'll leave tomorrow and have a try near
the waterhole by the Rugged Rocks where we saw those two
lions on the way up here. Maybe we'll find one. If not, we'll
go back to Nairobi and start over again — provided the rains
don't begin."

Through long hot days they retraced their steps.

Cameras were stowed in wagons. Ropes stayed coiled
at saddles. Men rode as they chose. Jones had set his finger
and put splints on it, and it was healing — probably it was
just a severe dislocation — but it was still paining him con-
siderably. There was an atmosphere of defeat. The white
hunters of the region had joined their voices to the skeptical
chorus. "It can't be done. Lasso a lion with a cowpony and
lariat? This isn't Buffalo Bill and his Wild West Show. This,
sir, is Africa."

At the Last Water they outspanned and spent a day
resting. Ahead of them lay twenty-four dry hours and then
the waterhole at the Rugged Rocks.

After the rest they inspanned and marched all night.
The air was still and the dust lifting from the feet of the
oxen drifted along with the wagons. Every so often the
wheels bumped on a rock and the brake beams shook and
rattled. As they crossed the top of the Mau the moon rose
and lit their way as they descended slowly toward the plain.
By dawn they were in the foothills. A cold wind sprang up
and they buttoned their jackets. "It was just about here that
we caught the giraffe that day," said Kearton, "remember
how hot it was?"

"I wonder what that old boy things of our necktie party
now?" Loveless said.

"One thing sure about a giraffe," said Means, "you got to get your rope on him in the first half mile. After that he can outrun any saddle horse living."

At sunup they entered the plain of the Rift. It quickly grew hot. Thirst increased. Toward noon they halted for a couple of hours. There certainly wasn't any sign of the rainy season here. Things were dry as the Sahara. They inspanned again and moved on, while the Colonel outlined his plans:

"We'll give the horses a good night's rest, then start hunting early in the morning. We've got enough horse-feed to last three days — if the water holds out. In three days we ought to get a lion if there's any there. If not, we'll go back to Nairobi. Now I'll ride on a bit and look for signs."

Baldy was a fast walker and drew ahead. Little by little the others began to string out. The land was baked white beneath the blazing sun, empty as mid-ocean, heat shimmers rising here and there.

Loveless presented his views to Means: "I been thinking about when we get that lion, seems to me that after the dogs stop him one of us had better go past him on the run, rope him, and keep a-going, and another fellow can catch him by the hind legs, and then we've got him!"

Means agreed.

Ulyate, who had never been too enthusiastic about strangers from another land coming and roping a lion in his backyard, shook his head.

"Just let me get straight what I'm to do," he said, "You want me to stand by as protection for the cameras and leave the Colonel and you two chaps free to do what you have to do? Is that it? And if the lion charges a rider, I won't fire. But if he charges the cameras, I will fire?"

"That's right. You don't fire unless he charges the cameras."

Ulyate had a .405 British Winchester that was popular for all-around use.

"We might find something at the Rugged Rocks," he said, "but if we don't, I don't think we'll find anything."

The safari moved more and more slowly as the heat increased. They had been twenty hours without water. The drivers no longer had breath to shout at their oxen, and the oxen moved with the blind patient instinct of suffering flesh.

Jones reached the Rugged Rocks ahead of them and they found him sitting on his horse, looking somberly at the ground.

"The waterhole is dry," he said.

Without a word they dismounted and turned their animals loose. If the waterhole was dry, words would not put water in it, so they now had to push on to Kijabe Station, if they could make it.

This was defeat as defeat is usually spelled: men, animals, weary, bone-thirsty — going beyond their second day without water except for the tiny amount carried in canteens, and now all of that was gone. But Jones was determined.

At dawn he set off with Loveless, Means, and Kearton to scout the country by the Rugged Rocks. At noon the next day the three of them rejoined the main body of the expedition which had straggled into Kijabe Station more dead than alive.

"We found lions," Jones announced cheerfully, "near the base of Longernot, the northern volcano, in a belt of lava that rises from the plain. A male and a female. We kept them in sight for a full hour. My guess is that they live in the neighborhood. And Ulyate agrees. He says no one has hunted that corner of the valley. There's no water there. Now, we've got to start back immediately and get them, or they'll be gone."

It was Means who rebelled. He'd strained his back,

reinjuring an old hurt sustained chasing a steer in the breaks at the head of the Verde River, and could no longer sit a saddle straight. Loveless had a festering thorn wound in his foot. Horses, dogs, oxen, porters, riders — all were utterly fatigued. "Colonel, we just can't make it," Means said, "and that's that. Look at the horses." Means wisely did not talk about the men. He knew Jones might not listen. Jones looked at the horses. He could nearly see daylight through some of them. Hard as they were, they had performed their last miracles of endurance and could not perform another — for a few days at least.

"You're right," he growled. "They'll need four or five days' rest. Well — we've got to chance it."

While they dawdled in camp, white hunters came out to visit them, asking if they had got a lion yet, and Jones said, "No, but we will." He never seemed to have the slightest doubt about it. But the inactivity made him irritable in the highest degree. Added all up, his frustrations came to something like this: he was contending against time, heat, flies, ticks, rain, distemper of dogs, sweats of horses, personalities of men, jealousies of the local population, finances, arrangements, a crippled finger, the pride of Jones which would never willingly stop short of victory and so he understandably paced nervously around the camp or went for long walks on the plain with John, the brown and white hound-dog with the scarred head. It was old John who had cornered Tom the big cougar, that day with Grey on the North Rim, and caught Kitty, too, and had his picture taken with Grey, and now he had become an international hound-dog and had visited Europe and Asia as well as Africa.

Jones felt John was his living talisman of good luck.[2] He reached down and scratched the old dog behind the ears, as they walked out toward a grove of fever trees — in this strange land that was threatening them both with defeat.

CHAPTER TWENTY-THREE

Lion

IT WAS JOHN who found the lion tracks. He found them near the carcass of a zebra that had been killed the night before, and he circled once, nose to the ground, hair shooting up along his back, as it did when he was after lion or bear, and then he lifted his head and bayed, and the pack joined in, all heads high, and Jones knew it was a hot trail.

He stifled the Comanche yell and let John lead him straight toward the nearby black volcanic mountain. This mountain was known as The Black Reef and it rose almost perpendicularly for about two hundred feet, honeycombed with caves, top covered with dense scrub and creepers and tall grass. On the south it ended sharply as though the lava had been cut off there suddenly.

Kearton and Ulyate had started the day together while Jones followed the dogs, and Means and Loveless had taken another route, and now, with the discovery of the fresh trail still unknown to him, Ulyate reined in, in the shadow of the Reef and pointed. Kearton focussed his field glasses.

"That's the Colonel," he said, "But I can't see the dogs."

As they watched, Jones rode straight for the Reef. Then they picked up the smaller black specks on the plain in front of him. The dogs were working a trail — lion? hyena? The pack had made a bend to the north, swinging back toward the Reef, and Kearton and Ulyate could hear them faintly.

Kearton got off and tore up some dry grass that grew in cracks between the rocks and piled it in a heap and wanted to make the smoke signal that would bring Loveless and Means and the rest of the party.

"Not yet," cautioned Ulyate.

Jones came toward them fast, now, along the southern toe of the Reef, and the dogs could be heard plainly, Old John with his Grand Canyon voice outstanding above the others. There was Sounder, too, also a veteran of the North Rim, and Rastus and the Rake from a pack of English fox-hounds, and a collie from a London pound, and Simba, a terrier. . . . A motley pack, chosen for effectiveness, not beauty. Jones was galloping close behind them leaning down, cheering them on.

"Light it!" Ulyate said, and Kearton touched a match to the pile of grass, blew on it and flame licked out. He threw green stuff on it, and a thin blue column of smoke rose.

"That will fetch the gang and tell the Colonel where we are."

Two quick shots sounded. Then there was a chorus of wild barking and baying. Then the heavy roar of a lion.

Kearton and Ulyate looked at each other and began to gallop toward the sound. It came from the top of the Reef not half a mile away. At the base of the rocky hillside, they left their horses and climbed on foot. The route was choked with rugged lava-rocks, creepers and bushes, so thickly overgrown that when Kearton lost sight of Ulyate and called, Ulyate answered from ten feet away. Nice country to meet a lion in face to face. Ulyate and Kearton climbed on toward the sound of the barking of the dogs and the sporadic roaring of the lion, till they came, out of breath, to the crest, and peering through the branches of a bush, this is what Ulyate saw: Jones who had apparently (and actually had) ridden up the nearly impassable hillside, sitting calmly on his horse within forty feet of a full-grown young lioness, who was crouched on a flat rock and seemed just about to charge him, while the dogs whirled around her.

Ulyate drew back with a start, and put finger to lips, almost afraid to move or whisper lest it set her off, "The dogs have got her bayed. . . . She's just the other side of that bush!" And when they had drawn back a step he added: "Jones is sitting on his horse right in front of her. Why she doesn't charge him, I don't know. And he hasn't even got a knife on him. He couldn't get away from her in this kind of ground. . . . Careful, don't disturb her."

Jones had been about a hundred and fifty feet from her when he first broke through to the top of the Reef. She was standing on a flat rock three feet above the ground and when she saw him she rose to full height and roared, opening her mouth wide, lashing her tail, and stamping at the rock with both forefeet in irritation, as much as to say: "How dare you disturb me in my sacred precinct?"

Intuition told him, however, that she was tired and winded from the run up the Reef and would not charge, yet. He moved forward to within thirty-five feet of her, being careful, because he knew the female is less predictable than the male. (In the graveyard at Nairobi he had been shown the graves of thirty-four big game hunters.killed hunting the animals he was attempting to lasso. Of the thirty-four, seventeen had been killed by lions, and eleven out of the seventeen by lionesses.) She snarled terribly but intuition told him, again, that she was bluffing, and he could see that half her attention was distracted by the dogs. He threw the lasso. It was falling over her head when a branch of a bush caught it and it fell in front of her on the rock. Even then, if she took one step forward he could catch her. But John nipped her rear end — one lion's rear end was as good as another to John, Africa, Arizona no matter — and she changed ends and took a swipe at John, but he ducked back.

Jones then recoiled his rope and threw again, this time hitting her on the back but failing to encircle her. She whirled and faced him, roaring terribly, and Ulyate, watching through the leaves, could not understand why she did not charge and obliterate him, because he wouldn't have much of a chance of getting away, in that thick growth, but she seemed just a trace uncertain; while Jones, on the other hand, appeared perfectly confident and Ulyate decided perhaps that was the answer.

From the lioness' point of view, this strange creature on the back of another creature, lashing out with its long thin paw, very likely appeared as something she could not at first cope with. But now she sank lower to the rock. Her roar changed to a growl. Her tail no longer lashed. Although she appeared more subdued and defeated, Jones knew she was growing more dangerous. She was rested and could mount a charge. Just the tip of her tail was moving as she crouched, and she was treading lightly up and down with her hind feet.

At this moment, Loveless and Means arrived, crashing through the undergrowth with their horses, and distracted her, and she ran off a short distance and jumped into a crevice between two rocks. The dogs followed her and she killed three and badly wounded Old John.

"We've got to get her out of there!" Jones yelled, "or she'll kill 'em all. Bring me the firecrackers."

For such an emergency he had included Fourth-of-July cannon crackers as part of their equipment. Lighting one he pitched it into the crevice, and the lioness left off mauling the dogs and departed.

"Ain't she a beauty, though?" called out Means as she ran.

"Don't you go a step nearer her than I do," Jones warned, "and if you do, go at a run so you'll have momentum!"

For two hours they drove her from one strong point to another along the side of the Reef, trying to maneuver her onto the plain where they could get a good throw. But she clung to the rocks and brush, and the day wore away. It was hot. The dogs were tired. The men were tired too. It was the story of the rhinoceros fight all over again. And the sun was beginning to go down. If dark came they would lose her.

"I'll get a pole," Jones said finally, "and I'll poke a noose over her head!"

At this moment she was crouched in a cave-like aperture halfway down the Reef. Ulyate made no comment but his face showed what he thought of poking ropes over lions' heads with poles, and of course these were the lions of fifty years ago, not the gentler ones of today, and this one was angry, with good reason. Loveless, too, objected. "It won't work, Colonel."

"Just the same we'll try it."

But without waiting for them to try it, she scattered the dogs and shot down the Reef and out across the plain.

John led the chase after her and the other dogs strung out behind, many of them trailing blood. John himself was bruised and clawed from head to tail, but he was in this fight to the finish, running almost as strongly now as in the morning.

She took refuge on a tongue of land extending into a gully, crouched at the base of a thorn tree, and waited for them to come up. She had chosen the spot well. With the gully on three sides, she could be approached only along the tongue of land. "Careful, now," Jones warned.

Means tried her first. Very slowly he maneuvered his raw-boned bay gelding, edging closer, watching for a chance to throw, but ready to spin and run, rope whining about his head, horse edging tensely under him, but the gelding was obedient and responded and was not paralyzed by the close proximity of the lion. They tell you horses go crazy at the sight or smell of a bear or a lion, but these didn't.

Means edged closer. She snarled warningly. Means spit and edged on. Again she snarled, and again he edged. The pony was sidewise to her. With a whirling jump, it could get into gear. . . . However nothing on four legs was supposed to be faster than a lion over a short distance, unless it was a cheetah.

She charged. Means spun and spurred. For thirty yards she gained rapidly. She was closing and within one more bound would have been able to reach the rear end of the bay, but — and here Jones and Loveless and Ulyate were holding breath for all they were worth — she never quite caught up that last bound. Means held steady one jump ahead of her. Then gradually he began to pull away. A Western cowpony had outrun an African lion, from a standing start. Photos showed later that she'd been about six feet from Means. . . . Of course the factor of head start made all the difference. How much head start? No one knew exactly. That was the whole question. Enough, was the answer.

The lioness quickly changed front, when she saw she couldn't catch Means, and made for Jones. As she had done with Means, she gained rapidly at first, but then Baldy began to draw away. Somewhere in the few scant yards of head start was the determining point.

When Jones too drew away, she returned to a thorn bush in the neck of land running into the gully, crouched low and waited as before. This new position, however, gave the ropers a better chance. There was room to make a quick dash past the bush and throw as you went. So: Means edged around on the north side of her, Jones moved in from the south. Tossing his rope and shouting he attracted her attention. He succeeded almost too well, because once she rose as if to charge, and he half wheeled his horse — he was within fifty feet — but she sank back.

From behind her Means shot forward at a run. Kearton began shouting, "Wait, wait — the camera's jammed!" But Means kept on. He raced by within twenty feet of her, roped her around the neck, but a lioness' neck is short and thick and with a quick twist she slipped the noose off.

Next Loveless tried. He caught her but she got the rope in her mouth and when it tightened it jerked a fang out as it slipped off. The jerking out of the fang appeared to unnerve her and she ran and hid in a thick clump of scrub and grass nearby. Nothing could move her from there. The dogs were exhausted now and couldn't generate much enthusiasm. The men and horses were running down too and it was growing late. Firecrackers and burning grass failed to budge her. Jones said, "I'll get her out of there."

He took a forked stick, old bearded man in white pith helmet, and fastened the stick to his rope and dragged the stick over her hiding place, passing within a few yards of her, partially uncovering her, but she didn't move. However he laid her head and neck bare for Loveless to make a throw. Loveless threw and the noose landed squarely above her head, but the stiff grass held it up, like a halo, above her head.

Loveless, without disturbing it, carefully passed the other end of his rope over the limb of a tree, and back onto his saddle. Now the trap was set. If she would only put her head up, he could yank the noose tight, set spurs, and drag her up to that tree limb, and hang her there. But she wouldn't put her head up.

"Hold on a minute," said Jones, and his voice had the tone of final authority.

He reached down and picked up the forked stick he had

been dragging back and forth. Riding forward with it in his hand till he was within a few feet of her, he reached from the saddle, and with the stick poked the noose around her ears.[1]

With a roar she sprang. Fast as he was — fast as Baldy was — they were not fast enough, and she seemed to the watchers to be landing squarely on them, when she was miraculously snatched away — dragged tumbling off across the ground, and up into a tree.

Loveless' loop had tightened on one hind foot as she shot through. Her entire body except that one hind foot had passed through the loop and she was flying fair for Jones — when Loveless caught her. Loveless' hand had been just fast enough.

Sinking spurs, he had galloped away, dragging her, off balance, across the gully floor and up against the tree limb. There she hung dangling and snarling. She tried to snap upward and reach the rope but could not.

"We got her!" Jones' Comanche yell arose in Africa one last time. "Great going, boys! Let the rains come! Now let it pour!"

Means went up to her and slipped his rope over one of her wildly kicking forelegs. Putting the rope over the branch of another tree, he stretched her in mid-air.

"Don't break her in half," Jones cautioned.

They slacked off a little. He got down and stood under her, directing things like the foreman of a construction crew.

"Easy, Means. Tighten a little on your line, Loveless. Lower away, now."

Slowly they lowered her to the ground. As she came within reach, Jones grabbed her and held her hind legs with both hands while Kearton tied them tightly together with a piece of strong short rope. Five minutes later she was muzzled, handcuffed, and secured.

In Jones' words: "The lion was no longer King, as it then and there abdicated to me on April 8, 1910."[2]

A month later she was in the Bronx Zoo, New York City, and Jones was saying to Doctor William T. Hornaday, Sc.D., A.M., director of the zoo, world-renowned zoologist and author of many books, who had been skeptical of his ability to capture wild African animals from Western cowponies, "Here's a lioness for you, Hornaday."

"Jones," said Hornaday, "I was never proved wrong in a fashion I liked better. I've been one of your strongest admirers since you caught those buffalo in the prairie thirty years ago, and I now accept your gift of the East African lioness, taken by the Buffalo Jones Expedition in Kenya. So far as I know, it's the first lioness ever caught by a man 65 years old riding a New Mexico cowpony wielding a grass rope."

The New York Times reported:

"BUFFALO" JONES RETURNS

Tells How He Roped and Branded
Wild Beasts in Africa

Colonel C. J., better known as Buffalo Jones, who has been in Africa roping wild animals, returned home yesterday on the Cunard liner Mauretania. The trip, he said, had been successful, and he had demonstrated that wild animals can be lassoed just like Western steers if one goes about it in the right way.[3]

The lioness was presented on June 15, 1910 and lived at the zoo, seen by millions, until her death on October 28, 1921.[4]

Before we take leave of Jones in Africa it might be well to listen to his leave-taking, as he remembered it years later:

When leaving Nairobi, the last person bidding me good-bye was the English philosopher, Lord Delmar. He stood at the "rickshaw," and when I approached to enter it to be driven to the depot, he said, "Buffalo, have you any more cowboys in the U. S. like these?" I airily but truthfully answered "Oh,

*about ten million of them!" "Well," he said, "there is one thing
I have settled in my mind, that there is not a nation on earth
that could buckle up against the U. S. A. in warfare." "Please,
your Lordship," I answered, "I hope that the United States will
never give any nation provocation to buckle up against the
peaceful, yet heroic, cowboy, if so you choose to call us, for
the Lord help them if they do."*

Lord Delmar added, wise man that he was, that "this
little handful of men in this expedition of fun and frolic, has
been more convincing of the greatness of America, her mercy
to the helpless, than had she sent a fleet of battleships around
the world."[5]

And finally the attitude of the natives toward Jones: *In
Africa today the heathen natives believe I was guided and
protected from those wild beasts by the Great Spirit. Just
before I left there they asked for a conference with me. I was
guided to a lonely grave where over an hundred natives were
assembled. They formed a circle about me and bowed to the
ground. The interpreter stepped up to me and said, "Great
Master, we have seen you catch the lion, leopard, rhino, and
we know you can do anything you want to do, as the Great
Spirit is surely with you.. Come with us to Somola Land (So-
maliland) and help free us from our enemies, and we will give
you all the camels in Somola and make you King." I told the
interpreter they all had the same power I had. But he whispered that he could not tell the people that, as they knew
better even as he and I knew better. Then I said to him loud
and distinctly, "I live in far-away America and I would rather
be a private citizen, just everyday Buffalo Jones, than to have
all the camels and wear a crown."*

*How easy it would be for me to proclaim that I was im-
bued with power from on high, as I have infallible proof,
recorded in motion pictures which do not lie. Even here, in
this enlightened land of America, many come to me and ask*

seriously if God has not chosen me especially to do these things. My answer is no, absolutely no; any other person can do the same things with wild animals if they are animal psychologists and have the nerve to back up their convictions. None but an imposter would deceive the superstitious, and credulous; just because Daniel emerged from the lion's den unharmed does not prove that God left his throne and descended to stand between his favorite and the jaws of death. It was Daniel's faith that saved him. He believed God had already given him power to tear the lions' jaws apart and destroy the brutes at his sweet will, and dashed into their den with a bravado equal to that of a bumblebee into a bathroom before the bather had donned his garments. Don't you know such a bather would take to a corner and be delighted when the intruder evacuated? Just so would the most vicious brute on earth escape if possible.[6]

CHAPTER TWENTY-FOUR

The Congo

JONES HAD HANDCUFFED more than a lion. His lion was the Great Outsize Thing, the Thing Beyond, the Beast, symbolizing brute-force Nature, the hostile environment wherein man was made to probe and bring his own order. For Jones, this probing, this order-bringing, was the great adventure, whether he met it in Kenya or Carnegie Hall. No matter how many beasts he brought home, there would be one more.

The year 1910 was a momentous one in the Old World's history and an exuberant one in the history of the young United States. The King of England died; Theodore Roosevelt sat horseback beside the Kaiser reviewing the mighty German Army; Glenn H. Curtis flew a biplane down the Hudson, duplicating in air the feat accomplished by Robert Fulton and his steamboat a century before; women suffragettes paraded Fifth Avenue; Buffalo Bill Cody staged his Wild West Show in Madison Square Garden and invited members of the graduating class of West Point to a reception afterwards; Caribou Bill Cooper, fifteen-thousand miles from Nome on a trip around the world by dog sled, drove his team of huskies down

Broadway; and Admiral Peary lectured after his return from the Pole. And Buffalo Jones lectured in Carnegie Hall, telling his adventures to a spellbound audience.

"One Night Only," the posters read. "BUFFALO JONES — in his thrilling account of — The Most Daring Expedition the World Has Ever Known, illustrated entirely with motion pictures taken in the field at great personal risk." People ate it up. Old Carnegie Hall at Seventh Avenue and Fifty-Seventh Street was packed.

Jones moved on. At Brooklyn he spoke at the Academy of Music. He entertained Mrs. Gertrude Vanderbilt Whitney and her friends with talks in her home. He renewed acquaintance with Buffalo Bill and Pawnee Bill who knew the old vivid days, and he posed with them in a famous photograph, all three wearing Wild West clothes. The two Bills had hit the show route.

And Jones, too, began lecturing about the States showing the African films. He drew enthusiastic crowds, but it appears that the movies were not shown extensively after the first weeks, giving some color of fact to the statement by Means that they were made and shown to discredit Roosevelt, a statement emphatically denied by Bird and by his son, the present Charles Sumner Bird.[1] In any case, whether the public tired of the lectures without films or whether Jones tired of the big cities, it is evident that he began to spend more and more time in the westlands, wandering back to nostalgic scenes of the eighties and nineties. He stayed at his daughter Olive's home in Topeka and on the ranch at Portales, New Mexico, where buffalo and sheep from his Kaibab ranch had gone into the building of substantial breeding experiments. He returned to northern Arizona and talked with Jimmy Owens and thrilled again at the sight of the House Rock Buffalo and the cattalo survivors.

He could have retired now. He had made his mark,

achieved his purpose, shown that it was possible to rule without killing, and that with high risk comes high triumph. Yet it was not like him to get up from the game while the cards were still being dealt. "I never did look forward to dying in bed as a great privilege to be looked forward to and prayed for," he said.[2]

And he was not well off. The African trip had not paid the great financial returns he had anticipated. He wished that he might do something for his daughters, Ollie and Jessie, and for his beloved six-year-old grandson, Toddie, in Topeka.

He began to think of doing the impossible again, and of the rewards that might be his. Still on good terms with Bird, he went to East Walpole, Massachusetts, and reminisced about Africa and Roosevelt and big game. "Wish I might have tied onto an elephant or a gorilla," he mused, "though I'm not sure but that the big apes could have chewed up our ropes as fast as we could throw them." The present Charles S. Bird recalls the meeting: "He wore his Western hat and dressed in civilian clothes. He was most entertaining, gentle and polite in every way. I was very much struck with his courteous and friendly character."[3]

The more Jones thought about it, the more determined he became to go after gorilla. Circus people whom he met assured him that a captive adult gorilla would draw the curious by the million. He recalled the fantastic interest of the Darwin-conscious public in the gorilla and in the problem of the "missing link" — more fantastic and more widespread than present-day interest in the "abominable snowman." He knew that the young gorilla that had been captured and brought to Boston in 1897 had lived for only a few days and that another young one which had arrived in 1911 had lived only twelve days.[4] He knew that older gorillas were said to be so elusive and so vicious that it was almost impossible to capture them without killing. He remembered how much the Congo gorilla country

was in the news now, how the Lang-Chapin expedition of the
American Museum of Natural History had been working in
the Congo for over four years with the cooperation of the
Belgian government.[5]

Jones' problem was the financing. He began contacting
various sources that might be interested: show people, museums, zoos, scientists.[6] He wrote to Bird and other acquaintances. Then one morning in September, 1913, a young friend
of Grand Canyon days, William A. Mougey, of Cleveland,
Ohio, received a letter which began with four stanzas of verse:
"My Dear Friend Mougey:

> *The call of the wild I've heard again,*
>   *As it echoes over the sea,*
> *It's as clear as the tom-tom's thrilling note,*
>   *Calling the braves to revelry.*
>
> *The call I heard when a boy of twelve,*
>   *And again at twelve times three.*
> *Each time I obeyed and reaped rewards,*
>   *More precious than gold to me.*
>
> *The summons is one I always obey,*
>   *One my soul can never deny,*
> *And the beasts may resolve, again and again,*
>   *They are masters, endowed from on high.*
>
> *But I am as sure as sure can be,*
>   *Will stake my life on conquering all;*
> *So bring my horse, saddle and rope,*
>   *And I will answer the call.*

"*How would you like to go with me to Africa? I
am after gorillas and other big game. Sincerely yours,*
                                        C. J. Jones[7]

Mougey was impressed. He and Arthur Mougey organized a company for which investors in Youngstown, Ohio, put

up $8,500. Jones was lecturing at the time in Wooster and Cleveland and, no doubt, used his spellbinding personality to promote the project.

He went on to the east coast to arrange details of the trip and to plan a new book on the whole adventure. In a letter from New York to his daughter, he comments, lending credence to the anti-Roosevelt purposes attributed to him, "If Roosevelt writes a page in the book, it should sell us many thousand copies. But I hesitate to allow him so to write. If we do, we would be expected not to call him down on his slaughter of animals. Mr. Bird will be here tomorrow and I will talk it over with him. They want Scull to write the articles under my name but I have positively refused. So Scull must use his own name. I am determined he shall not write the book."[8]

William Mougey tells of the elaborate preparations:

Jones' letter in September was the call of the wild to me and I have never rested a moment of the day until now and all is in readiness. . . . We are going for business, and when, over there in the French Congo country, we strike the trail of that ferocious demon of the forest, away will go the dogs and the hunt will be on.

If we can follow on horseback, well and good; if not, we will go on foot. Mr. Jones has provided all kinds of rope, chains, straps, cages, telegraph pole climbers, tackle, hooks, tongs, and muzzles. Heretofore he has always refused to carry firearms, but owing to the reputation of the terrible monster we are going forth to meet, this time a .405 Winchester is packed with the other paraphernalia. If Old Man Gorilla is an animal, ropes and human cunning will capture him, but if he is, as many claim, of the same origin as ourselves, it may be necessary to use firearms to prevent some terrible revenge from him.

The personnel of the party include Ambrose Means, the man most dependable in this sort of an adventure. He was the hero of the first trip and has achieved much notoriety as a cowboy. Mr. Means is a native of Oklahoma, with a trace of the Cherokee Indian blood in his veins; he is medium sized, dark complexioned, hair as straight and black as that of his swarthy ancestors; he has nerves of iron, is as cunning as his predecessors, fearless as a tiger, cautious as a fawn, and as tenacious as a bulldog, a real hero of heroes. Mr. Means has been all summer at the ranch at Portales, N.M., training the horses and dogs for the African trip. Having plenty of buffalo bulls to throw and tie, it has been the ideal place for training them to overcome fear, and to hold and throw any and all creatures their masters might tackle. Another cowboy of distinction, Dallas McDaniel of New Mexico, is also of the party. He has been selected by Mr. Jones as an ideal man for the work which requires courage as well as skill and endurance.

Doctor Hornaday, director of the Bronx Zoological, New York, and the greatest authority on natural history in the United States, does not believe it possible to save the adult gorilla alive, but Buffalo Jones is not to be daunted by any such conclusion. It is a well-known fact that the gorilla is passionately fond of music and will not leave the vicinity of a camp as long as the music continues, so Mr. Jones has taken advantage of his weakness and provided several talking machines with the records of the sweetest songs by women, and these, he is confident, will bring the old rascal up to the camp. It is also well known that the gorilla is a greater fool than the old fool over women, and many native women have been carried off by him and kept for years in his den. This fondness for the frailer sex may prove the downfall of the gorilla, just as it has of many a man. Jones figures that if there are women along to feed and cheer him after he is captured, it will be only a question of time until he forgets his companions of the forest. So Mrs. Means, the wife of the cowboy, and my own better *half are going along, and by their presence we hope to prevent his committing suicide or pining away.*

Mrs. Means will also be of great service in capturing animals, for she is the champion woman rider of the world, and is also an expert roper. For the past seven years she has been associated with the biggest Wild West shows, riding the Roman hurdles, wild steers, bucking bronchos, or any other wild or vicious animal that could be brought into the arena. Mrs. Mougey will act in the capacity of official stenographer and reporter of the expedition. . . .

We have had built in London two cages, large enough to hold the gorilla, even if he is seven feet tall and weighs six or seven hundred pounds, as some of them often do. There will be two picture machine operators join us there and they will record every move made, and the talking machines will record the terrible roar of the infuriated animal, of which we have heard so much. These will also report most faithfully the baying and bellowing of the hounds as they hunt the quarry.[9]

But, at the last moment, Jones, for once, lost some of his masterful touch. He had difficulty in making certain photographic and recording arrangements; and he was clearly upset at what he must have considered the intrusion of women into a "man's world." Just before leaving for Africa he wrote his daughter Olive from New York:

Dear Ollie: If we had plenty of money, I would not make the trip for I know it is a terrible trial for me. Yet I am trying to keep up courage and believe I can make it all right. . . . I sail on White Star Line Olympic at 12 noon, February 4th. Mrs. Mougey has finally got her way and is going with us. Am sorry we have the women along but it may come out all right. I am sure they will have no love for me for not a minute will I wait for man or woman. . . . I have erased Edison as they would not give me any show. We bought the recorder and will get the sounds in spite of them. I will also give a lecture so it will be of great value to you if I should never return. . . . The two buffalo robes I am taking to London to sell.[10]

On February 4, 1914, a few days after his seventieth birthday, Buffalo Jones boarded the steamship *Olympic* for Southhampton, England. Ambrose Means and Dallas McDaniel sailed on an American freighter along with eight horses and a pack of bloodhounds including Old John of Arizona fame. Mr. and Mrs. Mougey and Mary Means followed on the American liner *Philadelphia.*[11]

Once at sea, the old plainsman's confidence was restored. He wrote, *"Dear Ollie and Jessie: Now don't you worry. I am determined to keep all hands out of danger and return with the gorilla. You can handle all the business from Topeka and if we get the 'old man' then come and meet me. Tell Toddie I will soon be in Monkeyland and expect to rope a dozen or two. Love and kisses, Papa."*[12]

Because the freighter was late in arriving, the party missed planned connections for Africa and was obliged to spend a couple of weeks in London. Jones took advantage of the delay by completing the equipment for the expedition. This included two motion picture cameras, gramophones for recording the talk of gorillas and other animals, still cameras, rifles, revolvers, medical supplies, and other necessities for an equatorial safari. The guns were thought to be necessary for self defense in close jungle against leopards, gorillas, cobras, and other beasts but because of rigid French laws against the importation of foreign ammunition into the Congo, these American and British arms almost prevented the expedition from obtaining the necessary visas.

Jones also managed to arrange for various speaking engagements in Britain upon his return. He was promised twenty-four engagements and a minimum guarantee of two thousand dollars. And then disaster! In far-off Mexico, a British citizen, William G. Benton, was executed by General Francisco Villa and despite American efforts to obtain help for the widow, many Englishmen felt that the incident was a result of President Wilson's Mexican policies.[13] Jones wrote on February 24th.

Dear Jessie: I am out of luck. My dates have all been cancelled. The killing of Benton in Mexico has raised a great storm here. They appear to think the United States is responsible for it. . . . I have been overrun with reporters today and am going to give the press full details [of our trip] for nothing, so as to create as much sensation as possible. . . . Publicity is what we need. It will be like bread cast upon the water. Love to all, Papa.[14]

While in London, Jones was able to add to his pack of hunting dogs. He describes how he did it:

I learned of an extensive dog market, which was open every Sunday in East London. To be sure, I went and looked on. No one knew what was wanted until the third Sunday. With so many dogs mixed up, there were many pitched battles, and the dog which showed the most courage and ferocity I would either buy or send Mr. Means to obtain him. By working this way I accumulated nine champion "airedale" scrappers, which are considered the most ferocious dog in the world, excepting the bulldog. I also purchased four collies or shepherd dogs and one Russian boar hound. These, with our three American bloodhounds, gave us an imperial pack of seventeen ideal dogs. The last Sunday all the dog vendors were on to my game, and as soon as they saw Mr. Means or myself coming into the market they set their dogs to fighting. The police tried to separate them, but they were of no more avail than in a mixup with a bevy of "suffragettes," and the dog scrapping went right on. It was impossible to tell which of the dogs were the most savage, so I selected three of those I thought were "true grit," and find there was no mistake made.[15]

While this was going on, Means was entertaining the good citizens of London by riding about the narrow streets in boots and ten-gallon hat, astride his Arizona cow pony.

At last, on the fifth of March, Means and his wife and McDaniel sailed for West Africa from Liverpool with dogs, horses, and the whole elaborate array of expedition equipment. Jones and the Mougeys went on to Paris to see the American Ambassador about obtaining necessary customs authorization and gun and ammunition permits — the old plainsman carrying a letter from Secretary of State William Jennings Bryan. Having been assured that all would be taken care of, they left Bordeaux, France, on the French liner "Europe." They reached Cape Lopez, on the African equator on April 19, four days ahead of the slow freighter bearing Means and party from Britain.

Jones continues the story of the expedition:

On arriving at Cape Lopez we found the inhabitants of that little town (about one hundred white men) very cordial and accommodating. In fact, we fared sumptuously every day on the choicest game and most delicious tropical fruits of equatorial Africa. When Mr. Means and party arrived, all was hustle and bustle to get ashore. The decks of the great ocean steamer were set in motion. The horses were placed in hammocks and hoisted high above the hurricane deck and then lowered into very large surf boats, as it was impossible for the great ocean steamer to get within a mile of the shore. When Mr. Means arranged his gray steed in the hammock, he realized that there was no one below who could control and pacify his horse's ambitious spirit, so he himself leaped upon the horse's back and both shot up into the air and were lowered together far below into the surf boat. Next came Mrs. Means' horse, Squatty. When the hammock had been adjusted around the horse's body there was a real Wild West show, as Squatty pawed, kicked, and squealed like a wild beast, and, as he was hoisted from his mooring, Mrs. Means let go her hold on his nose and ear and leaped upon his back, like her husband, she and her horse went high above the upper deck, gracefully swung over the choppy sea and safely were lowered to the surf boat below. We managed to obtain pictures of this most thrilling and spectacular incident.

When the seventeen dogs were brought ashore, they were wild with delight. I took four of the most desperate scrappers and led them to a wire-netting corral; then six more were led in. The gate was closed and I inadvertently dropped the chains of three of my dogs, while I proceeded to chain the fourth one to a post. As soon as loosened, the three sprang at the other dogs like demons, and such a free-for-all fight I have never before witnessed. Fortunately or unfortunately, I held a rawhide in my right hand and a dog chain in my left. Instantly I realized if ever those ten dogs clinched in that humor, several of them would die then and there. Something had to be done and done quickly. Not only was my hat in the ring, but my soul and body, rawhide and chain, and I laid the missiles on the dogs as they came in, and the chain played upon those already clinched and they were soon separated.

As soon as we were temporarily settled in Cape Lopez, Mr. Mougey set about getting concessions arranged so as to land our horses, dogs, guns, etc., without duty, except those we intended to leave here. He found that there had been no advice to the commissioner here to admit our cargo, as promised by our ambassador in Paris. The cable was brought into requisition and after wrestling for a week with the high dignitaries, we were, by the good grace of his excellency, the Governor of the Congo, granted all the privileges and concessions we had asked for.

Weeks before we landed here, news was received that a band of American cowboys was to disembark at this place. A meeting was called by the citizens and a protest agreed upon.

It was claimed that the lonely town of Cape Lopez was to be invaded and "shot up" by desperados and spies, and that everyone would be obliged to dance the "tango" at the muzzle of the revolver, even these hot and sultry days. They really imagined we were spies for Great Britain in disguise and intended to turn over this rich and fertile region to their enemies. But after they had met us and learned the facts about the American cowboy, they almost fell upon our necks and received us with cordiality and real friendship.

At four o'clock on the morning of May 11, a tugboat took the Jones party's barge in tow loaded with supplies, dogs, and horses. For two days and a night, they headed up the river from Cape Lopez then southward, into the rain forest. The barge strained and swerved at the long rope cable. In the low swamp lands and the lagoons, the jungle was more riotous than anything Jones had known in his life. His earlier trip to East Africa had been in comparatively high, dry countryside, and he was not prepared for the exuberance of the Congo. At every turn along the river, new sights awaited him. Crocodile and hippos appeared in deep water and, along the banks, monkeys by the thousands, keeping up a constant chatter of comment, swung like acrobatic armies through the trees following the course of the tug. Orchids scented the steaming jungle and often provided the only accent in the endless green confusion that swept back from the brown waters of the vast and silent river.

At the end of the second day, the party reached its destination at Lake Fernan-Vaz, where they feasted on pineapples, mangos and other tropical delicacies. The lake was known as the center of the gorilla country and the men eagerly prepared for the great encounter. But five days of scouting and trailing ended in disappointment.

CHAPTER TWENTY-FIVE

Gorilla

JONES AND HIS PARTY returned disconsolate to the camp on the shore of Lake Fernan-Vaz. While they rested from the fatigue of those sorties into the heat and humidity of the jungle, they debated whether to try again or to move on to another base. Meanwhile, the gramophones broke the tropic stillness of each night with recordings of "I Dream of Jeanie With the Light Brown Hair" and "Believe Me if All Those Endearing Young Charms." But not a single male gorilla approached near enough to rouse the pack of dogs.

After four days of this, much of the time spent inside the tents, which gave the only shelter from frequent rain-showers, there came an unexpected break:

While lingering around the evening campfire, a well-dressed negro — a rarity indeed in that country — approached our camp. The seventeen dogs were on the alert, and only by quick action from all of us were they restrained.

The negro stood full six feet high, wore a Prince Albert coat, white trousers, a jockey hat, and Nature's boots. He spoke broken English and told us he had heard of the white hunters far away, and had come two days to tell them that in his country there were elephants, hippos, gorillas, and other wild beasts; that the French government had confiscated their guns and there was no way of killing them.

He said the gorillas destroyed their bananas and polluted the drinking water; that none had been killed for years and they had become very numerous. All of which was of interest to us.[1]

Two days later they went south again, traveling by powerboat to the country described by the negro, whom they learned was known as Chief Edembie and was well respected by his people. They set up a new base camp below Lake N'Gove and planned a new campaign.

The account continues:

Mrs. Mougey and Mrs. Means were entreated to stay at camp and protect our supplies and herd the horses, as the idea of roping gorillas from horseback had long ago been abandoned. At first the women protested, but when they realized that it was either that or no gorillas, they acquiesced, and they rode away for the lonely camp. Here they must rustle as it seldom falls to the lot of any American woman. No one can conjecture the dangers that hover around them, as very few white people ever pass through this isolated region. No one knows how many lions, leopards, hyenas, gorillas, rhinos, cheetahs, boa constrictors, pythons, hippos, crocodiles, cobras and hundreds of other reptiles, as well as scorpions, centipedes, tarantulas and other deadly insects, lurk in that locality. Yet, worst of all, they are in a region where cannibal negroes dwell. At least, they were cannibals not many years ago. I saw them eat chimpanzees' flesh and I feel sure they would devour human flesh now if they felt sure they would not be detected and punished. But the women are well protected. Each has a rifle, bowie knife, and revolver, but best of all, they have four of the most desperate dogs to be found in London. Each of the women has a trusty porter and they kept our best cook besides.

At 10:30 that night we were landed at a beautiful point high and dry on the banks of Lake N'Gove. The next morning our host set us down to coffee. We ate of the finest fish, of venison, pineapples, mangoes, and bananas, such as Americans never eat, except in foreign lands.

At the first peep of day, I crawled out of my blankets — yes, blankets, within two degrees of the Equator, and they were a luxury at that — and silently stole out to hunt the well from which the gorillas drank. The negro cook was up and showed me the path to the well. I led him into the dense jungle and told him, "Come on." "Oh massa!" he cried. "Wait, get a gun." I shook my head and darted into the bush. That was all I saw of the cook until breakfast time. After proceeding about two hundred yards, I heard a crackling in the brush which sounded about like a band of bears in the woods of Arizona. Then I turned and reported to our party what I had heard, but had seen nothing. I was for pursuing at once, but was reminded it was Sunday and no guide would hunt on Sunday in Africa.

In fact, I had not forgotten, as I had not reckoned on letting even a gorilla get away for the simple reason Sunday would interfere. Heretofore I always refused a guide, but in the Congo jungles one is indispensable.

Everything was made ready for Monday even if negroes refused to work, and when 4 o'clock came, I woke our cook and porters. By 5 o'clock we had drunk our coffee and eaten our "chop" meal as everybody here calls it. The Great Chief had arrived with his trusty guide and hunter. From every direction there were canoes headed to our landing to see the hunters who dare attack the most dreaded of all creatures, the gorilla. The power launch was at our command. I leaped in with our most hopeful dog, John, at the end of the string.

Mr. Mougey was punching up the porters, who were scared almost into fits. He finally rounded up fourteen of our twenty-seven. Mr. Means and Mr. McDaniel were looking after ropes, cameras, axes, etc., and just at sunrise, we landed at a banana plantation a mile away, where gorillas had been seen the day previous. As our guide started, he raised his hand and placed his fingers to his lips, which meant "Silence." It was only a few moments until he pointed to a banana tree eight inches in diameter lying on the ground, torn to ribbons. As he pointed, a faint sound came "engenies" — gorillas — and as we proceeded, we witnessed desolation and destruction. Acres and acres of magnificent banana trees strewed the plantation. It resembled the pathway of a southern cyclone. But no gorillas were seen. We passed into the jungle and found many beds in the trees. Invariably there would be also a bed at the roots of the tree, where the old man had waited and watched while his mate had slept. Finally, our dogs caught the scent of something, and we released them and the hunt was on. Old Drum, the Southern bloodhound, took to the east, while John and Blue, Mississippi bearhounds, took to the west. I felt sure the game had gone west and intercepted Old Drum. It proved the bearhounds had taken the back track, and the day ended in no game.

Our guide is a negro, tall and slender. I have hunted along with Indians from Mexico to the Arctic Ocean, and there with skillful Eskimos, and of all the guide hunters I ever met this negro has them skinned a mile. He knows every point of the compass even in the thickest jungle. Not a reed or leaf is out of place that he does not know it and tell us what has done it. Often the dogs would give tongue, and the guide would say "Bush pig, monkey, chimpanzee, hedgehog, python, bush buck, cat, etc."

Finally he whispered "Engenie." The Great Chief was called. They examined the trail through the little bushes.

The chief rose up and said, "Gorilla." The dogs were wild to go. They had already caught the scent. I unleashed John, and he darted into the jungle. But it was fully a minute before he opened up. Then Blue and Drum dashed away, and there was music in the air. I shouted to the guide, "Go, run!" and we all followed him with his "matcheo," a sharp cleaver about two feet long. Finally I heard a terrible commotion a couple of hundred yards ahead, and knew they had come upon the beast. The guide was not going fast enough, so I darted by him. The chief and Means both kept up with me, while the guide was far in the rear. Can anyone imagine an African jungle? I never could, before this occasion. It appeared every tree, every vine, every palm, and every reed was covered with the marks of cats' claws, and wild cats, at that. There was the fallen timber, bog holes, and swamps. Often one would go to his knees in mud. The water splashed all over. One place I ran into was covered with small sticks or dried weeds about three feet deep and twenty feet across. Every time I stepped, my foot would break clear through to the bottom, and the only way I could get through was to fall my full length again and again and break a pathway through. The dogs were yelling and fighting most desperately. Finally John turned to the right and the other two to the left. Mr. Means started to follow John, but I shouted, "come this way; let's keep together." As soon as we came near the dogs they would recede. Again and again we were almost up to them and away they would go. We could hear a great beast.

Bugh! Bugh! Wa! Wa! What moments of anxiety, what thrills, and counter thrills. The last chapter of a lifetime hunt. Would we ever reach the goal for which we had longed? The sun was high, but didn't touch us. The wind no doubt was blowing, but not where we were. It was like a bake oven, and perspiration was trickling over our bodies. Some ran into my eyes and nearly blinded me.

I could hear Mr. Means shout to encourage the dogs, and realized the quarry was notified of our coming and would struggle further on. Three miles had already been covered as near as I could tell. I was nearly exhausted. Then I stopped yelling, hoping to make a silent sneak up to the fight. I knew the dogs were about all in, from the tone of their voices and the longer intervals between their baying. My silence alarmed Mr. Means, as he thought I had fainted or given up the chase. Finally, I heard the dogs baying, treed at last. I gave a mighty yell and was soon up with the dogs. Mr. Means beat me there about thirty seconds. The old chief arrived simultaneously.

I looked up into the tree where the dogs stood with upturned noses, mouths wide open, and there sure enough was one of our ancestors, the dreaded of all creatures, the gorilla. Yes, no mistake. High in the branches it was passing from limb to limb, like some supernatural object. It kept going higher and higher until it had reached an altitude of one hundred and fifty feet. My moving picture camera was turned upon it as best it could be, and then for the first time in the history of the world, this almost obsolete species of animal posed for a picture. If this was the only one we were to see, I felt a thousand times repaid for all my toil and expenses. But this was only the beginning.

The forest was so dense and the underbrush so compact, it was almost impossible to get the monster in the moving picture finder. The creature never stopped except in a clump of leaves. Only as it passed from limb to limb or tree to tree was it possible to get a clear view of it.

I have witnessed wonderful feats on the trapeze, but here was something worth seeing. If I could only have one of these animals in a ten-acre tent one week in New York, I would have money enough to build a railroad across the continent. The somersaults it turned at the dizzy height *would have made the most noted acrobat in the world look like a thirty-cent piece with the figure "3" obliterated.*

After witnessing these wonderful performances, we dispatched the guide for Mr. Mougey and Mr. McDaniel and they joined us in short order with chains, ropes, tree-climbers, and all the other dogs, making seventeen all told. But it was too late, for the gorilla was in the dense forest, traveling at the rate of one mile per hour. All we could do was to watch and photograph the wonderful performance and listen to the shrill screams that made our heartstrings jingle. How wonderfully wise was the monster! Had it climbed a tree where we first started it, a rope could have been thrown high enough to catch it, but by standing the dogs off and running four miles it landed in the tallest and largest timber I ever saw. Many of the trees would measure fully seven feet in diameter. There was only one hope and that was to shoot a limb off under the brute and let it down by degrees; as it could catch limbs at frequent intervals.

Mr. Means shot and what a crash! Mougey shouted, "Stand from under, he has killed it." But not so. Just then, about thirty feet below the limb, the beast caught another limb with its left hand and the body swung a complete circle. A chatter from it indicated its contempt at such cunning tactics. Another shot brought it down about fifteen feet, where it caught a large limb and commenced the ascent through thick vines and limbs, completely lost to our sight. Finally it reached the topmost limb of a giant redwood tree about a hundred and sixty feet high. Means took aim again to cut the limb off, but for some reason, the gorilla stepped backwards and the ball hit and broke its leg and it swung helpless from the limb. Seeing the situation, I shouted to Mougey, "just as well kill the animal and put it out of misery."

He sent a ball into the body. It slipped off the limb

backwards and came sprawling through space to Mother Earth. The contact was terrible, breaking many bones. In an instant seventeen dogs were tearing away at the dead body, each one believing he had dispatched it. It is remarkable that the limbs of the tree were not cut off by the rifle balls, but the shock was so great it temporarily paralyzed the brute's feet and it gave way. The gun used was a .405 Winchester model, which has several thousands pounds striking power.

When we cleared away the dogs we found it a very old female, five feet, one inch high, measuring six feet, four inches around the chest, with a spread of arms seven feet, ten inches from tip to fingers. She was so old gray hairs were numerous. Her face was as black as a Guinea negro's. I took an impression of both hands and feet. The negroes pronounced her a fine specimen for a female and declared the average male is twice as large.[2]

Jones had found an "old woman" and she was dead. But he wanted a male gorilla, a chest-thumping, teeth-gnashing monster — alive.

After bagging the "old woman," they sent Mougey back to the base camp for supplies and he returned in a few days with Mrs. Mougey — Mrs. Means bravely consenting to look after the base alone. For the next week they hunted continuously. Gorillas were swarming about the lake jungles, alone, in pairs, and in families. And there Jones found the "old man."

It was Arizona's Old John who led Jones to the massive spreading tree standing isolated on a short tongue of land among the orchid-strewn bogs. The old plainsman had scarcely reached the scene before the entire dog pack in full cry was circling the trunk, searching out the dense shiny foliage of the branches overhead. Jones himself could see no sign of the gorilla but was confident that John was right this time. He noted with satisfaction that no other trees were near enough to tempt any gorilla to seek shelter and escape the dogs. In a few minutes, Means and McDaniel appeared, covered with bog mud and streaming with perspiration from their exertions. It was Means who spotted the beast high up in a limb crotch, beyond the reach of any lasso, even if the foliage had not made a throw impossible. After a brief council of war, Jones without hesitation began to climb, rope in hand. What a roaring and chattering broke out — dogs below and beast above produced a bedlam of dispute. But Jones climbed steadily, talking to the "old man" all the way.

A pair of native guides arrived and added to the din by shouting and gesturing to Means and McDaniel that the man in the tree was about to be torn apart by the infuriated ape. "No man must corner *engenie,*" they said and they begged Means to shoot before it was too late. At last Jones got a clear view of the dark brown mass of the great anthropoid. For a moment he hesitated. He could not believe his eyes. Was this man or beast? Standing there with one hairy foot in the crotch, it measured, he thought, about eight feet in height. Those eyes seemed almost human, dark, flashing defiance, anger, and perhaps fear. Had the Bible declared man to be lord of this, too? He was not sure. But he knew that this was the culmination of a lifetime search. Jones saw those knowing eyes take in the scene below, the men and guns and dogs, and he could sense the beast calculating the odds for escape or attack.

Carefully uncoiling the lasso, Jones swung the rope gently in a gap in the foliage and threw the noose over the great ape. He had hoped at best to snag an arm or leg, but at the first soar of the rope the brute sprang at Jones with unbelievable agility and the loop settled over the huge head and one outstretched arm. Almost at the same instant the old plainsman's boot slipped suddenly off the wet limb on which he was perched and he plunged headlong through the branches toward the dog pack below. He might well have broken a leg or his neck, but the rope he was holding had cinched tight on the gorilla from under one armpit to the other side of the beast's neck and the animal had been jerked off another limb by the weight of the man's body. Jones was thus caught up short in his mad plunge and the two — man and ape — dangled a few feet apart on the ends of the rope suspended from the limbs above. Despite the shouting and screaming below him, Jones had no intention of letting go that rope, now that he had the "old man of the jungle." "Don't shoot! Don't shoot!" he roared as Means raised the .405 Winchester. "Get more rope and more rope. I can hold him!"

But the next moment Jones was plunging again, right into the upturned faces of the dog pack below. He landed with a thud on the soft turf, still holding the rope for dear life. With an amazing display of sheer brute power, the gorilla had actually broken the "unbreakable" cord about his neck with a quick pull of his bulging biceps. At least, Means and McDaniel swore that they saw the feat performed but Jones said he was sure that the frayed end of the rope showed that it had been bitten through. Whatever the means of release, the gorilla flashed down through the branches so quickly that the dogs, panicked by Jones' fall into their midst, could not recover in time to seize the ape as he struck the ground and bounded away.

The gorilla had almost reached the thick jungle growth at the edge of the clearing when Means aimed the rifle and dropped him with a single shot through the heart. An enormous male, it was one of the largest ever taken in the French Congo. Jones was overcome with dismay when he saw the

recumbent form of the prize that had almost been his —
alive. They skinned out the massive beast for some museum
to stuff.[3]

The next morning was hot and breathless after the
tropical downpour of the night. But the old plainsman woke
cold. His face and hands were blue. His whole body shook
until he could barely stay on his cot. Within an hour the
rigors had ceased and the warmth came into him and he
could think. He thought of vague pains last night and a
strange headache yesterday that he couldn't shake. Yes — it
must be. He had taken quinine most of the time as a white
man should. But those days and nights in the swamp —
sometimes too intent on the chase to stop or remember —
and Jones had always been careless of body.

Perhaps he was just cold. The season was changing.
But then the warmth increased, and his body which had
shivered now burned with hot flushes. The heat increased
hour by hour until consciousness was mercifully suspended.

Like the great African hunter Carl Akeley who, unarmed
in mortal wrestle with an enraged leopard, saved his own
life by crushing the beast's chest with his knee, only to suc-
cumb later to malaria, Jones was felled by jungle fever
after surviving every hazard of tooth and claw.[4]

Still, he would not give up and insisted that the rest
of the party carry on the hunt while he return to the camp
where Mary Means had been guarding supplies and equipment in a solitary two-week vigil. In a few days he was
actually able to ride the fifty-mile distance through thick
jungle back to the base. He describes his experience:

*I was obliged to quit the hunt, having been stricken
with fever. The natives all knew that an American woman
was alone in that desolate land, and three burly men, scantily
clad, about an hour before sundown emerged from the dense*

forest a half-mile to the south of the camp with a firebrand in each hand and applied it to the grass, which was as dry as powder. In an instant the flames leaped skyward, as a stiff breeze was blowing directly toward the camp.

Our supplies were packed under a rude shed, and the horses under another close by. Mrs. Means was busy making ready for her evening tea. As soon as she realized fire was ignited, she snatched a gunny sack, soused it into a bail of water, then she grabbed a firebrand and ran into the grass and set fire clear along from east to west between the camp and the mighty conflagration which was sweeping in that direction. Then with the wet gunny sack she extinguished the blaze next to the camp, letting the other side of the fire keep burning. Then she ran about five rods south of the blaze, which was slowly backing up against the wind and ignited another blaze parallel to the one burning. The wind soon forced the last blaze across the burnt district. Just then the great billow-roaring conflagration arrived, and all was smoke and cinders, for it had no more fuel to feed the flames. But the sparks and cinders were swept across the burnt district into the rubbish around the tents and sheds. But Mrs. Means was anticipating this, and was there with the sack just out of the pail of water. This she hurled right and left until the last spark had been extinguished.

I was returning to camp and saw the blaze a mile away. By forcing my steed to his utmost I arrived in time to stamp out a few small jets of fire near the horse sheds. But Mrs. Means had it all under control and was master of the situation had I been shut out of the drama. When the natives saw me coming they ran for the forest and disappeared.

"It is needless to say I was proud of Mrs. Means and that we never left her alone in camp after that trying ordeal.[5]

That courageous trip proved too much for Jones. The continuous exertion with his high fever was more than his seventy-year body could stand. He appears to have suffered a severe and nearly fatal heart attack. On June 5 he wrote his family in Topeka:

*Dear Children — My hunting is ended. Never again will I join the chase. Not from choice but because nature has called a halt. My physical condition has become serious. My age is against me. My heart has become very unreliable and I blew a retreat on my horn and am through. . . . I am well repaid as we got a full-sized gorilla but was obliged to kill it. I have tramped from ten to fifteen miles per day, often running through jungles at full speed. Last night was a desperate time for me. My heart nearly failed all together. . . . But Mrs. Means was so faithful and attentive, I held out. I am feeling all right again today, and do not intend to tax my strength any more. The boys are out after gorillas but it is a hard proposition. The poisonous snakes are so bad they kill our dogs. We have lost four of them. Love and kisses for all. Papa.*⁶

After three weeks in camp with Mrs. Means, he returned to Cape Lopez on the coast and managed to book passage on a French ship for Bordeaux. His heart seizures continued and he was in a coma when placed on board the first day of July. He was well enough on the eleventh to write to his children again:

How rejoiced I am to be homeward bound. You will never know how sick I have been. I certainly was near unto death. The change came on the 7th. I left Cape Lopez on the 1st. The 4th and 5th I was very low indeed. I lost my mind and speech. The first name that came to me was Ollie. The next Jessie. The next Charles. But Whitmer I could not recall. Then Toddie. Then Thurston. Finally Whitmer came to me and so on. It worried me terribly trying to recall names . . . The others all stayed there. Have two gorillas but both

*dead. . . . I expect to land at Bordeaux the 18th, London the
20th, and remain there awhile. The Congo is the sickliest
place in the world and I was fortunate to get out. I am all
right now except weak . . .*[7]

But neither disappointment in the Congo nor the shadow
of death could stop the dreamer and the promoter in him. In
the same letter he concluded:

*I have a proposition from the proper authority in British
East Africa to start an experimental farm there. I asked them
for 200,000 acres for fifty years. But they don't want to give
up so much. Feel sure they would give 100,000. They have
agreed to give me all the wild animals I can catch, which
heretofore was forbidden to be sold for profit. I have orders
already for $40,000 worth of giraffes, two rhinos at $2,000
each, besides twenty-five zebras at $1,000. If Jones can sell
the sheep and buffalo [at Portales] for anything reasonable,
let them go and we will get the animals into money as soon
as possible.*[8] *I can sell 1,000 zebras at that price and they
are easily handled. I will write Jones and think he and Jim
Owens had better go there to look after things.*

One thousand zebras at $1,000 each! There was a cool
million in one swoop — and he could hardly wait to get
Uncle Jimmy Owens from Arizona and the rest of the boys
started on the new deal.

His good clothes had been left behind in Africa and he
arrived in Bordeaux on a weekend, too late to find any clothing stores open. He had to land in his old jeans and shirt
and "people looked at him as if he were crazy."[9] After re-
outfitting himself, he went on to Paris and thence to London,
which he reached on July 20. He waited there, hoping that
Ambrose and Mary Means and McDaniel and the Mougeys
would be able to find passage from Cape Lopez. But by mid-
August it became clear that his companions had been
stranded by the outbreak of war. He wrote Olive again:

I fear they are bottled up for a long time as my opinion is that the war will last for several years. The boats from Africa are all being stopped at the Canary Islands and I fear all our pictures on the trip will be spoiled. I have heard nothing from them about gorilla or anything else. Our horses are all dying off and we will lose the $1,000 that we depended on to bring them out. I wired Jones to send me the wool money. War is surely Hell. It is so heathenish and silly. I am terribly disgusted with humanity. To be sure, this war puts a stop to East Africa at present. Write me at New York. Love and kisses. Papa.[10]

He sailed the first of October for New York.

CHAPTER TWENTY-SIX

Trail's End

IT WAS A LONG WAIT for the Jones party at Cape Lopez. No passenger space was to be found and the expedition was soon short of money. Finally, in late September, with the aid of funds advanced by Jones before he left London, Ambrose Means and his wife and Dallas McDaniel sailed on the tramp steamer *Bornu* for England.[1] They arrived in Liverpool in October and after some further delays to procure funds, succeeded in reaching the United States. Means went back to Arizona where he became a guide for hunters, operating from the El Tovar Hotel in the Grand Canyon. McDaniel returned to his home at Portales, New Mexico.[2]

Meanwhile, Mr. and Mrs. Mougey were determined to carry on and bring back a live gorilla. Instead of leaving with the others, they left the coast on October 18, 1914, and returned to the jungle interior near Lake N'Gove. There they remained, hunting gorilla with the aid of native guides, until April of the following year. By that time they were financially destitute and being unable to obtain funds from America were forced to appeal to the French Governor of

Gabon for assistance in leaving the colony. The American Vice-Consul, McBride, reported to the Secretary of State that the Mougeys had been able to obtain the sum of $324.68 from the Governor and had left May 6, 1915 for Bordeaux on the French steamer *Afrique*.[3]

On July 1, the Kansas City *Star* carried the following report from New York City:

William Mougey of Cleveland, who shares with his wife, Helene, a love of wild creatures, particularly the anthropoids, returned yesterday by the French liner *Chicago* from a hunting trip of eighteen months in the French Congo, bringing with them a chimpanzee, known as Lindy, and a petite blue-faced monkey. They failed in the chief purpose of their exploration of the jungle, which was to bring to America one or more gorillas alive.

The expedition was undertaken under the protection of the French government and the Mougeys were liberally provided with guides and native hunters. They started from Cape Lopez and by canoe and foot traveled to Lake N'Gove.

Mougey and his gunmen got three young gorillas in the neighborhood of Lake N'Gove. They were in company with their mothers. Some of the full grown gorillas were nearly eight feet high, or would have been if they had stood erect, and weighed more than four hundred pounds. It would have been perilous to attempt to capture the mothers, so to get the baby gorillas, each several months old, it was necessary to shoot the mothers.

The finest specimen of the baby gorilla was the most savage and was named Demon. One died on the arrival of the party at Cape Lopez. Demon became quite affectionate, following Mrs. Mougey around like a dog. He died on the way from Cape Lopez to Bordeaux aboard the steamship l'Afrique. The last of the trio succumbed at Bordeaux.

Mougey says cannibalism is still practised in the French Congo, but that it is fast vanishing.

Not a word in the news story about Buffalo Jones or the cowboys. It is apparent that a breach had occurred among the expedition members. Had Mougey antagonized Jones by bringing women into a man's world? Certainly, the plainsman resented the presence of Mrs. Mougey. He complained in one letter that she was "kissing the nose of our best airdale dog which she has appropriated as a lap dog."[4] Perhaps his illness had made him irascible and difficult to live with on the trip. Whatever the cause, the break seems to have been complete. On April 11, 1916, U. S. Assistant Secretary of State, John E. Osborne, sent a letter to Jones at Portales, New Mexico, advising him that the Department of State had assisted Mougey in getting out of Africa and requesting Jones to advise as to the present address of the Mougeys.[5] Jones' reply of April 23 came from Denver on the stationery of the *Great Divide*, a weekly newspaper published by the Denver *Post*. It leaves no doubt of the strained relations between the former friends:

Hon. Sectr'y of State
Washington, D.C.

　　Yours of April 11th to Portales, N.M. overtook me here. I am astonished that Mr. Mougey asked for assistance in getting out of Africa, as he had all the finances of the expedition, also guns, ammunition, horses, in his possession. I was left without a dollar and so were Mr. Means, McDaniel, and Mrs. Means. I got out and succeeded in getting the others as far as London. But it broke me up financially.

　　As to Mr. Mougey's address, I do not know the number of the street but he resided in Cleveland, Ohio before leaving the U.S. No doubt you can find his address by the Cleveland directory of 1913-14.

　　We are proud of the Stand the President and Mr. Lansing have taken regarding to the U-boat warfare.

Sincerely yours,
C. J. Jones

P.S. It might be Mr. Ambrose Means could give you the address you want. He is at Fredonia, Arizona.

C. J. J.[6]

When Jones had returned to New York from London, he was well received and made arrangements to capitalize on his harrowing, if not too successful, Congo adventures. He even negotiated a deal concerning the controversial First African Expedition pictures.

I closed a deal with Bird today on the pictures. He releases all claim to America to me and I release Europe and all foreign territory to him except Canada. I was offered $10,000 for them two years ago and may be able to do some good business with them and mine and some other pictures I can add to them. Hornaday has a baby gorilla. He was offered $5,000 for it in Germany.[7]

The anticipated tour did not result in success — the U. S. was more interested in war than in gorilla talk — Jones suffered a recurrence of his jungle fever, and he gave up the show business and returned to his last stand in the West, the ranch at Portales where his beloved buffalo were.

More and more they loomed in his mind as identified with himself, and he began to write his memoirs — about them and him, and the other animals he had known and conquered.[8] In the foreword he gives us his philosophy of life:

I desire the world should know the wonderful power of man over wild beasts, and in order to make my assertions plain, must, with examples and illustrations tell what has actually been done. I cannot say that John Smith or Tom Brown did these things because they did not. So I am obliged to refer to my own experiences, which to some may appear as boasting. I have long since passed the age of boasting, and realizing that self-praise is half scandal, would avoid all allusions to self if possible.

When a boy I was made to believe as most children are today, that God stood between Daniel and the very jaws of death. That he shut the lions' jaws so they could not harm his favored apostle. The author of these biblical interpreta-tions was plainly not an animal psychologist or he would have told us no doubt that God also clipped the claws of the lions, for they are even a more deadly weapon than the jaws. As a matter of fact, if the mouth were shut and the claws clipped the animal could still despatch a man with one blow of his mighty paw.

The reader should remember that God's laws are "from everlasting," that man in the beginning was given dominion over every creature that moves upon the earth, and that if Daniel obeyed such laws he was by such obedience protected from all harm. The law that protected Daniel protects me in my encounter with wild beasts, namely the law of self-preser-vation. It is about the only law that the lower animal kingdom has to observe. When they disregard that law, then there will be an end to wild creatures, as they will fall prey to their natural enemies.

Daniel was a wise man who understood God's law and had faith in His promises. He knew in his own mind that he could annihilate the lions at his pleasure, and when cast into the den with those ferocious beasts, they felt that the stranger knew his power over them and they skulked away. Daniel occupied the same position as the victor of the two monster beasts which have battled for supremacy of the herd. Only one grunt from the victor sends all others into seclusion. Why? Because they know he has the power and will take their life. Then and there the law of self-preservation intervenes. [9]

Submarine and machine gun had come. Jazz, Prohibition, Communism were just around the corner. It was a long way back to the log cabin on Money Creek.

"One of his last efforts was to construct a hoist that would lift water to a higher level for the purpose of irrigation," wrote A. W. Stubbs, a friend of Garden City days. "He came to Kansas City where he built an apparatus operated by a gasoline engine. I secured permission for him to try it out at a lake in one of the city parks where it was an object of great interest."[10]

Never say die.

In 1917, a recurrence of the African fever forced him to bed at Olive's home in Topeka, and finally, on October 2, 1919, the Topeka *Capital* headlined:

BUFFALO JONES, HERO OF PLAINS AND DESERT, DIES

Big Game Hunter, Author, Lecturer, Farmer, Stockman, and City Builder, A Victim of Jungle Fever

HIS FAME WAS INTERNATIONAL

Followed Roosevelt in Exploration of Wilds of Africa — Founded Garden City in Unique Kansas Fight

Another of the sturdy pioneers who helped build the state of Kansas passed on yesterday when Charles Jesse Jones, internationally known as 'Buffalo' Jones, died at the home of his daughter, Mrs. Olive Jones Whitmer, 421 Topeka Avenue. A big game hunter in the American great west, in Arctic Alaska, and in the wilds of Africa, author, lecturer, farmer, and stockman, and founder of Garden City, Kansas, his life included such excitement and variety as falls to the lot of but few men. African jungle fever, contracted during his famous hunting trip to the Dark Continent five or six years ago, was largely responsible for his death.

The obituary, which is a lengthy one, went on to say:

At the conclusion of his African stay, he was stricken with the dreaded jungle fever and was unconscious when placed aboard ship for the return to civilization. He never regained his former health.

The account describes what it calls the unique feud between Stevens and Jones, which resulted in the skyrocketing growth of Garden City.

... Then hard times hit western Kansas, and for many years the big buildings erected by Jones and Stevens were inhabited only by the bats and birds. But for a good many years lately, Garden City has been booming solidly, and "Buffalo" Jones lived to see the town he helped found grow up to his early day hopes and plans.

"Buffalo" Jones also was one of the first to conceive irrigation plans for western Kansas, and the outgrowth of the irrigation system which he started near Garden City has made that section one of the bonanza farming spots of Kansas. ...

Though his two years' illness at the home of his daughter forced him to remain in bed most of the time, Jones' mind was not idle. When able, he worked on his new book, giving an account of the adventures of his two African expeditions. ...

When he was not at work on his book, he studied his design on a new centrifugal syphon pump. He later secured a patent on his new invention.

The funeral will be held at Garden City, probably on Friday in the Christian Church which Mr. Jones and his wife helped build, and his body will be laid to rest in the Garden City cemetery where his wife lies buried. Arrangements will be made today for Topeka friends to view the body before it is sent to Garden City.

The New York *Times* said:

Charles Jesse Jones, known throughout America as "Buffalo" Jones, famous cowboy and big game hunter and friend of the late former President Theodore Roosevelt, died today as a result of jungle fever contracted on his last trip to Africa in 1914.

"Buffalo" Jones became famous when he organized a band of cowboys in 1911 for an expedition to Africa to rope big game. He was for five years game warden at the Yellowstone National Park, having been appointed by President Theodore Roosevelt. While there, he built up a big herd of buffalo. Mr. Jones also won fame when he crossed the buffalo with domestic cattle and produced a hybrid animal known as the cattalo.

Garden City, Kan., in the heart of the sugar beet country in Southwestern Kansas, was founded by Mr. Jones. He was born in Bloomington, Ill., in 1844.

Garden City is today a flourishing community of eleven thousand people. Its wide streets invite you and its neat white houses are of the style common from the Atlantic to the Pacific. A solid sense of worth comes from it, and a statement that this is the heart of America. On a good year there are two million bushels of wheat in its grain elevators. Farmers glide to and from town in sleek cars, no longer sweaty and with chapped-cracked hands. Nobody picks up buffalo bones for a living. Garden City has the finest zoo in Kansas (containing a Jones Buffalo), the largest public swimming pool in the world (capacity three million gallons), and it sits on a gas-oil field, so that the time may come when oil-gas revenues will make the city so wealthy that taxes can be abolished. Wide green bottomlands are all around. The Arkansas River water, draining from the Rockies, brings incredible production to fertile soil. You think you are in a green garden. You feel Jones was right: all it takes is a little vision and the whole of western Kansas, the whole of the world, will be a garden. All it takes is the right man. And, in a garden spot called Valley View Cemetery, the man lies buried on top of a knoll outlined against the sky, as you come to it. His wife and the two sons are beside him. For many years his grave was unmarked. Today it has a simple granite stone.

A Pawnee Indian Legend says: "There was in old times a man who called the buffalo. He said that in surrounding the buffalo all the meat must be saved. He did not like the people to waste the buffalo. . . . When this man died, the people mourned him a long time. The Chief would ride around the village and call out, 'Now I am poor in mind on account of the death of this man, because he took pity on us and saved the tribe. Now he is gone and there is no one left like him.' "[11]

The Blackfeet said: "The Old Man can never die. Long ago he left the Blackfeet and went away to the West, disappearing in the mountains. Before his departure he told the Blackfeet that he would always take care of them, and some day would return. Even now, many of the old people believe that he spoke the truth, and that some day he will come back, and will bring with him the buffalo, which the white men have hidden."[12]

Zane Grey said there were three great types in the West: Buffalo Bill, hunter and scout; Wild Bill Hickok, gunman; Buffalo Jones, the preserver, who brought living things wherever he went.[13]

Jones was indeed the preserver, with a compassion that ran counter to the ruthless current of his times. And yet how typical that dedicated compulsion of the entrepreneur of the age of pioneer capital: to make of all nature his servant and means, to measure each landscape and beast in terms of utility and return on investment.

Now he is dead. And what shall we say of him? Shall we say that, to the sophisticated, he was a boy who wouldn't grow up? An incurable promoter and showman? An incorrigible romantic who went to Africa and lassoed a rhinoceros? Shall we say that he was a misguided Calvinist following literally the Biblical injunction to subdue the earth and "have dominion over the fish of the sea, and over the fowl of the air, and over every living thing"? That the buffalo are useless? That the Kaibab deer starved because he upset the balance of nature with his lion hunting? But if we note his foolishness, we note the foolery of an epoch. If we see his manhood, we see the manhood of a frontier that a softer age has relegated to the paperback and the viewing screen.

No, let us see him as William Mougey saw him at seventy:

He looks fifty. Straight as an arrow, robust and rugged, eyes as bright as an eagle's, muscles hard and sinewy, not an ache nor pain disturbs the old plainsman. He mounts the wild-eyed broncho as easily as of yore, swings and hurls the lasso as accurately as ever, throws and ties the giant buffalo bull as deftly and quickly as the best of them. . . . Breathing the free pure air and basking in the radiant sunshine; he is the ideal scout, and many of us sigh to be like him. With buffalo, cattle, and Persian lambs gamboling on a thousand hills, what cares he for Wall Street? King of the cowboys, conqueror of the animal kingdom, boy among boys, man among men, master of the chase, dauntless and more courageous than the greatest chief in his warpaint.[14]

No, let us say he played his destined role without fear, that he embodied "that restless nervous energy, that dominant individualism, working for good and for evil, and withal that buoyancy and exuberance which comes with freedom."[15]

CHAPTER TWENTY-SEVEN

Epilogue

AND WHAT OF THE MEN who rode with Jones? And what of the buffalo?

Charles S. Bird became an ardent admirer of Teddy Roosevelt, ran for governor of Massachusetts on the Progressive ticket in 1912, died in 1927. If he had any plans for discrediting T. R.'s hunting trip in Africa he changed them. "There was no question whatsoever as to trying to discredit Theodore Roosevelt who was a very warm and much admired friend of my father and my family," Charles Sumner Bird, his son, writes. "There is no truth either in the idea that the circulation of a motion picture was withdrawn."[1] Ambrose Means says the film was withdrawn from circulation at Bird's request, when Bird became intimate with Roosevelt, and was shown but little in the U. S.[2]

Zane Grey rose to fame with Jones, literally, acknowledging Jones as his mentor, the man who showed him the West and who, for Grey, was the West. The foreword to a recent

edition of Grey's book about Jones, *The Last of the Plainsmen,*
says that Grey had little success as a writer till he went west
on a hunting trip with Colonel Buffalo Jones. "Riding after
antelope, mountain lions, wolves, Grey got the feeling of the
land and the rugged men and women who tamed it. He
promptly put this feeling to use and in 1912, his novel, *Riders
of the Purple Sage,* was published. It became an immediate
success with an eventual sale of a million copies, and is still
being reissued."[3]

In the next twenty years, Grey wrote twenty-five novels
which had a total sale of seventeen million copies. At least
three readers per copy gave him an estimated audience larger
than any previous American author. Grey died in 1939.

Emerson Hough was among the first to write of the West
in popular terms, but was over forty before he became a success with *Mississippi Bubble* in 1902. He followed it with
54-40 or Fight and *The Covered Wagon,* standard works in
most libraries even today. Hough was on the scene for a long
time. As late as 1922, following a visit to the Kaibab and the
North Rim country, he wrote in the *Saturday Evening Post*
that the magnificent forest land should be designated "The
President's Forest" in the old-fashioned tradition of naming
certain forests "The King's Forest" or the "Emperor's Wood."
Incorrigibly romantic, Hough was a true believer in Jones and
things Jonesian. He died in 1923.

Marshall Loveless was, as late as 1949, living with his
hounds alone in a remote cabin in Arizona's Tonto Basin. He
was making his way as a guide and bear hunter. A later report
from the postmaster at Tonto Basin states that he moved to
Tucson in the early fifties and has since passed on.[4]

Ambrose Means, after making news with Jones in Africa

became a member of the 101 Wild West Show, a world's champion roper and rider, and later ranched in New Mexico and Arizona. He died in 1943.

Jimmy Owens stayed on as government lion hunter on the North Rim of the Grand Canyon until 1922. There was a sign on the trail leading to his cabin, "Lions Caught to Order, Reasonable Rates," and the outside of the cabin was so studded with lion claws that visitors could hardly see the logs. Jones' and Owens' inroads into the lion population of the Kaibab allowed the deer to increase in number to the point of starvation. Mass hunts were organized to reduce the deer population, and in the late 1920's, one massive attempt was made to drive them across the Colorado River to the South Rim. Zane Grey was present for this attempt but it failed. Jimmy Owens reached the end of the trail in 1936.

Theodore Roosevelt, friend and admirer of Jones, collected five hundred specimens of mammals on his African hunting expedition, including seventeen lions, eleven elephants, nineteen rhinoceros, and nine giraffe. He followed Grey and Bird in a camping-hunting sojourn in the Kaibab in 1913, this time with Jimmy Owens. Roosevelt died in 1919, as did Jones.

J. A. Stevens, Jones' partner and adversary in the founding of Garden City, and ultimate winner of the economic struggle between the two, died in 1902. "Little is known of the early life of John Stevens," says the Finney County History, "but it is definitely known that after his marriage he became one of the community's stable Christian characters."[5]

The Buffalo are now beyond danger of extinction. Those at House Rock have a saga all their own. In 1909, Jones rounded up most of them, drove them back to Lund, and shipped them to a ranch near Portales, New Mexico, where, after serving as practice targets for his ropers of the 1910 and 1914 African expeditions, they were sold to a man named Dunlap. The remaining were left to Jimmy Owens. By 1924, these, originally numbering fifteen or twenty, had increased to one hundred. The Grand Canyon Cattle Company then bought and shipped about a dozen calves to their fenced range in Old Mexico, and the resultant herd is still in existence in Mexico's northernmost state of Sonora. In 1926, Owens sold the remaining House Rock Buffalo to the state of Arizona for ten thousand dollars. These animals and their descendants were established in House Rock and nearby South Canyon areas on a permanent, controlled basis by the Arizona Game and Fish Department. Herds stemming from them were established at Raymond Ranch southeast of Flagstaff and at Fort Huachuca in Cochise County, southeastern Arizona. Part of the Fort Huachuca herd has been slaughtered and the remainder sent in part to Sonora and in part to Chapultapec, Mexico and in part to augment the Raymond Ranch herd. Buffalo are now permanently established in Arizona as one of the seven big game species open to hunting. The House Rock herd averages about two hundred head, and that at Raymond, one hundred fifty.[6]

The Yellowstone Park buffalo today number about eight hundred. They roam freely and they know the Park limits as well as the other animals and the birds do. (Wild ducks floating down the Madison River will rise when they cross the invisible Park boundary!) The buffalo keep to the hinterland much like their ancestors of the wild herd of old, with a result that few tourists see them. Jones caught two males and a female from the original wild herd, and two or three more calves were captured before that herd died out. Their strength was added to the tame herd. Yellowstone buffalo have furnished seed animals for many colonies — the Crow Indian Herd in Big Horn County, Montana, the Niobrara Herd in northern Nebraska, the Golden Gate Park Herd in San Francisco, to name a few. Still the Yellowstone buffalo have continued to increase, and each year it was found necessary to slaughter a certain number and distribute the meat to neighboring Indian tribes. So Jones' buffalo got back, in the long run of justice, to feed the descendants of the Indians deprived of their "cattle" by Jones and his fellow buffalo hunters. In the Park Museum at Fishing Bridge on the shores of Lake Yellowstone is the largest buffalo head on record.[7] Its horns measure 22 and ⅝ inches on the outside curve, their circumference at the base is 14 and ⅞ inches, and they have a spread of 35 and ⅝ inches. This is the head of "Old Tex," one of the three bulls bought by Jones from Colonel Goodnight at Palo Duro in the Texas Panhandle. Old Tex lived to the ripe old age of thirty-plus.

The Garden City buffalo herd was scattered across the United States, some to Michel Pablo and Charles Allard in Montana, some to Austin Corbin, Sr., founder of the Blue Mountain Forest Park near Newport, New Hampshire, where their descendants dwell today. From the Blue Mountain Park, some were sent to Pisgah Game Preserve in North Carolina, where Jones Buffalo continue to thrive. Incidentally Corbin paid Jones one thousand dollars apiece for ten animals in 1892, roughly the equivalent of $3,500 apiece today. One of the bulls Corbin purchased was sold to William C. Whitney and placed in his game preserve on October Mountain near Lenox, Massachusetts. This bull was one of the original wild calves captured by Jones in the Panhandle in '86. With others it was presented by Whitney to the Bronx Zoo, and from there its descendants, all Jones Buffalo, went to form the nucleus of herds in the huge Wichita and Wind Cave game preserves in Oklahoma and South Dakota respectively.[8]

Other Jones Buffalo went to General Harry C. Trexler who established a three-thousand-acre preserve on his estate at Allentown, Pennsylvania. When General Trexler died, his buffalo numbered more than seventy. He bequeathed them and the preserve on which they ranged to Lehigh County, leaving one hundred thousand dollars for their maintenance.

The establishment of the Montana Bison Range was a project of the American Bison Society, which came into being as a direct result of Jones' preservation of the buffalo at Yellowstone and elsewhere. The Montana Range was stocked in part with Jones Buffalo that had been to Massachusetts and New York first. Descendants of this herd were sent to Alaska and on last report were flourishing near Fairbanks. In the 1920's, a herd that contained Jones Buffalo was established on Santa Catalina Island off the coast of Southern California and Jones Buffalo are in the Moscow Zoo and in Mexico City at Chapultapec Park.

As for Canada: in 1906 there were less than twenty buffalo in all of the Dominion, except for the wild wood bison on their range near Slave Lake. The Canadian Government that year secured an option on the Pablo Herd in Montana and purchased it, including Jones Buffalo, for the vast sum of two hundred thousand dollars, thereby reversing the direction of the Jones-Bedson deal of a generation before. Seven hundred nine buffalo were transported to an enclosure of two hundred square miles near Wainwright, Alberta, and became known as the Wainwright Herd. They increased so rapidly that in order to preserve the range it was necessary to limit their number to *eight thousand*. The calf crop was from thirteen to fifteen hundred a year. To dispose of the surplus, it was decided to transport some of the younger animals to the Wood Buffalo Park, a range of ten thousand square miles in northern Alberta. For three years, 1925, 1926, 1927, the government sent north anually *two thousand* buffalo under two years of age. The limits of the Wood Buffalo Park were increased to 17,500 square miles. It already contained about twenty-five hundred wood bison (see Chapter 12, Note 4) and these crossbred with the newly-arrived plains bison. A conservative estimate in the mid-thirties put the whole number at ten thousand. In 1940, as a war measure, many of the Wood Buffalo Park Herd were slaughtered to provide meat for the Canadian-British war effort — Jones Buffalo going to provide the sinew and blood for the defeat of Hitler.[9]

Today throughout the world, buffalo total about twenty-two thousand: in the United States alone, nine thousand; in Canada, twelve thousand. Buffalo hunting, as well as buffalo, is back to stay, but in a way that would make old-time hunters turn in their graves. This is the manner in which shooting is allowed when the House Rock herd is "thinned," as it is annually. Chances are sold for forty dollars each. The animal is designated by the state gamekeeper and stands quietly in one corner of the fenced enclosure. The hunter shoots until the buffalo drops and is allowed to take the head, the hide, and one quarter of the meat. The rest of the meat goes to the state to be sold to the public for money to maintain the herds.

The biggest buffalo hunt in the United States takes place in the Black Hills of South Dakota every fall, but only two hunters take part in it. They are Boyd Perrigo and Fred Matthews who work for the state game department. Their kill is limited to the young bulls, and cows without calves, in the huge Custer State Park and Wind Cave National Monument herds, which must be thinned annually. When the hunt is finished one thousand animals are left in the herds, the number the range can readily support.[10] It is a far cry from Jones' skinning knife and pegged-out hides, or smokehouse for hams and tongues. Each animal is dressed where killed, loaded into a pickup by a special hoist, driven to the locker plant, skinned, chilled overnight, quartered, hung a few days for aging, and frozen ready for sale and shipment. Sale of such buffalo meat has netted as much as $118,000 annually. Proceeds go to Park upkeep. And the meat is bought by anyone interested, with sportsmen's clubs and supermarkets taking the lion's share.

A hunt to end all hunts took place not long ago on Santa Catalina Island where no hunting is permitted. Two boys set out secretly to stalk a buffalo with bow and arrow in true Indian style. They succeeded in killing a huge bull. When the carcass was found, the arrows were traced and the boys apprehended. The penalty was that they should replace the buffalo. This entailed going to Wyoming and finding a buffalo bull suitable to bring to Catalina. By the time they finished paying for the bull and paying for the crating and freight to California, they realized buffalo hunting on Catalina Island was not profitable.[11]

The buffalo were brought to Catalina in 1926 by a motion picture company filming the silent picture, *The Covered Wagon,* a box-office sensation of its day. There were about fifteen animals in the herd. When the picture was completed, the buffalo were left on the island. They increased and were augmented, now numbering about forty, and roam at will over forty-eight thousand acres fenced on all sides by the blue Pacific.

Jones' experiments with crossbreeding the American bison are of continuing interest. Cattalo are occasionally found in the United States, the result of some private breeder's fancy.[12] At Belle Fourche, South Dakota, for instance, Pierre Rosander is keeping the cattalo tradition alive. But in Canada development of cattalo has long been in government hands.[13] Authorities at Ottawa see in the cattalo the animal that can withstand the rigors of climate in the west and northwest provinces, just as Jones said, combining the hardiness of the buffalo with the meat-producing qualities of domestic cattle. Canadian experiments beginning in 1915 show that a hybrid 75 to 85 per cent domestic and 25 to 15 per cent buffalo is most practicable. There are over two hundred cattalo at the Dominion Range Experiment Station, Manyberries, Alberta; and the herd is gradually being increased and the project expanded. Jones' dream goes on.

Acknowledgments

To Jones' surviving daughter, Mrs. Olive W. Brown, and his grand-sons, Alexander H. Phillips and Charles R. Whitmer, go our special thanks and hopes that this work in some part does justice to their famous ancestor. In attempting to develop the whole story of the re-markable career of Charles Jesse Jones, the authors exhausted the known available sources rather early in the course of their researches. But these materials, exciting as they were, left blank whole periods of his life and left unanswered many problems dealing with key aspects of his character and purposes. We were able, at length, to contact Mr. Phillips and Mr. Whitmer. But, alas, it seemed that Jones was in many respects a legend to them as to others — the rumored existence of a manuscript of Jones' memoirs and of diaries and correspondence could not be substantiated despite months of correspondence. It was assumed by all concerned that the material had been lost or burned since his death, and the authors proceeded to attempt reconstruction of the "lost periods" by two years of search and correspondence with persons of every description who had known Jones or known of him. Then, just before this book was to go to press, we received word of a dramatic discovery, by Charles Whitmer, of the missing sources in the attic of a New Jersey beach cottage, a house that the family was on the point of selling. Thanks to this treasure-trove, we were able to solve, at last, various biographical and historical puzzles, but we were pleased to note that the extensive research we had already done had given us a portrait of the old plainsman and his career which was confirmed and enlarged by Jones' own papers. We are doubly grateful to the Jones family for their kind assistance and their generous permission to make use of the materials in the Jones papers.

We are indebted also to many in Garden City, Kansas, where so much of Jones began and where he lies in Valley View Cemetery, es-pecially to The Finney County, Kansas Historical Society, for permis-sion to use material from its outstanding collection: *The History of Finney County, Kansas.* In particular we should like to thank Ralph T. Kersey, historian, who has himself written about Jones, and Dr. L. A. Baugh, who knew Jones "when" and has labored tirelessly over the years to inflame his fellow townsmen in particular and Kansans in gen-eral with his own ardor for Jones, and Mrs. George O. and Rod Abbott.

To Nyle H. Miller, secretary, and F. R. Blackburn, research director, of the Kansas State Historical Society at Topeka we owe thanks for research in Kansas newspaper files and in the society's records.

We are indebted to Mrs. Mildred Smith Johnson of Sedona, Arizona, Zane Grey's literary secretary, for helpful anecdotes on Jones, and especially to the Grey family and Loren Zane Grey for kind permission to quote from books by Zane Grey about Jones.

We are also indebted to Lemuel A. Garrison, formerly at Grand Canyon National Park and now Superintendent of Yellowstone Park, and Mrs. Garrison, who not only threw open the files of the Park Headquarters to visitors from faroff, but cooked breakfast for them on a Sunday morning.

Charles Sumner Bird has kindly furnished recollections, books, and photographs, concerning the African expeditions; and Mrs. Eagle Smith and Mrs. Thomas Bowdon have provided much valuable information about Ambrose Means and the African expeditions.

To Lawrence Clark Powell, John A. Carroll, Horace M. Albright, Archibald Roosevelt, Hermann Hagedorn we owe thanks for their interest and encouragement, and the same to Frank Young of Roswell, New Mexico, who was to go on Buffalo Jones' first African trip but was so young that his mother wouldn't let him.

Also we wish to thank the chambers of commerce at Roswell and Las Vegas, New Mexico, McCook, Nebraska, and Garden City, Kansas, for putting us in touch with those who knew Jones, and the Arizona Game and Fish Department for its generous assistance in tracing Jones' Arizona days.

No words of gratitude could be complete without including C. J. (White Mountain) Smith, who knew Jones in Yellowstone Park and saw Jimmy Owens' cabin on Buckskin studded with lion claws. Bob Benson, in Santa Barbara, provided valuable information about firearms, and F. E. Wells checked the files of his Williams, Arizona, *News* and his memory for recollections of Ambrose Means and Jones.

Malcolm J. Renton of The Catalina Island Company and Buck Wharton of Sedona, Arizona, furnished the anecdotes of buffalo on Catalina, and Grace Davall traced the history of the lioness at the Bronx Zoo. We also thank Richard G. Van Gelder of the American Museum of Natural History and Theodore H. Reed, Director of the National Zoological Park, for their researches, likewise H. Bailey Carroll of the Texas State Historical Association. The editors of *Outdoor Life* and Ben East kindly allowed us to use excerpts from a recent article on modern buffalo hunting, and Mrs. Frank A. Wagner, Yellowstone Park librarian, was especially helpful. The Department of Agriculture at Ottawa provided material on Canadian cattalo experiments, and E. J. Warwick, chief of beef cattle research for the U. S. Department of Agriculture, helped us trace U. S. cattalo breeding to Mr. Pierre Rosander, Belle Fourche, South Dakota, twentieth century "cattalo man." The Liverpool Public Libraries provided important data on Jones and his buffalo in England as did the Zoological Society of London and the Cunard Steamship Company.

James de T. Abajian, Dr. Alexander T. Leonard, and especially Miss Frances M. Molera, daughter of the famous California pioneer, the late Andrew J. Molera, gave us helpful leads and information on the intriguing story of California's own buffalo and cattalo experiment of the early days.

Our friend and neighbor, R. N. Burgess, hardy cattleman and horsebreeder of the Grand Canyon country, who visited Jones at his cabin in the Kaibab days, provided many colorful descriptions of the old plainsman and his buffalo herd at House Rock and photographs of the cattalo.

W. H. Switzer, clerk in Jones' day of the Coconino County, Arizona, Board of Supervisors supplied anecdotes from his remarkable memory and fruitful leads on the Arizona period of Jones' life; likewise Elwin Pratt of Fredonia and Mrs. Edna Connelly of Salida, Colorado, niece of Dallas McDaniel, helped us with background material.

Our heartfelt thanks go to Jack L. Cross and Mrs. Elizabeth Shaw of the University of Arizona Press for their skillful editorial assistance, and to Mrs. Josephine Green for preparation of the manuscript.

To Charles Franklin Parker of Prescott, one of Arizona's own historians, and to Jack Schaefer of Santa Fe, lover and writer of the American West, we are indebted for helpful leads and discerning criticisms; likewise Paul Ellerbe and Jay Monaghan of Santa Barbara.

Last but not least we acknowledge our debt to C. J. Jones, Henry Inman, Guy H. Scull, and Zane Grey, without whose writings this writing would hardly have been possible.

There is not space to name all who have contributed to our book, but to one and all we tender appreciation and thanks.

Robert Easton and Mackenzie Brown

Notes

CHAPTER 1   YOUNG MAN, YOUNG NATION

[1] See Scull, *Lassoing Wild Animals in Africa,* p. 13.

[2] See Seton, *Wild Animals at Home,* p. 213.

[3] For this and other material on Jones' early life consult Jones, *Buffalo Jones' Forty Years of Adventure.* This episode is also dealt with in Jones' unpublished *Memoirs,* a copy of which is in the authors' possession.

[4] As for Noah Jones' friendship with Abraham Lincoln, there is, besides Inman's and Jones' evidence, the testimony of Jones' sister, Mrs. Nettie Jones Haulton: "Our father was a great friend of 'Abe' Lincoln and had him for his lawyer." Finney County, Kansas, Historical Society, *History of Finney County, Kansas,* vol. 1, p. 115. However, the well-known Lincoln scholar, Jay Monaghan, curator of the Wyles Lincoln Collection at the University of California, Santa Barbara, finds no reference to Noah Jones among those persons who retained Lincoln for legal services during this period.

[5] *Genesis,* Ch. I:28.

CHAPTER 2   WESTWARD

[1] Osage orange seeds resemble ordinary orange seeds, though somewhat rougher and larger. The plant was native to the Osage Indians' territory in Missouri, Arkansas, Oklahoma. Hence its name. It was later used as a decorative hedge plant as far west as California but has gone out of fashion. It is also known as the bodark (*bois d' arc*) apple.

[2] Material in this chapter is largely drawn from *Buffalo Jones' Forty Years of Adventure,* pp. 30–36.

CHAPTER 3   BUFFALO AND INDIANS

[1] Jones' estimates are higher than Hornaday's (*The Extermination of the American Bison,* pp. 469–499) but in line with Seton's thinking (See *Life Histories of Northern Animals,* p. 294). Jones gave no estimate of his own kill other than that it was "thousands."

"It has been claimed by some authors that the Indians killed with more judgment and more care for the future than did the white man," says Hornaday (*The Extermination of the American Bison,* p. 398) "but I fail to find any evidence that such was ever the fact. They all killed wastefully, wantonly, and always about five times as many head as were really necessary for food. It was always the same old story, whenever a gang of Indians needed meat a whole herd was slaughtered, the choicest portions of the finest animals were taken, and about

75 per cent of the whole left to putrefy and fatten the wolves."

The Indians had been mass-slaughtering buffalo for centuries before the white man arrived. Lewis and Clark as they ascended the Missouri River in 1805 observed: "On the north we passed a precipice about 120 feet high, under which lay scattered the fragments of at least one hundred carcasses of buffaloes although the water which had washed away part of the hill must have carried off many of the dead. These buffaloes had been chased down a precipice in a way very common on the Missouri, and by which vast herds are destroyed in a moment. . . . The Indians then select as much meat as they wish, and the rest is abandoned to the wolves, and creates a most dreadful stench." (Lewis and Clark, *History of the Expedition*, I, 210).

Did these slaughters by the Indians materially reduce the herds? "From time immemorial the tribes had lived off the herds, but never lessened their numbers" (Collins, *The Unvanquished Buffalo*, p. 8).

It was the white man with a money motive and a rifle that almost exterminated the species. Hornaday says that for every hide successfully taken there were four or five dead buffalo, due to careless or wanton methods of killing and skinning.

[2] *Forty Years of Adventure*, p. 256–257. The dimensions of the average full-grown buffalo bull were:

Height	5'10"
Girth at heart	9' 3"
Length	10' 2"
Weight	2,000 pounds
Width between eyes	13"
Length of hair on forequarters	4"
Length of beard	12"

The beards often dragged the ground as they walked.

[3] *Ibid.*, pp. 261–262. The horseback method of hunting, as employed by Buffalo Bill Cody and others, was to ride to the right of the running herd and as near the front as possible, shoot to the left as a man on horseback would naturally shoot. This caused the herd to circle to the left, or to "mill." Keeping it milling you killed as many as desired and left them handy in one spot for skinners and meat wagon. See Wetmore and Grey, *Last of the Great Scouts*, pp. 324–327.

The horseback method was more dangerous, strenuous, required top marksmanship and plenty of available buffalo to be effective.

"On horseback it took 15 to 25 hunters to kill 1,000 buffalo a season. A still hunter could kill 3,000 single-handed." Collins, *The Unvanquished Buffalo*, p. 10.

[4] Stuart Cloete reports elephants doing the same. (See *The Curve and the Tusk*, p. 280). Similarly, musk ox are described as defending *even the dead members of a herd,* so that a hunter wishing to possess himself of animals he has shot must kill the entire herd. See Freuchen and Salomonson, *The Arctic Year*, p. 323.

⁵*Forty Years of Adventure,* p. 234–235. The guilt of buffalo hunters has been dealt with in *The Last Hunt,* by Milton Lott and in Mari Sandoz' *The Buffalo Hunters.* Jones seems to have been the first to state the idea.

⁶*Forty Years of Adventure,* pp. 92–94.

⁷*Ibid.,* p. 92.

⁸*Ibid.,* pp. 84–91. The Indians' attitude toward the plainsmen, the other side of the coin, is exemplified in the remark of Little Robe, Chief of the Cheyennes, following a fruitless trip to Washington to try and curtail whiskey traders and buffalo hunters on Indian lands: "Your people make big talk, and sometimes make war, if an Indian kills a white man's ox to keep his wife and children from starving; what do you think my people ought to say when they themselves see their cattle killed by your race when they are not hungry?" Branch, *The Hunting of the Buffalo,* pp. 179–180.

To the Plains Indian the buffalo was sacred because he depended on them for his livelihood. From them he derived food, shelter, clothing. He used every part of the animal: hair, skin, flesh, blood, bones, entrails, horns, sinews, contents of the bladder and paunch, kidneys, heart, liver, trachea, and pericardium, even the stones of the gall bladder which were used as "medicine" paint. And the foetus cooked in its enveloping fluid was considered a special delicacy.

The Pawnees, in explaining their religious customs, said: "Through the corn and the buffalo we worship the Father."

The Blackfeet asked: "What one of all the animals is most sacred?" and the reply was given, "The buffalo." Roosevelt and Grinnell, eds., *American Big Game Hunting,* p. 179.

⁹See Cook, *The Border and the Buffalo,* p. 194.

¹⁰For an eyewitness' account of the Pocket Canyon Fight, consult the volume by Cook cited above. The dramatic escape of Black Horse, or Nigger Horse as the plainsmen called him, from Fort Sill with his band of Comanches is also dealt with by Wellman in *The Indian Wars of the West,* pp. 187–198. Wellman bases his account largely on Cook. See also Grey, *Raiders of the Spanish Peaks,* pp. 54–56. Grey, who knew Jones well, says emphatically that he was the hero of the Pocket Canyon Fight. Cook mentions Jones and Pat Garrett as being present on the buffalo range at the time of the killing of Sewall, and the implication is that they rallied with the others to avenge their friend. Some liberty has perhaps been taken in giving Jones a leading part in the fight.

Jones also appears in *The Thundering Herd,* Grey's novel about buffalo hunting, and in a number of other works by Grey.

¹¹Cook, *The Border and the Buffalo,* p. 159.

CHAPTER 4   PRAIRIE TOWN

[1] Anecdotes in this chapter concerning Jones in Garden City come largely from the *History of Finney County, Kansas* and from personal interviews in Garden City (August 6, 1958) with Dr. L. A. Baugh, Cap Burtis, Ralph T. Kersey, and others.

[2] The Model 76 Winchester was an immediate favorite with plainsmen. Theodore Roosevelt, for example, ranching in Dakota Territory in 1884, gave up his Sharps .45-120 and his .50 caliber double-barreled English Express because better than either .was "a .45-75 half-magazine Winchester. The Winchester is by all odds the best weapon I ever had, and I now use it almost exclusively, having killed every kind of game with it, from a grizzly bear to a bighorn." There is a well-known photograph of the President-to-be, dressed in fringed buckskin clothing and holding his .45-75 at high port.

The Model 76, known as the "Winchester Centennial Model" because it was first exhibited at the Philadelphia Centennial Exposition in the summer of 1876, had a 28-inch barrel and a tubular magazine that normally extended the full length of the barrel. It took a Winchester centerfire cartridge with a powder charge of 75 grains and a bullet weighing 350 grains in a 1⅞-inch case. The carbine had a barrel 22 inches long and a wooden stock extending almost to the end of the barrel; this carbine was the official weapon of the Royal Northwest Mounted Police until 1914. The regular military version of the 76 had a 32-inch barrel, a 13-shot magazine, a saber bayonet, and weighed nine pounds.

In all, 123,211 Model 76s were produced in a 21-year period. See Williamson, *Winchester, The Gun that Won the West*, pp. 69, 189; Sharpe, *The Rifle in America*, p. 234.

[3] George Earp later became town marshal, according to one account, but was not always so successful as his famous brother in keeping the peace. One time some Garden City boys were selling pickles boiled eggs, and other provender to passengers when the train stopped at the station. A young Easterner, off the train, made a derogatory remark about the local edibles. George Finnup hit him with a pickle. The young Easterner ran after George and was spanking him on the station platform when adult Garden City-ites intervened. "You can't do this to a boy of our town!" was their attitude. A friend of the Easterner got off the train with two .45 guns. A shot appears to have been fired. The train began to pull away. Marshal Earp came running up, pistol in hand, but it failed to go off (at whom it is not clear) so he said to H. M. De Cordova who was standing near: "Shoot him, Hank."

"I haven't any gun," was the only justification De Cordova gave for not shooting.

"Here's mine," said Squire Worrel, solving the difficulty and threw De Cordova a .38.

A drop shot caught the young Easterner low in the left shoulder about 130 yards away while he was running to catch the train. He died on the station platform. Finney County, Kansas, Historical Society, *The History of Finney County, Kansas*, vol. 1, pp. 47–48.

[4] *Ibid.*, p. 63.

[5] Wetmore and Cody, *Last of the Great Scouts*, pp. 321–322. Possibly Jones meant McPherson (Walsh, *The Making of Buffalo Bill*, 162–163; Russell, *The Lives and Legends of Buffalo Bill*, 190). However, Wild Bill Hickok, who apparently got Bill Cody a job as peace officer in either Abilene or McPherson or both, was marshal of Abilene and Cody was associated with him there at the time Jones names.

[6] Once Jones lassoed a rattlesnake. He'd very nearly put his hand on it while crawling on his belly stalking an antelope. Jumping to his feet he saw the rattler slithering toward a prairie dog hole. He stuck his gun butt-downward into the hole to block the snake. The snake promptly coiled up at the gun butt. Jones couldn't get his gun. Neither could the snake get down the hole. Jones ran to the top of the nearest rise, signaled the wagon, got his lasso, and: "I . . . threw a noose over the head of the serpent, and endeavored to keep it alive for museum purposes; but drew the rope too tightly around its neck and choked it to death." *Forty Years of Adventure*, pp. 178–179.

[7] Jones' *Memoirs*, Ch. 7, pp. 2–3.

[8] He built the Nickel Plate railroad grade from Garden City to Dighton, Kansas.

[9] *Forty Years of Adventure*, p. 48.

[10] *Ibid.*, p. 50. Jones might have added that the manure was mighty useful. "In the early days of travel over the treeless plains, the droppings of the buffalo, known as 'buffalo chips' (*bois de vache*), often furnished the only fuel that was to be had. The dry chips burned slowly and made a hot and fairly lasting fire over the coals of which cooking was done with a great deal of comfort. The snows of winter did not change it, the spring rains merely dampened the surface, and even a long storm hardly wet through the sixteenth part of an inch; its surface remained, year after year, unaffected by the weather, except that annually it became a little harder until at last it was almost impossible to cut it with a knife. The underside, . . . retained . . . moisture longer, and was never quite so hard.

"No one would suspect that so inconspicuous an object would be of any benefit to humanity, yet it has saved many a life by furnishing heat with which to prepare warm food and drink, and often gave the fire which kept men from perishing in the bitter cold of winter.

"The Indians held the buffalo chip sacred. In many of their

ceremonies it was used as a support to keep some sacred object from
... the ground." (Garretson, *The American Bison,* pp. 168–169).

CHAPTER 5 LASSOING BUFFALO CALVES

[1] The strenuous nature of these hunts — hours upon hours, miles upon
miles — is almost unbelievable by modern standards which include
few such activities in their frames of reference. The Indians, however, had set the example with their buffalo running ponies — used
for killing, not for lassoing. These were usually pintos, "either black
and white or liver and white. They were carefully trained and all
those that proved satisfactory had their ears slit to distinguish them
from the common stock. They were never used for any other purpose than running buffalo. . . . There is a record of one belonging to
a noted Comanche buffalo runner which ran for four hours, at high
speed, among an immense herd of buffalo. Its meandering course
covered an estimated distance of between forty and fifty miles,
during which its rider lanced no less than one hundred buffalo."
Garretson, *The American Bison,* pp. 176–177.

Jones' will to victory drove him in a fashion that seems superhuman today but was well within the context of his times.

[2] Jones' herd became the largest and best known but was not the
only one. An Indian of mixed blood named Walking Coyote had
driven a band of thirty buffalo from Alberta to the Flathead Indian
Reservation in Montana. Another Indian of Latin blood named
Michel Pablo bought the herd for $2,000. Pablo formed a partner-
ship with Charles Allard and the herd became known as the Allard
herd, or the Pablo herd, or the Flathead herd. Meanwhile in Texas,
Colonel Charles Goodnight at his ranch in the Panhandle had begun
catching calves in a small way, and at Ft. Bennett, Dakota Territory,
and at Stony Mountain in Manitoba there were herds, which with
Jones' helped to preserve the species. See Branch, *The Hunting of
the Buffalo,* pp. 228–229.

CHAPTER 6 COLONEL JONES

[1] As quoted in Jones, *Forty Years of Adventure,* p. 113.
[2] *Ibid.,* p. 129. This is a paraphrase.
[3] *Ibid.,* pp. 159–160.
[4] *Ibid.,* p. 143.

CHAPTER 7 THE BUFFALO RANCH

[1] *American Big Game Hunting,* pp. 172–174. The first known attempt
to domesticate the buffalo was made by Vicente de Zaldivar in 1598.

From San Juan on the Rio Grande north of the present site of Santa Fe, New Mexico, he traveled to the buffalo range. He built cottonwood corrals near a river, tried and failed to corral adult buffalo, succeeded in catching calves, but they all "died of rage" within an hour. He brought back none. Horgan, *Great River, The Rio Grande in North American History*, p. 199.

[2] Jones, *Forty Years of Adventure*, pp. 236–237. Hornaday says the price was $50,000 for 83 head. (See *Extermination of the American Bison*, p. 458.) $50,000 would be the equivalent of about $200,000 today.

[3] Jones, *Forty Years of Adventure*, pp. 237–238. As for the difficulty of handling buffalo bulls: "One of the hardest jobs I ever tackled," Zane Grey quotes Jones as saying, "was that of supplying the buffalo for Bronx Park. I rounded up a magnificent 'king' buffalo bull, belligerent enough to fight a battleship. When I rode after him the cowmen said I was as good as killed. I made a lance by driving a nail into the end of a short pole and sharpening it. After he had chased me, I wheeled my bronco and hurled the lance into his back, ripping a wound as long as my hand. That put the fear of Providence into him and took the fight all out of him. I drove him uphill and down, and across canyons at a dead run for eight miles single handed, and loaded him on a freight car; but he came near getting me once or twice, and only quick bronco work and lance play saved me." *The Last of the Plainsmen*, pp. 49–50.

[4] "Three years ago," writes George Bird Grinnell in 1892 in *American Big Game Hunting*, (p. 53), "there were in this country about two hundred and fifty domesticated buffalo, in the possession of about a dozen individuals. Of these the most important herd was that of Hon. C. J. Jones, of Garden City, Kansas.... Next came that of Charles Allard and Michel Pablo, of the Flathead Agency in Montana . . ."

Hornaday lists the following herds as existing in 1887: Jones — 57 head; Allard-Pablo — 35; Bedson (later purchased by Jones) — 83; Buffalo Bill Cody — 20 head, comprising part of the Wild West Show (they all died of pleuro-pneumonia while performing at Madison Square Garden in the winter of 1886–'87); Charles Goodnight, Clarendon, Texas — 13; Frederick Dupree, Cheyenne Indian Reservation near Ft. Bennett, Dakota Territory — 9. (Dupree was asking $650 for a cow and a bull.)

In addition there were a few smaller herds and individual animals in captivity here and there. (See *Extermination of the American Bison*, pp. 387–388.)

[5] Jones, *Forty Years of Adventure*, p. 242.
[6] *Ibid*, p. 251.
[7] *Ibid.*, p. 263. "Colorado and Kansas passed laws in 1875 to protect

the bison, but by then the herds were virtually gone. A similar bill came before the Texas legislature. But General Phil Sheridan, then commander of the Southwest, successfully opposed it. He said that the hunters by destroying the redskins' food supply were doing more to solve the Indian 'problem' than the Army had done in 30 years. 'Let them kill, skin and sell until the buffalo is exterminated, as it is the only way to bring about a lasting peace and allow civilization to advance.' In Washington a bill to protect the bison passed both House and Senate. President Grant refused to sign it." From Collins, *The Unvanquished Buffalo*, p. 11.

The first protection ever given the buffalo by the United States Government came after the buffalo were dead, for all practical purposes. It was a law passed by Congress in 1894 and signed by President Cleveland making it unlawful to kill a buffalo in Yellowstone Park, the penalty being a fine of $1,000 or imprisonment in a penitentiary.

CHAPTER 8   THE LAST HUNT

[1] Seton, *Life Histories of Northern Animals*, p. 295.

[2] Quotations used in this chapter are from *Buffalo Jones' Forty Years of Adventure*, pp. 201–224.

[3] As happened to four cows Jones didn't catch. The fate of these cows is graphically described by Seton in *Life Histories of Northern Animals*, pp. 295–296. "The very last individuals I have knowledge of were found in 1889. The account of them I got from W. Allen, cowboy . . . of Clayton, N. M., four years after the event. I give in full.

"About August 20, while out with a party hunting mustangs, in the neutral strip about twelve miles northeast of Buffalo Springs, the riders saw four animals, which they supposed were mustangs, as they were rolling in the dust. They were about three miles away, on the south side of a little knoll. The hunters rode around on the north side and got within seventy-five yards, to learn that these were four Buffalo.

"They took alarm at once and started off westward, closely pursued by the hunters for about three miles, and then met another man driving a bunch of mustangs. The two bunches, mustangs and Buffalo, joined, and the men chased them for two miles, when they parted, the mustangs turning to the left, keeping up with the X I T fence, and the Buffalo going to the right. Allen chased these about five miles farther and right into two of his own party. The Buffalo circled from them south and west three miles back, then right back to the X I T fence again. He fired four shots into a cow. She quit the bunch and went two miles to a lake, while he chased the three right through the X I T fence and left them. The men then returned to the cow at the lake; she ran into the deepest water, and stood at bay. After resting a short time she came out of the water and they shot her. A photographer, who was with the camp, took the pictures of the part with the skin and meat in view. That was the last Buffalo Allen ever saw. He learned that the three were killed later on. This ended the last stragglers of the southern herd."

The murders were over. The buffalo could rest in peace.

Though Garretson adds (*The American Bison*, p. 155): "As late as 1897, a small herd of wild buffalo, numbering between twenty and thirty animals, ranged in Lost Park near Bison Park, Park County, Colorado. They had been protected by ranch and cattle men, but occasionally some unprincipled person would kill one, and the increase was less than the loss. Through the work of these vandals, the herd dwindled until there were but four left; two bulls, one cow and one calf. They were all killed in February, 1897. These are believed to be the last wild buffalo killed in the United States."

According to Hornaday there were 256 buffalo in captivity in 1889. Approximately 150 of these were Jones'. There were in addition an estimated 200 that had taken refuge in Yellowstone Park, making a grand total of 456 buffalo in the entire world. *Extermination of the American Bison*, p. 387.

[4] Jones, *Forty Years of Adventure*, p. 224.

CHAPTER 9   THE BUFFALO KING ABROAD

[1] They still remember him around McCook. Arthur B. Wood, who was a young delivery boy for the local superintendent of the Burlington Railroad, recalls that he had a herd of 50 buffalo a mile or two northeast of town. Wood and Bill Brown and two or three other boys used to ride their bicycles out to the buffalo pasture on Sundays, when the cowboys who took care of the buffalo for Jones were usually sleeping off their Saturday night drunk, and ride the buffalo calves, which were of about the same explosive nature as a modern Brahma calf. Letter of H. P. Sutton, Sept. 26, 1958.

[2] Jones, *Forty Years of Adventure*, p. 227. The *Runic,* with her sister ship the *Cuthic,* were the first all-cargo steamers ordered by the White Star Line. Each was 4,700 tons gross. Both were fitted with special facilities for the shipment of live cattle and are thought to be the first so-called "cattle boats." They make further claim on the marine historian's attention by being the first White Star ships installed with triple expansion engines, pioneering this type of power plant for several large liners then under construction. Letter from The Cunard Steamship Company Limited, March 13, 1961.

[3] *Ibid.,* p. 229. As to the fate of the buffalo delivered in England, the

Liverpool Courier for Monday, Nov. 9, 1891, reports: "The White Star steamer Runic, which arrived in the Mersey on Saturday from New York, had amongst her cargo ten pure-bred Western buffaloes. They are magnificent specimens obtained from Nebraska and arrived in first-class condition. They were in charge of Mr. C. J. Jones, the owner of an extensive ranch in McCook County, Nebraska. . . . The ten animals in question, the price paid for which is stated to be £500, are consigned to a Liverpool gentleman." And the *Liverpool Mercury* of the same date adds: "He (Jones) has made buffalo breeding a specialty for some years past and states that as the animal in its natural and wild state is almost extinct, the only way to keep the species in existence is by means of partial artificial raising. Some time ago Mr. Jones visited this country and secured orders from several noblemen and gentlemen for young buffaloes to be sent over, to be placed in their parks."

CHAPTER 10   CHEROKEE STRIP

[1] Finney County, Kansas, Historical Society, *History of Finney County, Kansas*, vol. 1, p. 110.

[2] Jones, *Forty Years of Adventure*, pp. 266–272. Henry S. Johnston, who still lives in Perry, Oklahoma, recalls that Jones was among the settlers of legal entry and got a quarter section of land. "Jones was a very active politician," Mr. Johnston says, "and was chosen Sergeant at Arms of the Populistic House of Representatives of the Oklahoma Legislature in 1897, that is the Fourth Territorial Legislature of Oklahoma. He made GOOD. He moved away soon thereafter but I do not remember where." Letter of Feb. 18, 1961.

CHAPTER 11   ARCTIC ADVENTURE

[1] For this information we are chiefly indebted to Mrs. George O. Abbott of Garden City, whose husband was associated with Jones in the construction of the Populist Railroad.

[2] These and other quotations of Jones in this chapter are from *Forty Years of Adventure*, pp. 287–290.

[3] *Ibid.*, p. 301.

CHAPTER 12   WHITE WOLVES

[1] Jones, *Forty Years of Adventure*, p. 306.

[2] *Ibid.*, p. 306–307.

[3] *Ibid.*, p. 307.

[4] *Ibid.*, p. 310. No question but that Great Slave Lake was famous for storms. See Mackenzie, *Voyages From Montreal On the River St. Lawrence Through the Continent of North America to the Frozen and Pacific Oceans*, pp. 233–235. See *ibid* for buffalo having ranged even this far north, though Jones does not mention the fact, they being gone in his time. These would have been the "Woods Buffalo." Although only one species of American bison is known to science, early explorers and writers tell of three kinds: 1) mountain bison, 2) woods bison, 3) plains bison; but the distinction is now thought to be merely the result of environment. The mountain bison, inhabiting the eastern Rockies, were more active, vicious and wilder than the plains bison, its legs were thick and stronger, its body lighter and shorter, its robe darker. The woods bison was the largest and finest of the three varieties. Its robe was thicker and darker. Bulls weighed as much as 2,500 pounds. See Garretson, *The American Bison*, pp. 5–6.

   Of course in the strictly scientific sense, bison are not "buffalo" — buffalo being the term reserved for the water buffalo, African buffalo, etc.

[5] Conditions were such that they found it impossible to send a shepherd dog to Ft. Resolution with word of their whereabouts, and Martha, the girls, and the outside world remained without news of Jones for this entire winter.

CHAPTER 13   NAZZULA! NAZZULA!

[1] The standard maneuver of musk ox at the approach of danger was to run into a group and form a circle, heads and horns outward. This accounts for their action when Sousie Barromie spoke to them. The musk ox employed this maneuver so effectively against wolves, forming a circle with calves and young stock inside, that the wolves did not as a rule bother to make them "form up" but by-passed the herds. See Hornaday, *The Minds and Manners of Wild Animals*, p. 55.

   As to *why* Sousie should talk to the musk ox, listen to what Jones says. "One lovely day in May I heard an old Indian, La Pierre, who was considered the head of the Yellow Knife tribe, teaching a group of children, who were seated on a beautiful carpet of moss. He was narrating to them a story, similar to that of the flood, yet vastly different in characters and circumstances. As near as I could understand, the story ran something like this:

   Many, many years ago, the birds and beasts were fighting for supremacy. They fought great battles, and the beasts were always victorious. Finally the birds had a big talk among themselves, and agreed to adopt a new method of warfare. The eagle and the crane were sent to intercede with the Great Spirit, and implore him to withhold the rain until vegetation was all dead, and thus starve the beasts into subjection. They made the ascent by continually circling upward, for one moon. From that time on, the rain did not fall until all the vegetation had died, and the animals were without food. They too would have died of thirst, had not the Great Bad Spirit caught a beaver, and laying its tail on a flat rock, took another rock and pounded it until it was flat. And from that time until this, the beaver's tail has retained that shape.

The Great Bad Spirit told him to make a dam, from sticks and stones, and to use his tail as a trowel and plaster it with mud. This he did, and thus a reservoir was formed that furnished water for the beasts. But the animals could not live on water alone, and many died of hunger. The fish were all dead excepting those in the reservoir. . . . At last things became desperate, and the loon rebelled, and cried mightily for rain. The Great Good Spirit bent his ear to listen. Then came the rain in torrents. It was in the spring of the year. The ice on the reservoir had melted from the shores, and as the rain came down, the water washed from the hills, great stones upon the ice. *As soon as the beasts saw that a great flood had come, some of all kinds congregated on the ice, and thus floated without seeing land, for two moons.* The rocks were so wet that moss grew on those that had lodged on the ice, and the animals ate it and lived. *Finally the raven left the ice for one whole day, and came back with a piece of reindeer meat in his mouth.* Then the animals knew that the flood had nearly subsided. . . . While the animals and birds were upon the ice, the musk ox was chosen king of all, and where it goes, all the other animals are in duty bound to follow for protection. The musk ox understands all animals, also the Indians, who must always address that animal if they are compelled to kill one for food, as it can intercede with the Great Spirit for or against them. Therefore the little Indians ("yahzas," as they are called) are taught to reverence the musk oxen, and to speak gently to them. That when an Indian observes this rule, no harm will ever visit him or his children." *Forty Years of Adventure*, pp. 431–432.

[2] "In all the words of the Slave language with which I am familiar, the accent is placed on the ultimate, which gives a sad intonation," says Jones. "Their language comprises very few words, and upon the emphasis depends the meaning. For instance, a word meaning a short distance will be soft, without any accent; while if meaning farther away, the same word is accentuated — so that by varying the accent, all known degrees of distance may be conveyed by the same word." *Forty Years of Adventure*, p. 379.

[3] *Ibid.*, p. 378.

CHAPTER 14   MUSK OX CALVES

[1] Some of the material in this chapter is from Jones, *Forty Years of Adventure,* pp. 380–395, some is from his *Memoirs,* and some is imaginative recreation.

[2] See Hornaday, *The American Natural History,* pp. 103–107. Jones' economic incentive is clearer when one reads that a musk ox calf sold in New York a few years later for $1,600 ($5,000 today).

[3] Jones said he knew a man could live 39 days on meat alone because he'd done it on this trip. *Ibid.,* p. 394. Vilhjalmur Stefansson redemonstrated the idea years later.

CHAPTER 15   PRESIDENTS AND GRIZZLY BEARS

[1] Fred Meyer Schroder, author and sourdough, reports seeing exactly such a sight in the Yukon at this period. Interview of September 11, 1956.

[2] "In 1907," says Seton, "I took a canoe trip down the Mackenzie River to the Arctic Region, covering the country north of the Great Slave Lake, and there had the joyful privilege of checking up and confirming the main events of Buffalo Jones' own trip. During more than one storm I lived in the cabin which he built on Great Slave Lake; and lying about the door of that cabin I found the skeletons of nine large wolves that had been killed there at short range, and thus gave an answer to certain critics who questioned the tale." Finney County, Kansas, Historical Society, *History of Finney County, Kansas,* vol. 1, p. 128.

Hornaday was also impressed. See *Camp-fires in the Canadian Rockies,* p. 112.

[3] Lemuel A. Garrison, Superintendent of Yellowstone Park, writes the following in a letter of March 8, 1961:

I have had the Army records searched for information which might bear on your problem, without finding a direct statement to the effect that Buffalo Jones was appointed by President Roosevelt. There is, however, some material which suggests that was the case.

The correspondence file indicates Major Pitcher contacted Buffalo Jones in the spring of 1902 in an attempt to purchase animals from his Kansas herd. None were obtained, but that may have alerted Jones to the possibility of obtaining a position managing the Yellowstone buffalo herd. The next item in the file was a copy of a letter (R-IV: 92, C. J. Jones from E. A. Hitchcock, Secretary of Interior, Jul. 8, 1902), sent to Major Pitcher to inform him of Jones' appointment as Game Warden in Yellowstone Park. The part which is pertinent here reads as follows:

"Sir: Immediately upon receipt hereof you will proceed to the Yellowstone National Park and report to Major John Pitcher, U.S.A., Acting Superintendent of that reservation, for duty as Game Warden in the reservation; it is distinctly understood that your employment as warden is to be at the pleasure of the Secretary of the Interior."

Two things make it unlikely that Jones was selected by Major Pitcher. He was just then attempting to get the job for a man of his choice, who had been employed in the Park for some time, and there is the statement in a letter explaining the events leading to the resignation of Jones (R-VII: 25–28, Maj. Jno. Pitcher to Military Secretary, Department of Dakota, Nov. 28, 1906), in which the Major says:

"Mr. Jones was sent to the Yellowstone National Park on July 8, 1902, for the purpose of assisting in establishing a new herd of buffalo, on account of his supposed knowledge and experience with these animals. He did very good work in building the necessary fences and corrals, and in looking after the purchase and transportation of the twenty-one head of buffalo shipped to this place, but here his usefulness in the park ended absolutely."

In President Roosevelt's book, *Outdoor Pastimes of an American Hunter* (New York: Charles Scribner's Sons, 1923), he covers his Yellowstone trip in 1903, but gives only a passing mention to Buffalo Jones, " . . . a famous old plainsman, who is in the Park taking care of the buffalo." (p. 329). He also makes his friendship with Major Pitcher quite evident. [Authors' note: Roosevelt describes Jones as "Buffalo Jones, a famous old plainsman" who is managing the hounds which keep the cougars under control and "tending with solicitous care" the buffalo at the Mammoth enclosure. (See *Outdoor Pastimes*, ed. 1905, pp. 295, 298.)]

Despite that, there is the article in the Butte *Miner*, July 3, 1903, indicating President Roosevelt's continuing interest in the Yellowstone game situation.

The rapidly worsening situation between Buffalo Jones and Major Pitcher, finally led to the Secretary of the Interior placing Jones in direct charge of game in the Park (Letters, R-VI: 58–9, Maj. John Pitcher from Secretary of the Interior, Jul. 6, 1905). The following excerpt is pertinent:

"At the time of the appointment of Mr. C. J. Jones as Game Warden of the Yellowstone National Park, no specific instructions were given as to his duties, but you were ad-

vised that his work would be performed in the park under
your general supervision."

" . . . I deem it best that you should be no longer burdened
with the details of the preservation of game in the reservation, and hereafter this work will be held to strict account-
ability for the care, preservation and management of the
game within the Yellowstone National Park."

To the evidence furnished by Mr. Garrison's letter, can be added
the statement which appears often in *The History of Finney County,
Kansas,* and which is common oral tradition in Garden City and elsewhere, that Roosevelt appointed Jones game warden. These may
have the fallibility of local tradition. However, the New York *Times*
of Oct. 2, 1919 states unequivocally that Roosevelt appointed Jones
game warden at Yellowstone National Park, and so does Jones in his
Memoirs, Ch. 3, p. 1.

[4] Garretson, *The American Bison,* p. 197.

[5] Annual Report of the Superintendent of Yellowstone Park, dated
October 15, 1902. The Pablo-Allard herd had been divided at the
death of Charles Allard and a portion had passed to Howard Eaton
at Mendora, North Dakota.

[6] Letter of J. N. Hulpieu, dated August 28, 1958. Jessie Jones says her
father drove a herd of "about 26 head" overland to the Park, Finney
County, Kansas, Historical Society, *History of Finney County,
Kansas,* vol. 1, p. 109. I. L. Diesem and others speak of his drives to
Yellowstone, *Ibid.,* pp. 113–114. Epic drives were by no means un-
common at this time. One of Jones' neighbors helped drive 400 wild
horses from Winnemucca, Nevada, over the Rockies to western
Kansas where they were sold to settlers, *ibid.,* p. 164.

[7] From *The Independent,* June 7, 1906.

[8] Opinions differ on how close friends Jones and Roosevelt were.
In 1930 Newell Joyner took down this reminiscence from Judge
Meldrum, U. S. Commissioner in Yellowstone Park in the early
1900's who said he knew Jones then and earlier: "Roosevelt, Jones
and I (Meldrum) were delegates to the same convention in 1884.
It was the convention at which Blaine was nominated. This seemed
to be sufficient excuse to Jones to consider Roosevelt as an old
'buddy' and when he learned of Roosevelt's coming to the park, he
came to me and said 'Judge, now that the President is going to come
into the Park, I think we ought to get together and talk over old
times.' I replied, 'Well, I don't make a habit of bothering Presidents
of the United States.' Jones said, 'Aren't you going out in the park
with him?' And I told him that I wouldn't unless I was asked and
I had not been asked yet but I hoped he enjoyed it. Well the long
and the short of it was that when Roosevelt came into the park he
left all of his aides and his secretary at headquarters and gave orders
to Pitcher that he would be accompanied only by Pitcher, Burroughs

and the smallest number of men necessary to take care of the camp. When the cavalcade started out Jones took his hounds and went along in the hope that he might tree a mountain lion and thus provide a little entertainment for the President. The first evening in camp Roosevelt called Pitcher to him and told him to send the hounds and their owner back stating that he did not want them. This word was given to Jones and he suggested that Scout McBride take the hounds back but the result of it all was that Jones and his hounds returned to Mammoth. I met him down at the Post Office shortly after he came in and said, 'Hello Jones, I thought you were out with the President.' Jones was so mad that he never said a word." Photostat furnished by Lemuel A. Garrison, Superintendent of Yellowstone Park, Mar. 8, 1961.

In refutation of Judge Meldrum and those who considered Jones a charlatan and cheap hanger-on, there is the fact that by Meldrum's own testimony Jones and Roosevelt may have been personally acquainted as early as 1884. Certainly Jones must have been known to Roosevelt by 1890 when George Bird Grinnell (co-editor with Roosevelt of the Boone and Crockett Club's publication, *American Big Game Hunting*) visited Garden City and did the article on Jones and his buffalo and cattalo; nor is it likely that a man of Roosevelt's interests could have missed the significance of Jones and his buffalo-capturing-and-preserving exploits. Finally there are: Roosevelt's own laudatory statement on Jones in the introduction to *Lassoing Wild Animals*, and the article in the New York Globe for April 1, 1910, which treats the intimacy between the two men as generally accepted, and the New York *Times* statement that Roosevelt appointed Jones game warden of Yellowstone (see Note 3), Jones' own account of the President's visit to Yellowstone, which follows: "President Roosevelt, when he entered the Park for his memorable camping trip, left all the grandeur and panoply of his position at the Park gates. Inside he was just the simple, wholehearted big boy that we who knew him best realized him to be. One little incident, showing his gentle consideration for his brother man, comes to my mind, and my eyes grow misty as I remember it. The party was made up of Army officers, Mr. William Loeb, and myself with an orderly to look after the horses, arrange the luncheon and keep the camp. We were seated about the luncheon, when Roosevelt noticed the orderly standing in the distance, not eating nor doing anything in particular. 'Where's your lunch?' called out our Chief. 'Oh, Sir, I did not bring anything.' 'Well, sit down here and share with us.' The orderly's eyes grew big with horror: 'Sir, I cannot sit at table with my superior officers.' The Colonel's voice fairly roared as he said, 'Well, as the commanding officer of the United States Army, I bid you sit right there and eat.' Needless to say, the orderly ate.

"It was a rule of the Park that not a gun could be fired, but on the visit of our distinguished guest, the Park officers decided to waive the rule that Colonel Roosevelt might have a shot at the lions. This he gently but firmly refused. He asked no privilege denied his friends.

"Several kegs of whiskey were sent by Park officers to our camp but the next day they were returned, unopened, to the Post.

"On one day's ride, we came to Hell Roaring River, and found two logs across it. These the horses must walk or be left behind. Now the going was none too good at best, and the prospects of the struggle through brush and tangled thicket did not please Colonel Roosevelt. The guide shouted 'everybody dismount.' President Roosevelt was next the guide and waving his hand, calling gaily, 'Stand aside.' The Rough Rider applied his spurs vigorously, and the horse carried his fearless rider safely across the roaring chasm." See Jones' *Memoirs*, Ch. 3, p. 5.

9 Interview with L. A. Garrison at Yellowstone Park, Aug. 8, 1958.

10 Interview with Mrs. Frank A. Wagner, Yellowstone Park Librarian, Aug. 8, 1958.

11 Interview with C. J. Smith at Santa Barbara, California, July 18, 1958; interview with Jack Haynes at Yellowstone Park, Aug. 9, 1958.

12 Letters bearing on Jones' official relation to the Park, and the Park to Jones, are in the files at Yellowstone Park Headquarters, Yellowstone Park, Wyoming.

13 "The moving picture," wrote William T. Hornaday, "that Col. (Buffalo) Jones had taken in the Yellowstone Park showing him thrashing an angry grizzly bear with a bean pole while the grizzly bear was suspended by the leg, wildly swaying between heavens and earth, swinging and clawing in every direction was the one tremendously amusing thing that Col. Jones did with wild animals, and that film always excited roars of laughter. I expected that when the bear was let down to earth, and turned loose, it would at once turn upon Col. Jones and rend him from limb to limb; but instead of that, he struck a bee line for the tallest timber that he could find, wildly rushed into it, and there turned over a new leaf." Finney County, Kansas Historical Society, *History of Finney County, Kansas*, vol. 1, p. 122.

14 A transcript of this news item is in the files at Yellowstone Park.

CHAPTER 16   ARIZONA WILDERNESS

1 "The Bird in the Bush" in *Redbook Magazine*, April, 1917, pp. 16–27.

2 Wooley's son, Joseph A. Wooley, tells of this and later incidents in Roscoe G. Willson's fascinating account "How the Buffalo Came to Arizona." Wooley's story seems to date the first entry of the buffalo earlier than Garrison since the animals are described as spending the winter of 1905-06 in the Kaibab.

[3] Letter from Elwin Pratt of Fredonia, Sept. 10, 1960. Elwin is the brother of Ernest Pratt, Vice-President of the "company."

[4] "Siwash," also known as Sowats Creek. "Buckskin" is an early designation of the Kaibab.

[5] Consult *Arrington Report,* Arizona Game and Fish Dept., 1934.

[6] Letter from the Secretary of Agriculture to the Secretary of the Interior, Washington, Jan. 3, 1906. (In the Yellowstone Park files.)

CHAPTER 17   THE CATTALO RANCH

[1] *Last of the Plainsmen,* p. 34. For reference to the drive from Texas see *Arrington Report,* Arizona Game and Fish Department, 1934, and, more recently, Roanna H. Winsor, "Time Over Coconino" in *Arizona Highways,* Feb. 1961, p. 9. The latter records, "Buffalo Jones takes almost a year (1905) to drive a herd of 50 buffalo from Texas to Coconino County — ." Rancher R. N. Burgess who was prominent in the development of water resources in Coconino County related to the authors the details given on the reputed swimming of the Colorado by the buffalo.

[2] Interview with L. A. Garrison, Yellowstone Park, Aug. 1958.

[3] Authors' correspondence with James de T. Abajian, Dr. Alexander T. Leonard and Miss Frances M. Molera, granddaughter of E. J. Molera, 1958. See also Garretson, *The American Bison,* p. 219.

[4] A detailed account of the buffalo drive is given in "The Buffalo Hunt" by Charles C. Niehuis, in *Arizona Highways* for Feb. 1945. Niehuis' well written story gives a humorous description of the renegade bull's attack on a horse-drawn hay wagon resulting in a dead horse and a farmer buried in the hay. Niehuis concludes, "There is no record of what eventually happened to the buffalo bull that returned to Lund (Utah)."

Elwin Pratt of Fredonia, who had personal acquaintance with Jones in that area at the time, disagrees with both of the accounts in certain details. He writes (letter of Sept. 19, 1960):

"The story about the old Buffalo Bull charging the team and the hay wagon is partly true. The bull got away at Pintura, or Anderson ranch as it was then called, and made several trips back and forth, and wherever he was met, the teams would always give him the road and that is what happened when he was met by the load of hay. The team ran away and the wagon tipped over, but the horses were not killed. The bull ran at large until some one killed him on the Lund desert west of Cedar City.

"My father was Lorum Pratt Sr. and was Forest Supervisor for seven years on the Kaibab, but never had any connection in the Buffalo Company (formed by Jones to promote the Cattalo project). Rather, it was my brother, E. B. Pratt. The Company was not incorporated and finally broke up. J. T. Owens finally became the owner as he purchased the others out, one by one getting the remainder of only about twenty buffalo. My brother told me many tales about Buffalo Jones. He said Jones was a great promoter and had many good ideas but they didn't always work out. Ideas to cross the buffalo with native cattle, cross Persian sheep with the deer and cats with the white-tail squirrels."

[5] Letter of June 19, 1958, from Lawrence E. Powell, Chief of Game Management, Arizona Game and Fish Department.

[6] For a comment on the problem of the hump see Roscoe G. Willson, "How the Buffalo Came to Arizona", p. 52. For Goodnight's report see below chapter XXVII, note 12.

CHAPTER 18   WILD STALLION

[1] *Last of the Plainsmen*, pp. 3–6.
[2] *Ibid.*, p. 6.
[3] *Ibid.*, pp. 30-31.
[4] *Ibid.*, 32–33.
[5] *Ibid.*, pp. 49–50.
[6] *Ibid.*, p. 232–233.

CHAPTER 19   ZANE GREY GETS AN EYE-FULL

[1] Finney County Kansas Historical Society, *History of Finney County, Kansas*, vol. 1, p. 114.
[2] *Last of the Plainsmen*, p. 7.
[3] *Ibid.*, pp. 300–302.
[4] Grey had frequent cause to marvel at Jones' understanding of animals ... as when the plainsman insisted, against the advice of everyone else present, that a certain bay stallion would carry two live, snarling mountain lions, the very smell of which had driven other horses mad. Jones explained that the stallion would not bolt over the Grand Canyon rim from terror because, "he's helping us out. He's proud to show up the other nags." Grey commented: "Jones was always asserting strange traits in animals and giving them intelligence and reason. As to that, many incidents coming under my observation while with him, and seeing with his eyes, made me inclined to his claims, the fruit of a lifetime with animals."

As it turned out, the stallion proudly packed the captured and bound cougars to camp without turning a hair! See *Tales of Lonely Trails*, p. 74.

⁵ Letter of W. H. Switzer of Flagstaff, Arizona, Mar. 15, 1957: "During 1909 to 1911, inclusive, I was Clerk of the Board of Supervisors of Coconino County, and at that time we were paying bounty on mountain lions. Mr. Jones killed a mother lion with nine unborn kittens. He skinned out the entire bunch, and sent in for the bounty and collected ten payments."

⁶ This letter is dated Nov. 30, 1907.

⁷ N. C. Jones had come from Illinois to Garden City and been for a time Jones' assistant at Yellowstone Park, later succeeding him as keeper of the buffalo.

⁸ *Last of the Plainsmen*, pp. 308-309.

CHAPTER 20   THE GREATEST CHALLENGE

¹ Garden City *Imprint*, Nov. 2, 1907.

² Jones' *Memoirs*, Ch. 4, p. 1.

³ Scull, *Lassoing Wild Animals in Africa*, p. vi.

⁴ Ambrose Means' account of the trip, written in collaboration with his wife, and kindly furnished the authors by his daughter, Mrs. Eagle Smith. Means' account of the trip as reported by F. E. Wells, publisher of the Williams (Arizona) *News*, appeared in *Scenic Southwest Magazine*, Winter Edition, 1935-36. Selections from the latter account follow:

> ROPED AFRICAN LIONS TO DEFEAT ROOSEVELT
> True Reasons For Buffalo Jones' Trip to South Africa Published For First Time — Editor Tipped Off By Head Of Big Printing Company On Long Island, New York — Cowboys Were To Steal Famous Teddy's Thunder — Were To Rope Every Species of Big Animal Roosevelt Shot.
>
> Tipped off by LeRoy Latham, head of the Latham Litho and Printing Company of Long Island, the editor of the *Northern Arizona Magazine* secured from Ambrose Means, lone survivor of the celebrated Jones Expedition to Africa, the true reason for which that novel hunting party was sent to Africa. Mr. Latham wrote in part as follows:
>
> > Mr. F. E. Wells,
> > Northern Arizona Magazine
> > Williams, Arizona
> >
> > Dear Mr. Wells:
> >   Ambrose Means has sent me a couple of copies of your magazine, and I just want to tell you that they afforded me a most enjoyable evening of reading, and much of the contents took me back to several trips that I have made in your section of the country.
> >   One excellent trip was in the Kaibab with Ambrose

Means before that section was damned with its improvements.

What I am particularly writing you about is to suggest that you try to get from Ambrose a story that I wormed out of him one night over a camp-fire, a story of the real reason for the first Buffalo Jones trip to Africa.

It is a story with a lot of political significance and shows that the whole trip was conceived for political purposes and to thwart the danger that a big Democratic politician foresaw in Theodore Roosevelt's proposed trip.

Sincerely,

(signed) LeRoy Latham

Acting on Mr. Latham's tip, the editor cornered Ambrose Means one day a few weeks back when he was in from his trap lines, for a short stay in town, and is pleased to report that he secured the story. Here it is in Means' own words:

First Buffalo Jones Trip To Africa

Yes, there was a political reason back of Jones' first trip to Africa. You see Roosevelt had recently handed the presidency of the United States over to Taft and there was much discontent among the progressive element of the country and much talk that Roosevelt was the only man courageous enough to cope with the reactionary interests in the country. They wanted Teddy's Big Stick back in the White House and were open in saying so. . . .

Mr. Bird had seen the ease with which the Arizona cowpunchers could rope a big mountain lion and tie him up and it occurred to him, that if he could send a couple of cowboys over to Africa to rope every ferocious animal that the redoubtable Roosevelt might shoot, Roosevelt's feat would look like small potatoes by comparison.

Buffalo Jones was picked to lead the party and he chose Marshall D. Loveless and myself for the two cowpunchers who were to toss the twines. Charles Sumner Bird financed the entire trip and we boys jumped at the chance. . . .

When the Englishmen there in Nairobi heard that we really intended to make a try at a rhinoceros we became the center of some lively betting. They didn't tell us at the time, but we learned afterwards that the betting odds against our success were 5 to 1 on the rhinoceros.

Roosevelt had been there just a little before us and when asked by the Englishmen whether we would succeed, he said, "I wouldn't be surprised if they do. Those cowboys are a reckless care-for-nothing bunch."

One Englishman amused us by asking how we could throw a 300-foot rope. He said it wouldn't be safe to venture closer than that to a rhinoceros or a lion without a good heavy gun.

They didn't make us feel any easier about it when they took us up to the cemetery where they bury their big game hunters. They had 34 of them buried there at that time, all killed by the big game they were hunting. . . .

The authors are indebted to the foregoing in its entirety for numerous details that appear in Chapters 20, 21, 22, 23. See also p. 270.

[5] Charles Sumner Bird enjoyed a reputation for integrity and fair dealing in his home state. For a commentary on the man and his work at the time he became a candidate for governor of Massachusetts on the Progressive Party ticket, consult Needham, "The Massachusetts Campaign." Regarding the reasons for the African trip, Bird wrote, "It has been asked by some what the object of the Buffalo Jones African Expedition was. I will tell you.

"You know my friend Colonel C. J. Jones broke his rifle a generation or so ago and vowed he would never again kill game save for food or in self-defense. Since taking that oath he has subdued or captured all kinds of wild animals in North America, including the musk ox, buffalo, grizzly bear and cougar.

"I discovered that it was his dream to go to East Africa to prove that with American cowboys, horses and dogs he could lasso and capture the savage animals of that country as readily as he has the wild animals of our country. As a sporting proposition, it seemed to me unique and fascinating, and so, as a small tribute to Colonel Jones, I volunteered to finance the expedition.

"I somewhat doubt whether there is another man in the world who has the courage, skill, and determination to do what he has done in the animal kingdom, and he well deserves to be called "The Preserver of the American Bison." Letter of Charles S. Bird to Guy H. Scull, July 8, 1910. Quoted in Scull, "Lassoing Wild Animals in Africa," *Everybody's Magazine,* Sept., 1910, p. 310.

Jones himself said: "Well, the African lion is a difficult problem: it's got to be solved. I'll catch him all right, but what will happen after that I don't pretend to know, being a hunter and not a prophet. I am taking my branding irons, and the lions I don't want I'll brand and turn loose to fight another day.

"I believe in giving these wild things a fair sporting chance. . . ." (from the New York *Globe,* Friday, April 3, 1910). The *Jones Papers* make no mention of any deliberate attempt to discredit Roosevelt but reveal strong opposition to his killing of African game.

[6] Jones' *Memoirs,* Ch. 4, p. 5.

[7] For a detailed account of Jones' activities in Africa, see Scull, *Lassoing Wild Animals in Africa.* For how a modern cowboy does it, see the following:

John Wayne has proved himself a real cowboy — even in Africa.

Big Duke is in Arusha, Tanganyika, East Africa, making "Hatari" for Howard Hawks.

He recently roped and caught a fleet wildebeest weighing 450 pounds. The wildebeest resembles the American bison but is vicious and as fleet as a deer.

Wayne made the capture from the front of a catching car, speeding up to 65 miles per hour over rough terrain. Strapped to a seat on the front fender, he had the animal subdued in 30 seconds from the time it started to run. The local white hunters called his feat sensational, but a friend who wrote here about it said Wayne pooh-poohed it. "A real range-riding cowboy would have bagged it in 15 seconds," said Wayne. "And I would have, too, back in the days when I was making those eight-day westerns for Monogram." (AP dispatch datelined Hollywood, and appearing in the Santa Barbara, California *News-Press,* March 12, 1961.)

CHAPTER 21   RHINO

[1] New York *Globe,* Friday, April 1, 1910.
[2] New York *Times,* Friday, April 1, 1910.

CHAPTER 22   HOUND-DOG

[1] Scull, *Lassoing Wild Animals in Africa.*
[2] John may have hunted buffalo calves in the snow of Yellowstone Park and been among "the lion hounds" that Jones hitched to the makeshift sled on which he sledded the calves to captivity. . . . John going with his master from Yellowstone to Grand Canyon, and finally to Europe, Asia, and Africa.

CHAPTER 23   LION

[1] Scull, *Lassoing Wild Animals in Africa,* p. 132. See also Kearton, *Wild Life Across the World,* p. 193. Jones' own account of the hunt is in *Collier's,* March 11, 1911, p. 46, and in his unpublished *Memoirs.*
[2] Jones' *African Journal,* p. 34.
[3] New York *Times,* Saturday, May 28, 1910.
[4] Letter from Grace Davall, Assistant Curator, New York Zoological Society, Aug. 22, 1958. Ambrose Means' account of the capture of the lioness continues from his interview with F. E. Wells, as reported in *Scenic Southwest Magazine,* Winter Edition, 1935-'36, pp. 1–88:

We were three hours driving that lioness out into the open country, where we could use our horses and ropes, and we paid dearly for it in dogs. Nearly every one of our 21 dogs were either crippled or killed, by the huge beast, before we got her where we wanted her. Some of the wounded were in such bad shape they died later.

I got the first rope on that lioness but it didn't do any good. She charged me at a distance of 40 feet and all I could do was drop the rope and spur my horse trying to get away from her.

I was on just about the fastest saddle horse and the quickest on the get-away I ever saddled, but as I looked back I could see that lioness gaining on me at every jump.

She got so close I thought it was all up with me. It looked as though the next jump would land her right on top of me and that horse.

I jerked my six-gun and figured I'd pump her full of lead anyway, though lead would never stop her. I waited to pull the trigger and then I realized that my horse was gaining. The Englishmen's pictures showed that lioness had lacked less than six feet in reaching my horse.

We both got ropes on her after that and it wasn't long before we had her stretched out and Jones tied her.

"What a fine specimen you are," Buffalo Jones exclaimed as he stood back and looked at that big lioness. "We'll take you back to the USA for a souvenir."

We did just that, that being the only animal we attempted to bring back with us. That night we were given a champagne supper by an English lord in celebration of our triumph and it wasn't until later that we learned he had lost 5,000 pounds on us.

We played around at roping a few more wild animals and then sold our horses and dogs and set out for home. We arrived in London to find the city so full of people who had come to attend the funeral of King Edward VII that we couldn't get a bed.

We reached New York on the seventh day of June 1910 and turned the lion over to The Bronx Zoo.

Strange as it may seem those pictures which were designed to dampen the enthusiasm for Roosevelt had not more than been started to circulate in America when Mr. Bird got better acquainted with Mr. Roosevelt, and ordered them withdrawn, so that to this day they have never been shown to any extent in the United States. They were sent to England and shown there for a time and then withdrawn altogether.

Buffalo Jones, who had killed thousands of Buffalos just for their hides, broke his old buffalo gun after this trip, captured 30 wild buffalo and started the herd that now roams wild in House Rock Valley.

"Man was made to rule over animals," he said, "not exterminate them."

[5] See Jones' *Memoirs*, Ch. 8, p. 1–2.
[6] *Ibid.*, Ch. 8, p. 3.

CHAPTER 24   THE CONGO

[1] See Scull in "Lassoing Wild Animals in Africa," *Everybody's Magazine*, Sept. 1910, p. 310.

[2] New York *Globe*, April 1, 1910.

[3] Letter of Charles Sumner Bird, April 17, 1961.

[4] Letter of Grace Davall, Assistant Curator of Mammals and Birds, New York Zoological Society, March 23, 1961.

[5] See New York *Times*, April 4, 1914.

[6] The niece of Dallas McDaniel writes (letter to authors, April 28, 1961), "It seems to me, the best I can remember, the expedition was financed by a circus company for their show, but of course I was very young at the time, and it's been so many years ago, I could be wrong." Mrs. Eagle M. Smith, daughter of Ambrose Means, says (letter of March 7, 1961) that it was rumored "Jones was offered $250,000 to bring back an adult male gorilla. The alleged reason for the large amount of money was because some research unit wanted to see if a male gorilla would mate with a woman. They had heard of gorillas carrying off women, but the natives had never known of this." Despite extensive correspondence with the New York Zoological Society and other scientific organizations and individuals who might have known of the Jones expedition, it has not been possible to identify specifically the financial backers of the trip. Nor have checks of the New York *Times* and other papers yielded any evidence. Jones' correspondence does not mention a $250,000 offer. The organization of the company to which investors contributed $8,500, noted in a following paragraph, is described in Jones' letter to his daughter, Jessie (January 9, 1914).

[7] Kansas City *Star*, March 22, 1914.

[8] Undated letter in the *Jones Papers* from New York to Topeka (probably January 1914).

[9] Kansas City *Star*, March 22, 1914.

[10] Letter of February 3, 1914. To simplify the text the authors have added here excerpts (beginning with "I have erased Edison") from Jones' letter to Jessie of February 4, 1914.

[11] Manuscript in the *Jones Papers* entitled "Second Article of the Buffalo Jones Expedition," dated April 28, 1914, Cape Lopez, West Africa, p. 1. The term "Congo" popularly included this region.

[12] Letter of February 4, 1914.

[13] Letter of February 20, 1914. For the story of the Benton incident see Gruening, *Mexico and its Heritage,* p. 579.

[14] Jones had apparently counted rather heavily on speaking engagements to complete the financing of his expedition. The loss of this source of income accounts in part for his later financial difficulties.

[15] "Second Article of the Buffalo Jones African Expedition," pp. 3–4.

CHAPTER 25   GORILLA

[1] Manuscript in the *Jones Papers* entitled "Our First Gorilla," undated, but written approximately June 1, 1914, p. 2.

[2] *Ibid.*, pp. 3–13.

[3] The above account of the taking of the second gorilla has been imaginatively recreated by the authors. Jones' correspondence simply states (Letter of June 5, 1914, to his daughters), "I am well repaid as we got a full-sized gorilla but was obliged to kill it" and (July 11, 1914, to his daughters), "Have two gorillas but both dead." The Topeka *Capital* (November 9, 1914), states, " 'Buffalo' Jones finally captured a full-grown gorilla, a feat never accomplished before, using only the cowboy's weapon, the lasso, according to information received from him. However, he did not go into further particulars." A letter from Mrs. Edna Conelly, niece of Dallas McDaniel, to authors (23 April 1961) states: "They did capture a live gorilla but due to the war conditions were unable to bring it back and had to kill it." Although the Jones expedition failed to bring back a live gorilla, an adult female was given to the Bronx Zoo on August 24, 1914, by Professor R. L. Garner. She became famous as "Dinah," but lived less than a year, dying August 2, 1915. See New York *Times*, December 21, 1914; August 2, 1915. W. L. Hornaday writes of her in his *Minds and Manners of Wild Animals*. For an interesting history of the gorilla and of attempts to bring him into captivity, see Zahl, "Face to Face with Gorillas in Central Africa." Modern capture-methods rely on the group technique of beaters and nets, not Jones' individualistic lasso approach.

[4] "Jungle Fever" was a popular name for malaria.

[5] Letter to Kansas City *Star*, November 8, 1914.

[6] Jones' death certificate lists "Jungle Fever" as cause of death.

[7] Most of this material is from Jones' letter of July 11, 1914 but the authors have taken the liberty of inserting relevant material from his letter of August 17, 1914 to his daughters from London beginning with "I lost my mind" and ending "to recall names."

[8] This "Jones" at Portales, New Mexico, was manager of the ranch there and apparently no relation to C. J. Jones.

[9] Letter of July 19, 1914 to his daughters.

[10] Letter of August 17, 1914 to his daughters.

CHAPTER 26   TRAIL'S END

[1] Cablegram: American Vice-Consul McBride, Boma, Africa, to the Secretary of State, October 15, 1914 (U. S. Department of State Decimal File, 1910–29).

[2] The daughter of Ambrose Means by his second wife is now living at Grand Canyon, Arizona. She is Mrs. Eagle M. Smith.

[3] Dispatch of October 11, 1915, Boma, Africa, (U. S. Department of State Decimal File, 1910–29).

[4] Letter to his daughters June 5, 1914.

[5] U. S. Department of State Decimal File, 1910–29.

[6] *Ibid.*

[7] Letter to his daughter, Jessie, October 10, 1914.

[8] Jones' *Memoirs* consist of 43 single-spaced, typed, legal-size, pages annotated in his own handwriting and would be equivalent to approximately 175 standard-size pages, double-spaced. They end with the following sentence closing the first African trip, "It would not take long to conquer the animal kingdom if all hunters would go after wild beasts as we went after them in British East Africa." The *Memoirs* provide details not found in any other source but contain major omissions, such as the record of his Arizona buffalo experiments.

[9] The *Memoirs*, p. 1.

[10] *History of Finney County, Kansas*, Vol. 1, p. 112.

[11] Adapted from Grinnell, *Pawnee Hero Stories and Folk Tales*, pp. 132–141.

[12] Grinnell, *Blackfoot Lodge Tales*, pp. 257–258.

[13] *Last of the Great Scouts*, pp. vii–viii.

[14] Kansas City *Star*, March 22, 1914.

[15] Turner, The "Significance of the Frontier in American History," *Academic Reprints*, Jack L. Cross, Ed., El Paso, 1960, p. 28.

CHAPTER 27   EPILOGUE

[1] Letter of Charles Sumner Bird, Nov. 5, 1958.

[2] Letter to authors of Mrs. Eagle Smith, Aug. 19, 1958.

[3] *The Last of the Plainsmen*, New Bantam edition, 1958, facing p. 1.

[4] Letter to authors of Jesse H. Ratliff, Postmaster, Mar. 13, 1961. See "Arizona Sheep Trek" in *National Geographic*, April 1950.

[5] *The History of Finney County, Kansas*, vol. 1, p. 15.

[6] For further information on the buffalo, consult Arizona *Arrington Report*.

[7] According to Garretson, *The American Bison*, p. 202.

[8] "The year 1934 will long be remembered by the Crow and Sioux Indians as the time when the buffalo returned to their former range, this time in full possession by these tribes, to be unmolested and free from the danger of the white man's rifle. . . . For several years the herd in the Yellowstone Park had been increasing beyond the limits of its

grazing facilities and it became a problem to dispose of the surplus. Each year it was found necessary to slaughter a number of the buffalo, the meat being distributed among the various tribes of Indians. This donation aroused a strong desire on the part of the Indians to own herds of their own, which finally resulted in the 'Indian Experiment of establishing herds on the Crow and Sioux Reservations." *The American Bison,* p. 226.

[9] *American Wild Life,* p. 28. A full account of various private and public buffalo herds is given in *The American Bison.* See especially pp. 228–230 for the Canadian herds.

[10] See *Outdoor Life,* October 1958, pp. 31–32. Perrigo and Matthews use 150 or 180-grain soft-nose bullets and .30-.06's. Range: 100 yards or less. Most animals drop dead in their tracks.

[11] Letters of Malcolm J. Renton, Vice-President Catalina Island Co., Oct. 28, 1958 and Buck Wharton, Sedona, Arizona, Aug. 17, 1960.

[12] Jones was not the only one breeding cattalo in the U.S. Colonel Charles Goodnight, famous Texas rancher, was also an experienced breeder. Here are his comments: "I can summarize my experience in crossing Texas buffaloes with native cattle, as follows:

I take a male buffalo calf, put him with a native cow and let him suck her until weaning time. I let him run with common cattle until large enough to serve. He will then cross with any kind of domestic cattle. In making the first cross, no male calves have ever been born; cows conceiving them either suffer abortion or die, hence I only get heifer calves and a small per cent of them. There is no trouble whatever in giving birth. The cause of abortion and death is unknown to me. The heifer calves obtained breed readily to either the buffalo or the cattle. When bred to the buffalo, the males, which are three-quarters, are not fertile. The females are perfectly fertile and will breed to either race. I breed them back to the polled Angus stock from which they come, and get males which are fertile and which are half-breeds.

The type or race of hybrid cattle is now virtually established in a small way and I herewith give you a few of the points of advantage which the "Cattelow"* have over common cattle.

First, they are immune from all diseases as far as I have tested them. I know they are immune from Texas Black-Leg and Texas Fever. I have shipped three bulls, one-eighth buffalo, to our coast, the worst tick-country we have. One did die and two are living, so I have reason to believe that if they were a little higher in the buffalo blood, they would be entirely immune.

Second, the "cattelow" are much greater in weight, eat much less and hold their flesh better under more adverse conditions. They will easily cut about 70% net of their gross weight. They have a better meat, clear of fibre, and it never gets tough like beef.

They have long and deep backs, enabling them to cut at least 150 pounds more meat than other cattle. More of them can be grazed on a given area. They do not run from heel flies nor drift in storms, but like the buffalo, face the blizzards. They rise on their forefeet instead of their hind feet. This enables them to rise when in a weakened condition. They never lie down with their backs down hill, so they are able to rise quickly and easily. This habit is reversed in cattle.

When a herd on range gets weak and poor towards spring, their lying down with their backs toward slopes and on sides of hills causes a loss of from 1% to 6%. Every weak cow which so lies down can never get up, unless she is found by the herder.

The buffaloes have 14 ribs, giving them a longer and deeper loin. As we get them higher and deeper in the buffalo we get the extra rib on the "cattelow" They can exist on less food or salt than cattle, as before stated.

They could do without water much longer than cattle, without inconvenience. They are docile, easily broken and never fight. They put on flesh faster than any cattle and will live and appear to do well where cattle will perish. They have many other points in their favor too tedious to mention. — from *The Journal of Heredity*, Vol. V, No. 5, May 1914, pp. 197–199.

[13] Consult Deakin, *Hybridization of Domestic Beef Cattle and Buffalo* and Logan, *Hybridization of Domestic Beef Cattle and the Bison.*

---

*The word is so written in Col. Goodnight's manuscript. The spelling "cattalo" has now been generally accepted, after some years of confusion, and is adopted by practically every authority. It is the preferred spelling of the American Breeders' Association.

Bibliography

THE CHARLES JESSE JONES PAPERS

Journal of the First African Expedition

Manuscript Articles on the Second African Expedition

Memoirs of his Life to the Year 1910

Correspondence, 1910–1917

BOOKS AND ARTICLES

Akeley, Carl E. *In Brightest Africa,* New York: Garden City Publishing Co., 1923.

Branch, E. Douglas, *The Hunting of the Buffalo,* New York: D. Appleton and Company, 1929.

Catlin, George, *North American Indians,* London: 1841, 2 vols.

Chittenden, Hiram Martin, *The Yellowstone National Park,* Cincinnati, The Robert Clarke Co., 1904.

Cloete, Stuart, *The Curve and the Tusk,* New York: A Signet Book, New American Library, 1954.

Collins, Henry H. Jr., *The Unvanquished Buffalo,* Bronxville, The Blue Heron Press, Copyright, 1952.

————, *1951 Census of American Bison,* Bronxville, The Blue Heron Press, Copyright, 1952.

Cook, John R., *The Border and the Buffalo,* Topeka: Crane Co., 1907.

Croy, Homer, *Jesse James Was My Neighbor,* New York: Duell, Sloan & Pearce, 1929.

Deakin, Alan; Muir, G. W.; Smith, A. G.; and MacClellan, A. S., *Hybridization of Domestic Cattle and Buffalo (Bison Americanus),* Ottawa: Department of Agriculture, 1943.

Dobie, J. Frank, *Tales of Old-Time Texas,* Boston: Little, Brown & Co., 1955.

East, Ben, "Big Buffalo Hunt," *Outdoor Life,* October 1958, p. 34.

Finney County, Kansas, Historical Society, *History of Finney County, Kansas,* Garden City, Kansas: 1950, 2 vols.

Freuchen, Peter and Salomonsen, Finn, *The Arctic Year,* New York: G. P. Putnam's Sons, 1958.

Garretson, Martin H., *The American Bison,* New York: New York Zoological Society, 1938.

Goodnight, Colonel Charles, "My Experience With Bison Hybrids," *The Journal of Heredity,* May, 1914.

Grey, Zane, *The Last of the Plainsmen,* New York: The Outing Publishing Co., 1908.

————, *Raiders of the Spanish Peaks,* New York: Grosset & Dunlap, 1938.

————, *The Thundering Herd,* New York: Grosset & Dunlap, 1925.

————, *Tales of Lonely Trails,* New York: Harper & Brothers, 1922.

Grinnell, George Bird, *Blackfoot Lodge Tales,* New York: Charles Scribner's Sons, 1923.

————, *Pawnee Hero Stories and Folk-Tales,* New York: Charles Scribner's Sons, 1920.

Horgan, Paul, *Great River, The Rio Grande in North American History,* New York: Rinehart & Co., Inc., 1954.

Hornaday, William T., *Camp-Fires in the Canadian Rockies,* New York: Charles Scribner's Sons, 1923.

————, *The Extermination of the American Bison,* Report of the National Museum, Washington, 1887.

————, *The Minds and Manners of Wild Animals,* New York: Charles Scribner's Sons, 1923.

————, *The American Natural History,* New York: Charles Scribner's Sons, 1926.

Inman, Colonel Henry, *The Old Santa Fe Trail,* Topeka, 1916.

————, and Col. William F. Cody, *The Great Salt Lake Trail,* New York, 1898.

Jones, Charles Jesse with Colonel Henry Inman, *Buffalo Jones' Forty Years of Adventure,* Topeka, 1899.

Jones, Charles Jesse, "Capture of Mountain Sheep," *Harper's Weekly,* January 12, 1901, pp. 45–46.

————, "The Cattalo", *Farmer's Review,* Aug. 22, 1888.

————, "Breeding Cattalo", *American Breeder's Association Annual Report,* vol. III, p. 161, 1907.

————, "Roping a Lion," *Collier's,* March 11, 1911, p. 19.

————, "My Buffalo Experiments," *Independent,* June 7, 1906, pp. 1351–1355.

Kearton, Cherry, *Wild Life Across the World,* London: Hodder & Stoughton, c. 1915.

Kersey, Ralph, *Buffalo Jones,* Garden City (Kan.): The Elliott Printers, 1958.

Lewis, Henry Harrison, "Managing a National Park," *Outlook,* August 29, 1903, p. 1039.

Lewis, Meriwether and Clark, William, *History of the Expedition Under the Command of Captains Lewis and Clarke to the Sources of the Missouri, etc.,* prepared for the press by Paul Allen, New York: Harper & Brothers, 1876, 2 vols.

Logan, V. S. and Sylvestre, P. E., *Hybridization of Domestic Beef Cattle and Buffalo,* Ottawa: Department of Agriculture, 1950.

Lott, Milton, *The Last Hunt,* Boston: Houghton Mifflin Co., 1954.

Mackenzie, Alexander, *Voyages From Montreal on the River St. Lawrence Through the Continent of North America to the Frozen and Pacific Oceans,* London: Cadell & Davies, 1801 (reprinted Toronto 1927).

Needham, Henry Beach, "The Massachusetts Campaign", *Colliers,* Oct. 11, 1913, pp. 9–15.

Niehuis, Charles C., "The Buffalo Hunt", *Arizona Highways,* February 1934, pp. 7–9.

Rhodes, Eugene Manlove, "A Bird in the Bush", *Redbook Magazine,* April 1917, pp. 16–27.

Roe, Frank Gilbert, *The North American Buffalo,* Toronto: 1951.

Roosevelt, Theodore, *A Booklover's Holiday in the Open,* New York: Charles Scribner's Sons, 1916.

————, *African Game Trails,* New York: Charles Scribner's Sons, 1910.

————, *American Big-Game Hunting,* edited by Theodore Roosevelt and George Bird Grinnell, New York: Forest & Stream Publishing Co., 1893.

————, *Outdoor Pastimes of an American Hunter,* New York: Charles Scribner's Sons, 1905.

————, *The Wilderness Hunter*, New York: G. P. Putnam's Sons, 1893.

————, *Theodore Roosevelt*, An Autobiography, New York: Charles Scribner's Sons, 1920.

Russell, Don, *The Lives and Legends of Buffalo Bill*, Norman: University of Oklahoma Press, 1960.

Sandoz, Mari, *The Buffalo Hunters*, New York: Hastings House, 1954.

Scull, Guy H., *Lassoing Wild Animals in Africa*, New York: Frederick A. Stokes Co., 1911. Also published in *Everybody's Magazine*, Sept.-Nov., 1910.

Seton, Ernest Thompson, *Wild Animals at Home*, New York: Grosset & Dunlap, 1913.

————, *Life Histories of Northern Animals*, New York: Charles Scribner's Sons, 1909.

Sharpe, Philip B., *The Rifle in America*, New York: Funk & Wagnalls, 1938.

Vestal, Stanley, *Dodge City: Queen of Cowtowns*, New York: Bantam Books, 1957.

Walsh, Richard J., with Milton S. Salsbury, *The Making of Buffalo Bill*, Indianapolis: The Bobbs-Merrill Co., 1928.

Wellman, Paul I., *The Indian Wars of the West*, New York: Doubleday & Co., 1954.

Wells, F. E., "Roped African Lions to Defeat Roosevelt", *Scenic Southwest Magazine*, (Williams, Arizona) Winter 1935-36, pp. 1–8.

Wetmore, Helen Cody and Grey, Zane, *Last of the Great Scouts*, New York: Grossett & Dunlap, 1918.

Williamson, Harold F., *Winchester, The Gun That Won the West*, Washington: Combat Forces Press, 1952.

Willson, Roscoe G., "How the Buffalo Came to Arizona", Arizona Days and Ways Magazine, *Arizona Republic*, Oct. 16, 1960, pp. 24–25 & Oct. 23, 1960, p. 52–53.

Works Progress Administration of the City of New York, *American Wild Life*, Wm. H. Wise & Co., Inc., 1947.

Zahl, Paul A., "Face to Face with Gorillas in Central Africa", *National Geographic*, January 1960, pp. 114–137.

DOCUMENTS AND NEWSPAPERS

Arizona Daily Sun
Arizona Republic
Butte Miner
Chicago Times
Garden City Imprint
Garden City Herald
Illustrated London News
Kansas City Star
Kansas City Telegram

Liverpool Courier
Liverpool Mercury
London Telegraph
London Times
New York Globe
New York Herald
New York Times
Santa Barbara News-Press
Topeka Daily Capital

Arizona Game and Fish Department, *Arrington Report,* Phoenix, 1934.

Arizona Game and Fish Department, *Buffalo* (Big Game Bulletin No. 9–58) Phoenix: 1958.

United States Department of Interior, *Management of Buffalo Herds,* Washington, 1955.

————, *Yellowstone Park Files.*

United States Department of State, Passport Office Records, 1914.

United States National Archives, Department of State Decimal File, 1910-1929 (Charles Jesse Jones) Files 355a.11/-; 355a.11/11; 355a.11/14.

Index

For text and chapter headings in *Lord of Beasts,* Designer Douglas Peck selected two modern typefaces: Caledonia, created by Borzoi's W. A. Dwiggins in 1940, and Times Roman, designed by Stanley Morison in 1932 for the London *Times*. Killgore of Phoenix set type and Tyler printed the book on Warren's Arizona Eggshell textstock. Joanna Duro buckram, an impreglin linen, was the bookcloth used by the Arizona Trade Bindery.